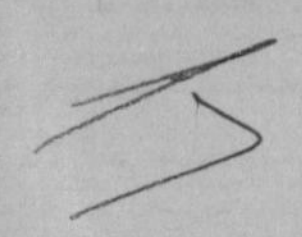

D0772760

The Encyclopaedia of

FLY FISHING

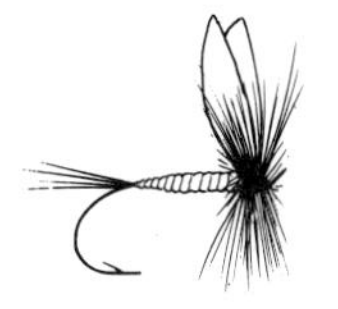

The Encyclopaedia of
FLY FISHING

CONRAD VOSS BARK

B.T. Batsford Ltd London

First published 1986

ISBN 0 7134 4557 2 (cased)

Typeset by Servis Filmsetting Ltd, Manchester
and printed in Great Britain by

Anchor Brendon Ltd
Tiptree, Essex
for the publishers
B.T. Batsford Ltd
4 Fitzhardinge Street
London W1H 0AH

Introduction and Acknowledgment

Detailed information on fly fishing in England, Scotland and Wales appears in alphabetical order within this book. The various entries include: descriptions of our major rivers, lochs, lakes and reservoirs and where and how to fish them; the flies, tackle and techniques that can be used for salmon, sea trout, and brown and rainbow trout; fishermen's knots; diagrams and descriptions of fly casting; some 150 fly dressings of the most popular and widely used flies; short summaries of many of the major books that have been written about fly fishing, their significance and importance, and biographies of their authors. Longer entries give advice on the best ways to fish for salmon, trout and sea trout, the techniques of the dry fly, nymph, upstream and downstream wet fly fishing and dapping. There are essays on the history of fly fishing on the waterways of Britain and details of some of the major angling organisations and clubs.

In preparing this book I have been fortunate in having access to the library of the Flyfishers' Club which has some 2,500 volumes as well as a number of unpublished papers. I would like to thank the club's President, Committee, Secretary and Honorary Librarian for their invaluable help. I have also been fortunate in that I have been able to draw on my own experience of fly fishing over some 50 years along with those experiences of my father and grandfather which have proved very useful in providing information which would not otherwise have been available. I have also made use of many of my articles which have appeared in *The Times*, *The Field*, *Trout and Salmon*, and *The Flyfisher*. I would like to thank the editor of *Trout Fisherman* along with the editors of the above publications for their help and encouragement.

Many good friends, experts in their own particular subjects, have spent considerable time and trouble in providing information for special sections and I am profoundly grateful for their help. Their names are acknowledged in the text but I would like to express my gratitude especially to: Peggy Baring, David Barr, Peter Borenius, Allen Edwards, P.K. George, Gerald Hadoke, Jack Heddon, Ron Holloway, Mick Lunn, Alastair Nicholl, Donald Overfield, Peter and Val Rennie, Geoffrey Snutch, Ken Sutton, Don Thompson, Jack Thorndike, Peter Tombleson, the Hon. Aylmer Tryon, Bernard Venables, Major John Walker, Nancy Whitlock and Dermot Wilson.

I would also like to acknowledge how much I have learnt about salmon fishing from Thomas Kenny and the late Dick Levinge, about sea trout fishing from Hugh Falkus, and about entomology from John Goddard.

Many people have helped in research; looking for photographs, reading old papers and fishing books, and making valuable suggestions. They include: Sir Edwin Arrowsmith, Alex Behrendt, Derek Bingham, Raymond Blacklaw, R.A. Brooks, Dr R.B. Broughton, Donald Carr, Elizabeth Carter, Jack Chance, Brian Clarke, Sir Christopher Cockerell, E.J.M. Davis, Peter Deane, Gerald D'Sousa, Hugh Falkus, Alan Finch, Norman Fox, Norman Fuller, the Rev. Donald R. Geddes, Paul Gibson, Irvine Hall, Steve Hare, John Hillaby, Jean Howman, T.C. Ivens, Joy Jacques, Norah Kite, Peter Lapsley, Art Lee, Nick Lyons, Joy Parboosingh, David Martin, Alick Newsom, Alison Opyrchal, Jean Parrington, David Pilleau, Reg Righyni, Bill Sibbons, George Tyler, Dr Norman Tricks, Mike Weaver, Anthea Williams, Richard Williams, Jean Williams, John Wilshaw, Laurie Williamson, Colin Wilson, Tony Witherby and Frank Woodcock.

My thanks also to many fishing friends and ghillies, to the secretaries and river keepers of the Hungerford Club, to the Piscatorial Society, and to Roy Buckingham and David Pilkington for their expert advice on fishing moorland streams.

For the delightful photographs and drawings I am deeply grateful to the artist, Gerald Morton, and to John Goddard, Graham Swanson and Dermot Wilson for the colour slides. Their contributions were quite invaluable. So too was the work of Janet Munns, who typed and checked the script. I am also most grateful for the care and attention given to the production of this book by William Waller, Editorial Director of Batsford, and his staff.

I must also thank the publishers, authors and the holders of copyright for permission to quote extracts from the following books:

In the Heart of the Country, H.E. Bates, Country Life Publications, Hamlyn; *The Management of Angling Waters*, Alex and Katharine Behrendt, André Deutsch; *Sunshine and the Dry Fly*, J.W. Dunne, A and C Black; *Going Fishing*, Negley Farson, Clive Holloway Books; *Salar the Salmon*, Henry Williamson, Faber and Faber; *Reflections on a River*, Howard Marshall, H.F. and G. Witherby; *Fishing for Salmon*, Charles McClaren, John Donald, Edinburgh; *Trout From Stillwaters*, Peter Lapsley, Benn Books; *Torridge Fishery*, L.R.N. Gray, Nicholas Kaye; *Sea Trout Fishing*, Hugh Falkus, H.F. and G. Witherby; *Nymph Fishing in Practice*, Oliver Kite, Herbert Jenkins; *A Year of Space*, Eric Linklater, Macmillan, A.D. Peters; *Famous Flies and Their Originators*, Donald Overfield, A and C Black; *Bright Rivers*, Nick Lyons, Lippincott, New York; *Fisherman's Fly*, David Jacques, A and C Black; *Reservoir Trout Fishing*, Bob Church, A and C Black; *Still Water Fly Fishing*, T.C. Ivens, André Deutsch; *Modern Salmon Fishing*, Antony Bridges, A and C Black; *Catching Salmon and Sea Trout*, Balfour Kinnear, Nelson and Co; *A Salmon Fisher's Odyssey*, John Ashley Cooper, H.F. and G. Witherby; *The Way of a Trout with a Fly*, G.E.M. Skues, A and C Black; *A Man May Fish*, T.C. Kingsmill Moore, Colin Smythe Books; *The Guileless Trout*, H.B. McCaskie, Cresset Press; *Where the Bright Waters Meet*, Harry Plunket Greene, Philip Allen and Co; *What the Trout Said*, Datus C Proper, Knopf, New York; *A History of Fly Fishing for Trout*, J. Waller Hills, Philip Allan and Co; *The Floating Line*, Anthony Crossley, Methuen and Co; *The Trout*, Frost and Brown, Collins New Naturalist Series; *Fishing in Print*, Arnold Gingrich, Winchester Press, New York; *Fishing From the Earliest Times*, William Radcliff, John Murray.

But above all else I am deeply in the debt of a very fine dry-fly fisher, my wife Anne, who first encouraged me to write this book and gave continual support and advice during the several years it took to produce.

Conrad Voss Bark
Lifton, Devon

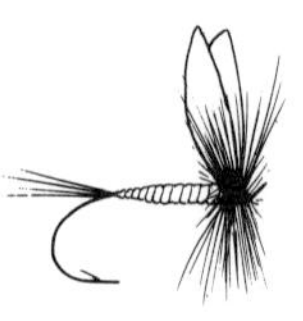

The Fly

Fly fishing has always been, and we believe always will be, the favourite method of angling; and deservedly so. Few who have once owned its sway are capable of resisting its attractions.

W.C. Stewart, *The Practical Angler*, 1857

Around the steel no tortur'd worm shall twine,
No blood of living insect stain my line;
Let me, less cruel, cast feathered hook,
With pliant rod athwart the pebbled brook,
Silent along the mazy margin stray,
And with fur-wrought fly delude the prey.

John Gay, *Rural Sports*, 1720

Ace of Spades A reservoir wet fly, designed by David Collyer, popular in the 1970s and 1980s, a nice balance of the matuka and black lure styles.

Body: black chenille
Rib: oval silver tinsel
Wing: matuka style wing, black hen, tied down by the silver rib
Tail: black hen fibres
Overwing: dark mallard blended over the black hen
Hackle: beard style Guinea fowl
Hook: 6 to 10, long shank

Acid Rain *See* Pollution.

Adamson, W.A. *Lake and Loch Fishing for Salmon and Sea Trout* (A and C Black, 1961) is memorable because in it Adamson gives the description by David McNaught of the take of the 19½lb sea trout on the dap on Ash Island beat of Loch Maree on 25 September, 1951:

To this day I can still remember the expression on the gillie's face when he found he could not lift the net out of the water at the first attempt . . .

The fish was taken on a Black Pennell which McNaught said was dressed 'like an inverted umbrella' on a 1/0 salmon hook, 14lb b.s. nylon, a mercerised cotton floss line and a 15ft split cane rod.

Aelian (AD 170–230) A Roman writer of natural history who gave the first surviving description of fly fishing. William Radcliff in *Fishing From the Earliest Times* (John Murray, 1921) gives the full text of the Lambert translation:

I have heard of a Macedonian way of catching fish and it is this: between Bercea and Thessalonica runs a river called the Aestraeus and in it there are fish with speckled skins; what the natives of the country call them you had better ask the Macedonians. These fish feed on a fly peculiar to the country which hovers on the river. It is not like flies found elsewhere nor does it resemble a wasp in appearance, nor in shape would one justly describe it as a midge or a bee, yet it has something in each of these. In boldness it like a fly, in size you might call it a midge, it imitates the colour of a wasp, and it hums like a bee. The natives generally call it the hippouros.

These flies seek their food over the river but do not escape the observation of the fish sunning below. When the fish observes a fly on the surface it swims quietly up, afraid to stir the water above, lest it scare away its prey; then coming up by its shadow it opens its mouth gently and swallows down the fly, like a wolf carrying off a sheep from the fold or an eagle a goose from the farmyard; having done this it goes below the rippling water.

Now though the fishermen know of this they do not use these flies for bait for fish; for if a man's hand touches them they lose their colour, their wings wither, and they become unfit food for the fish. For this reason they have nothing to do with them, hating them for their bad character; but they have planned a snare for the fish and get the better of them by their fishermen's craft.

They fasten red wool round a hook and fix on to the wool two feathers which grow under a cock's wattles, and which in colour are like wax. Their rod is six feet long and their line of the same length. Then they throw their snare and the fish, maddened and excited by the colour, come straight at it, thinking by the sight to get a dainty mouthful; when, however, it opens its jaws, it is caught by the hook and enjoys a bitter repast, a captive.

Aelian is untrustworthy. The flies he describes are unlike any known insect and the information clearly came to him secondhand. Dr J.M. Elliot of the Freshwater Biological Association suggests that hover flies (*syrphids*) might possibly fit though he points out that they are nothing like a midge.

Although the ancient Egyptians used short rods for bait fishing in fish ponds, a 6ft fly rod and a 6ft line for river fishing raises doubts.

The colour of the wings of the artificial pattern being 'like wax' suggests a dun colour. Roman wax candles were not made from purified wax. The hook sizes are not mentioned. The smallest Graeco–Roman hooks in the British Museum are about size 10, Redditch scale.

Mrs Laycock, of the information staff of the Greek Embassy in London, writes:

> The river Astraeus in Macedon is now known as the Kotichas. It is now a small river passing through the villages of Arkohorio and Monospita. Some rather unimportant species of fish can be found in the flatlands at Monospita . . . [but] in the mountainous area of Arkohorio there is trout fishing. Two methods of fishing are normally used, casting nets, or using rods with either a dummy fish bait or a plume.

Aldam, W.H. A Victorian fisherman with a sense of humour who produced a book in 1875 entitled, *A Quaint Treatyse on Flees and Artyfichall Flee-Making*, based on a manuscript of a hundred years or so earlier. It contained not only the details of the tying of about 25 Derbyshire trout flies but mounted specimens of the flies themselves and of the materials of which they were made. A rare and curious book much sought after by collectors. Aldam was among the first members of the Flyfishers' Club. He died in April, 1888.

Alder A rather dark fly, somewhat like a sedge, but with very dark black-veined wings which fold into a roof shape, shaped like a sedge but shiny like a stonefly. The alder frequently lands on hands and clothing and stays there for some time unless disturbed. The natural alder fly is not often found on the water but an artificial pattern, highly praised by Charles Kingsley, often fished wet, will take fish when alders are about. Goddard suggests this might be because the trout take it for its resemblance to an emerging mayfly nymph or even a sedge. Harris suggests a sedge, a large heavy fly of the blue-bottle type, or even a beetle. Artificial patterns are often localised – the Herefordshire Alder, the Derbyshire Alder – but the following is a reasonable compromise:

Body: purple or dark brown floss silk
Wings: roof shape; matched pair of slips taken from pheasant, grouse or partridge wings, speckled, and as dark as possible, lying flat and close to the body
Hackle: black cock
Head: black tying silk
Hook: 12 or 10

Alexandra A wet fly for trout and sea trout, designed by George M. Kelson, mostly used on lakes for trout, on rivers for sea trout, suggesting in appearance a spawning stickleback. The fly was named Alexandra after the Danish princess who married Prince Edward of Wales, later King Edward VII, in 1863:

Body: flat silver tinsel from tail to head
Tail: originally ibis, now generally bright scarlet floss
Wings: strands of green peacock herl
Cheeks: originally ibis, but now bright red or scarlet feather fibres
Hackle: black
Hook: sizes from 6 long shank for sea trout down to ordinary size 10 for lake trout, but the startling effect of bright green, scarlet and silver is inclined to be lost if the hook is too small

Allen The River Allen is in Dorset, rising near Sixpenny Handley and winding its brief way through lovely country into the Stour at Wimborne.

One of the most beautiful of the chalk streams in miniature, those who have rods on the Allen try to keep it a secret. Though in part stocked, the wild brown trout grow large and cautious, and must be approached with due care, fine nylon, and small flies. Beacon Beige, Pheasant Tail, Black Gnat, are popular in sizes from 14 to 18 or 20.

Quite apart from producing wild and beautiful trout, the Allen holds the official record for the biggest English grayling, not quite up to Austrian standards but by no means bad at 3lb 10oz, taken on fly by Mr Iain White on 28 August, 1983.

Rods are difficult to get, as on most of the smaller chalk streams, but the Shaftesbury Estate Office at Wimborne St Giles does occasionally let.

Alness A short salmon and sea trout river which runs into the Cromarty Firth. A great deal of work has been done to attract visitors by the Highlands and Islands Development Board and the Novar Estate. Alness Angling Club lets rods. Fishing can be had by residents at Dunraven Hotel, Strathpeffer and the Coul Hotel, Contin.

Amber Nymph An imitative wet fly, almost entirely used for reservoir and southern lake fishing, first dressed at Blagdon, Somerset, by the local doctor, Dr Bell, at some time in the 1920s or 1930s. It suggests a sedge pupa. Richard Walker's Chomper patterns have affinities. Dr Bell's original Amber Nymph was lightly dressed:

Body: amber seal's fur
Back: a strip of dark feather fibres from the head of the fly to the tail, sometimes though not always varnished
Hackle: one or two turns only of a dark reddish hackle at the head
Hook: generally 14

The Amber Nymph, 50 or 60 years later, is still a favourite for bank fishing at Blagdon. Most modern dressings are too heavy and have strange additions, such as a peacock herl head. One of Dr Bell's original dressings is in the Flyfishers' Club museum in London.

Andrews, Ted An artist and fly-tyer, a contributor to *The Anglers' Mail* and other journals, Ted Andrews' book, *Basic Fly Tying in Pictures* (Stanley Paul, 1983), is a good way for beginners to learn fly dressing with matched drawings and captions illustrating the tyings stage by stage.

Anglers' Co-operative Association An organisation formed in 1948 to fight pollution on behalf of anglers. The first statutory law against pollution (Rivers – Pollution Prevention Act, 1876) was well-meaning but ineffective; in fact pollution increased after the passing of the Act. Little or no action was taken until shortly after the Second World War when a leading barrister, John Eastwood K.C. doing research on common law, discovered that every riparian owner or tenant of a fishery was entitled to have water flowing past his land in its natural pure state. This law had seldom been tested because of the high costs of taking action in the courts. Eastwood formed his co-operative association on the basis that many anglers contributing a little to a common cause would provide enough money to fight cases from which all would benefit. Within months Eastwood was proved right, winning his first case, gaining damages and an injunction against the defendant.

The famous case which made the reputation of the A.C.A. was fought on behalf of the Pride of Derby Angling Association in 1951. Their river, the Derwent, was badly polluted by British Celanese, Derby Corporation, and East Midlands Tar Distillers, who were pumping millions of gallons of untreated sewage and tar products into the river. The water was then being used by a power station which was returning the water into the river in an even worse state than before.

The A.C.A. took action on behalf of the Derby anglers. The case lasted 13 days in the High Court, went to the Court of Appeal, where it lasted six more days, before the A.C.A. finally triumphed, winning substantial damages and costs and a cleaning-up of the river.

The director of the A.C.A. (1984) Allen Edwards, writes:

> Hundreds of cases have been fought since those early days and many miles of waterway cleaned up. In the past ten years alone £300,000 has been obtained as damages on behalf of members. The A.C.A. never has less than two dozen cases on its book and has seen a remarkable change in the face of pollution. In the early days the giants of industry were at fault. Today pollution is as likely to come from mismanaged farms as ever more stock is crowded into smaller and smaller space. Whatever the source the A.C.A. will fight the battle. Ironically, one of the latest in a long line of injunction proceedings is against a trout farm. This takes pure chalk stream water and returns it to a river in a condition which is equivalent to that of the treated effluent of a town of 65,000 people.

See also Pollution.

Annan A salmon river in Dumfrieshire, noted for its big back-end fish during the first two weeks of November. Worming and spinning takes place but Hallsheath Estate has many miles of fly-only water. The Newbie Estates at Annan have a beat just above the estuary which is good for the early run in February–March. Rods are at times available from Castle Milk and Annandale estates. Tackle shops at Moffat and Lockerbie are helpful with information.

Ants At times there can be a heavy fall of winged ants on rivers which attracts the attention of trout. Dressings of artificial ants have been largely neglected. Here is Charles Cotton's:

> *Red Ant:* the dubbing of brown and red camlet [wool] well mixed, with a light grey wing
> *Black Ant:* the dubbing of the black-brown hair of a cow, some red warped in for the tag of his tail, and a dark wing. A killing fly

There is a version some 230 years later by F.M. Halford:

> *Body:* split into two parts, a thicker and longer abdomen, a smaller thorax, made up of red or black floss silk
> *Wings:* white or blue grey hackle points tied between abdomen and thorax

Appetiser A reservoir lure designed in 1973 by Bob Church which might well double as a night sea trout fly:

> *Body:* white chenille ribbed silver tinsel
> *Wing:* large spray of white marabou herl
> *Overwing:* natural grey squirrel tail
> *Throat hackle and tail:* a mix of dyed feather fibres – orange, green and silver

Arndilly Fancy An excellent salmon fly, named after the Arndilly beat of the Spey. The origin is recent, somewhere in the 1950s, but it is said to have inherited characteristics of an earlier trout fly pattern. There was confusion about who first dressed the Arndilly, which is discussed by C.P. Wagner, former President of the Anglers' Club of New York, in Vol. 60 of the Club Bulletin (Winter 1981/82). He gives John Macdonald's dressing:

> *Tag:* silver oval tinsel or wire
> *Tail:* golden pheasant crest
> *Body:* yellow floss with silver tinsel overlay
> *Hackle:* bright blue wound around behind the head forming a 'muff' under the wing
> *Wing:* black or dark brown fur, stoats tail or black bear or equivalent
> *Eye:* jungle cock or omit
> *Head:* red lacquer or red thread

Ashmere Two well-stocked trout lakes in Felix Lane, Shepperton, Middlesex, with a devoted following of Londoners who make up the majority of the season ticket holders for bank and boat fly fishing. The lakes were opened in 1948, expanded in 1958, and another lake is being developed. One interesting point about Ashmere is that the fishing season is divided into two halves, 1 March to 15 July and then from 15 September to 15 November, the reason being that water in the London area heats up in mid-summer and the fishing goes off until the cooler weather arrives again by September.

The Association of Stillwater Game Fishery Managers was set up in 1984 by the Salmon and Trout Association to protect and promote the interests of private proprietors of stillwater fisheries. It will:

> seek to iron out some of the existing anomalies in stillwater fisheries legislation and will also set about the establishment of a code of operation designed to protect the interests of the fly fishing public.

Atlantic Salmon Trust The main objectives of this organisation are to collect and disseminate new knowledge and facts about the Atlantic salmon, to identify dangers and potential threats to its stocks, and to work closely with all bodies worldwide that are striving for salmon conservation.

Gerald Hadoke writes:

Being a registered charitable organisation we are prevented from exerting pressure on the Government or Members of Parliament, but this does not mean we refrain from giving considered views on any Government publication which concerns the well-being of the Atlantic salmon.

It is an important aim of the Trust to ensure that the true economic and social benefits arising from the country's salmon resource are assessed so that the runs of salmon may be cropped in a manner which provides the optimum benefits to the community and yet allows for the resource to be sustained and developed.

The Trust has long realised it must concern itself with the international regulation and conservation of stocks. Thus it has been involved in the organisation of international conferences, the most recent of which gave the impetus for the holding of the International Convention for the Conservation of Salmon in the North Atlantic which formed the basis for the establishment, in Edinburgh, of the Atlantic Salmon Conservation Organisation. On the European front, the Trust has been in constant touch with the Commission and its officers and in addition has been able to maintain very close links with the European Parliament through its Working Group on Fisheries. The Trust helped to organise and participate in the European Parliament's first 'Hearing' on Atlantic salmon and presented a paper on the management of salmon in E.E.C. waters to the meeting.

Examples of the Trust's work in the international field include the reports it has published on the Faroese and Greenland commercial salmon fisheries and on the fisheries of Iceland. At home the Trust has continued to stimulate discussion on matters of importance, has caused action to be taken to improve the publication of the nation's salmon statistics, and is preparing economic evaluation schemes for consideration at national and regional level.

Austin, R.S. A West Country fly dresser, R.S. Austin had a tobacconist business at Tiverton, Devon *c.*1880 onwards for a number of years. Fame came from G.E.M. Skues for Austin's creation of the Tups. Austin called it originally the Red Spinner, which indeed it was, and first tied it *c.*1900. Skues fell in love with the pattern and christened it the Tups Indispensible – tups because that was a name for a ram and some of the dubbing was taken from a ram's private parts, and indispensable because it took fish when other flies did not. It became the rage and Austin was inundated with orders and consequently became sick of the Tups, longing to go back to tying his other famous Devon patterns – the Blue Upright and Pheasant Tail. After Austin's death in 1911, the fly tying business was carried on by his daughter for many years.

Avington A lake fishery near Winchester which specialises in producing large trout and is the haunt of anglers hoping to catch a record fish. Avington already has two records, a brook trout of 5lb 6oz in 1979 and a rainbow of 19lb 9oz in 1977, both caught by Alan Pearson. The theories of the owner of Avington, the late Sam Holland, on breeding have been widely publicised.

Avon England has five river Avons and Scotland has two (Avon, from the Celtic *Abh*, *Abhain*, meaning river), but the one most fishermen think of is in the Vale of Pewsey, running through Netheravon – famous as Frank Sawyer's water – and on to Salisbury, Fordingbridge, Ringwood, and the sea at Christchurch, where you can see the netsmen at work.

It is difficult not to fall in love with the Avon, not only because it is a beautiful river, but because it is also generous and prolific. It breeds large fish of all kinds, roach and barbel and chub as well as grayling, trout and salmon. The insect life is abundant and bushes along the bank are sometimes covered with flies, especially during a good hatch of grannom.

The Salisbury Anglers have trout water on the Avon – some of the cheapest chalk stream fishing anywhere in England – and there were vacancies for members in 1983. The Piscatorial Society, more expensive, has excellent water and a fine club house. Day permits for salmon and sea trout fishing are obtainable at the Royalty Fishery, Christchurch, but the best salmon water is held by estates such as the Somerley Estate water at Ibsley. There is a waiting list.

Some mixed trout and coarse fishing on day tickets can be had from the Bull Hotel, Downton, and the Bat and Ball, Breamore. The upper river and tributaries are fairly closely preserved for trout. **Sources include:** *Nymphs and the Trout*, Frank Sawyer, A and C Black, 1958; *Nymph Fishing in Practice*, Oliver Kite, Jenkins, 1963; and the *Haig Guide to Trout Fishing in Britain*, edited by David Barr, Collins Willow, 1983.

Axe The River Axe comes down from the Mendip Hills in Somerset past Wookey Hole, and into the Bristol Channel south of Weston-super-Mare. Trout are to be caught here on the fly but it is largely a coarse fish river, more so than the other Axe, not all that far away, which rises near Beaminster in Dorset, passes Axminster and enters the sea at Axmouth on the south coast, having been joined by the Yarty. The Dorset–Devon Axe could be said to be the home of the dry fly for it was here that G.P.R. Pulman fished, at Slimlakes Bridge, just above Axminster. There is a sea trout run but fishing is largely preserved by clubs; however it might be worth making enquiries at the George Hotel at Axminster for trout or the White Hart at Colyford for sea trout. In 1983 there was bad pollution of the Axe by farm effluent, many thousands of fish died, and the river may take a few years to recover.

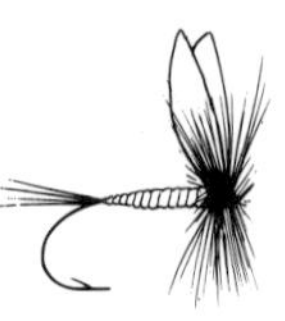

The Lure of the Fly

Nelson was a good fly fisher and as proof of his passion for it continued the pursuit even with his left hand.

Arnold Gingrish, *Fishing in Print*, Winchester Press, New York, 1974

Lord Grey would have risen to great heights if he had not wasted his time fishing.

Lloyd George commenting on Viscount Grey of Fallodon, Secretary of State for Foreign Affairs, 1905–1916

How can we be expected to take an interest in a country like Canada where the salmon do not rise to the fly?

Lord Melbourne, British Prime Minister, *c.* 1835

B

Babingley A small self-contained Norfolk river that rises in the Hillington–Harpley area and flows straight into the Wash seven miles to the west, joined on its journey by three tiny tributaries, one of which is the Congham. David Barr writes:

The Babingley is Norfolk's nearest imitation of a chalk stream and produces a steady number of brown trout, some reaching two pounds, though the average is much less. It is also, for much of its length, the boundary of the Sandringham Estate. Mostly private, part of its waters are in the hands of the King's Lynn Angling Club. If access were made easier, or indeed possible, this little river could easily become a host for sea trout.

Baby Doll A reservoir lure designed by Brian Kench in 1971 and still a favourite for three reasons: it is simple to tie, has an attractive name, and attracts fish. Now tied in many colours, the original was white:

Body: white nylon wool shaped like a small fish
Tail: strands of wool shredded out to look like the tail of a fish
Head: black tying silk or nylon varnished black
Hook: almost any size from a longshank 12 upwards

Although a lure, it can often take fish when fished quite slowly, especially when trout are herding sticklebacks.

Baigent Dr Baigent had a practice at Northallerton in North Yorkshire around the early 1900s and designed a fly for the Swale known as Baigent's Brown. It was what is now generally known as a variant – very little body but with long hackles that are about twice as long as the hook shank.

Body: yellow floss silk
Hackle: large dark furnace standing out well all round
Hook: 10 to 16

Various explanations have been given why these large hackles on a fly attract the trout, for they often bring up a fish which has refused a more conventional pattern, no one can be certain why.

Barker, Thomas The great Izaak Walton, not himself a fly fisherman, gleaned his knowledge of flies and fly fishing for the first few editions of his *Compleat Angler* (1653), from Barker's *The Art of Angling* (1651). In fact, Barker was quite an important figure in the development of fly fishing, the first writer to give details of how to tie flies and wind hackle, notable for his emphasis on the need to find materials that would float well, and the first writer to mention the use of a reel and gaff in salmon fishing.

Barker came to London from Shropshire and lived in Westminster at the same time as Walton was running his ironmonger's shop and general store in Fleet Street, but whether they met is doubtful. This was the time of civil war, Walton was a Royalist, Barker a Parliamentarian. Walton took what he wanted from Barker's book and acknowledged his debt.

Barker's mayfly dressing is surprisingly modern: a chamois leather body ribbed with black hair. He wrote well. His palmer flies . . . 'will serve all the year long, morning and evening, windie or cloudy . . .' His instructions on how to dress flies have a charming assurance:

Now to show how to make Flies: learn to make two Flies and make all; that is the Palmer, ribbed with silver or gold, and the May Flie; these are the ground of all flies.

For salmon fishing, the reel should be able to hold a horsehair line 26 yards long and his salmon flies, on large hooks, had to have 'six wings or four at least'. Barker's description of salmon flies suggests they might have been tied to imitate the big dragonfly but there is no certainty about this.

Barr, David Wisbech solicitor, contributor to *Country Life*, general editor of the *Haig Guide to Salmon Fishing in Scotland* (Macdonald, 1981), and its companion, *Haig Guide to Trout Fishing in Britain* (Collins Willow, 1983). These two books marked a new approach to the concept of guide books. They contain evocative essays on the character of the rivers and lakes they describe, as well as information on how they may be fished and when and where to obtain the fishing: two unique reference books, widely praised.

Bates, H.E. (1905–1973) One of the great English novelists and short story writers, Bates was an accomplished fly fisherman; and fishing frequently came into his writing, particularly in the character of Uncle Silas. Born at Rushden, Northamptonshire, Bates went to Kettering Grammar School, and at an early age began fishing the Nene. Later he made his home in Kent. He married and had two sons and two daughters. Bates's writing about the countryside is probably among the most perceptive of our time:

As the afternoon went on and the sun grew warmer and the voices of the girls drowsier under the warm-scented apple trees, and the light more vivid on the white and crimson corn-barn and the claret lily-leaves, I began to understand something of what fishing is about – why it has remained so deeply in the affections of men, why it has never become an expression of collective social snobbery, why it brings out the best and not the worst in a man's nature. (*Tunnicliff's Countryside*, Clive Holloway Books, 1983, chosen by Ian Niall.)

Best Fishing Stories, an anthology edited by John Moore (Faber and Faber, 1965) contains two written by Bates. His major works included *Fair Stood The Wind For France*, *The Purple Plain* and *The Scarlet Sword*; the comic *Darling Buds Of May* with the Larkins family; and his three volumes of autobiography, *The Vanished World*, *The Blossoming World* and *The World In Ripeness*.

Bayham Abbey Lake and Sundridge Lake Two well-stocked trout lakes within easy reach of London – Bayham Abbey being situated at Lamberhurst and Sundridge at Sevenoaks, both in Kent.

Beacon Beige One of the Wills family, on leave from the Somme in 1917, designed a fly called the Beige which was popular in the Dulverton area. Some 30 years later another fly dresser, Peter Deane, made improvements to the Beige and called it the Beacon Beige after Culmstock Beacon which was near his home, then by the banks of the River Culm. The Beige and the Beacon Beige are very much West Country patterns, both admirably suggest an olive, and some say a BWO and an Iron Blue as well if you are careful. Here is Peter

Deane's dressing of the Beacon Beige which must be dressed as lightly and delicately as possible:

Body: stripped peacock quill from the eye feather with clearly defined markings so that it produces a nice ribbing effect. One has seen the quill over-tied on a floss base but this is not in the original dressing
Whisks: four or five fibres from a stiff grizzle cock
Hackles: grizzle, with a dark red cock wound through it. The original dressing specified a very springy Indian red game hackle, dark, and rather long in the fibre

Popularised by Dermot Wilson in recent years, the Beacon Beige is now widely used on the Hampshire chalk streams.

Beauly A salmon river in Inverness with good runs, not only in the main river but in the tributaries, the Glass and Farrar. The Lovat Estate at Beauly lets rods. The Glen Affric Hotel at Cannich has good fishing for residents on the Glass and Farrar, where the glens, in autumn, are said to be among the most beautiful in the Highlands. The Glass and Farrar fish from July to mid-October.

Behaviour From time to time in sporting journals one reads criticisms of anglers' behaviour. Alex Behrendt made the point light-heartedly but pungently in his *Management of Angling Waters* (André Deutsch, 1977). Behrendt started life as a fish farmer, then switched to running a fishery:

It was a revelation. I had always understood that fishermen are a special breed of human: honest, law-abiding, peace-loving, helpful, generous-minded, self-critical, unselfish, modest and kind. Then I had to deal with them and found that they are just like everyone else – some good, some not so good. Some of them are not in the least ashamed of cheating if the opportunity arises. What can you think when you find a tin of maggots underneath the seat of a boat in a trout fishery with a rule 'fly only'? Or when you see a man casting and with every cast the sunlight catches the brilliant flash of a fly spoon? Then there is the fellow who sneaks to his car before he comes to weigh in the fish. Should you . . . look into his creel to admire his catch you would find that the chap could not count to five, the correct bag limit. There are seven trout in his creel . . .

Behrendt and other fishery managers know that when a group of people work or play together certain codes of behaviour must be observed; yet the problem of making rules also raises the spectre of enforcement. A ghillie at Blagdon, Donald Carr, had a list of some of the worst offences:

Playing radios
Parking cars close to the water's edge
Peeing in or near the waters
Ground baiting
Unhooking small trout by tearing out the hook and tossing them back into the water with a splash
Cruelty in other ways: letting trout suffocate in the air flapping about in a boat or on the bank
Net stakes: a recent habit of coarse fishermen, who are used to staking out a swim, and do the same with landing nets on a reservoir

Alex Behrendt

Keep nets: in use to hold trout until the end of the day when the big ones will be kept and the others returned
Bunching: when one bank angler catches a fish the others on either side draw in close and cast over his water
Walking close behind other anglers and risking a fly hitting one's face on their backcast.

Behrendt, Alex A pioneer of lake fishing. Alex Behrendt established the first major trout lake fishery in England at Two Lakes, in Hampshire, in 1951. The son of an eastern European carp farmer, Behrendt was conscripted into the German army in the Second World War, was taken prisoner in Italy and brought to a prisoner of war camp in England. Allowed out for farm work, he found that he liked England and as well as that fell in love with an attractive widow, whose husband, a Captain R.N. had earlier been killed in action. After the war they worked together to start what Behrendt had originally envisaged as a carp farm at Two Lakes, but finding that the English did not eat carp, as the Germans do, Behrendt turned it into a trout fishery. It quickly established a reputation for the skill of its management, the size and quality of its trout, and the beautiful landscaping of the lakes and the surroundings.

By 1980 the two lakes that Behrendt had started with had become seven. The estate and the fishery have been willed to the Hampshire College of Agriculture whose fishery management students have trained there under Behrendt and his staff for a number of years. Two Lakes was also a centre for the annual Fishery Management Conference which brings scientists to this

Dr Bell of Blagdon

country from many parts of America and Europe. The standard work on lake fisheries is *The Management of Angling Waters*, André Deutsch (1977), by Alex Behrendt, with sketches by his wife, Katharine.

Bell, Dr H.A. (1888–1974) Although he never wrote a word about fishing and shunned publicity, Dr Bell of Blagdon had the greatest formative influence of any man on the development of reservoir fishing in the first half of this century.

Howard Alexander Bell served in the First World War with the R.A.M.C. and after his return to civilian life opened a practice in Sussex, but from 1920 onwards, whenever he could, he fished Blagdon. In 1935 he was able to buy a practice at Wrington and a few years later opened a surgery at Blagdon village, as close as he could get to his beloved lake.

In those days Blagdon was fished with spinners or with traditional sea trout and low-water salmon flies. Fly fishing was carried out from boats and bank during the evening rise. Daytime fishing with the fly was thought to be of little use.

Bell had read Skues and, following his example, used a narrow spoon to spoon out the trout he caught. One of his friends said 'He would scoop out his grandmother if he thought there was anything in her.'

The stomach contents of the Blagdon trout were a revelation. There was nothing there but small larvae and pupae, among them the pupae of the famous black midge. Bell realised that the natural food of the trout had no relationship at all with the Jock Scotts, the Mallards and the Peter Rosses which were being fished by his friends. He was a good fly dresser and began to tie patterns that imitated and suggested these food insects. Success came at once. Fishing during the day, often in bright sunlight, he would come back with a limit of eight trout, many of which he gave to his patients. His friend, Alick Newsom, described his methods:

A typical cast would be a Worm Fly on the tail, a Grenadier on the first dropper, and a Buzzer on the top dropper. The flies were not leaded. They were quite small. He fished from the bank, using a standard 1X gut cast and cast out as far as was comfortable. He made no attempt to go for distance but let the flies sink slowly, waiting for some time, but judging the time so that the tail fly did not get snagged on the bottom. He used the knot at the end of his greased silk line as a bite indicator. When the flies were fully sunk he would gather them in slowly. He had a pear-shaped landing net attached to a cord slung over his shoulder. He liked to fish over sunk ditches and holes and moved slowly along the bank, searching for weed beds. During the Second World War, for example, a German bomb exploded just off the north shore and he often fished the crater because of the good growth of weed. He was a shy man and liked to fish alone and when he became so successful he hated anyone writing about him. An article about the way he fished appeared in *The Field* and I showed it to him and he was so angry he tore it up. He would never fish anywhere near a crowd. Typically, Bell's Bush is named after him and this is at the far end of the lake, right away from everyone. He was really in some ways a recluse though he was a marvellous doctor. He never wrote anything at all about fishing. When he was not on the lake or in his surgery he was at home in Wrington, gardening or listening to music.

Bell's reputation grew and was perhaps even increased by his reluctance to have anything written about him. There was a legend that he put a magic oil on his flies which was why he always caught more than anyone else. Willie Cox of Bristol, who knew Bell well and was influenced by him, said that people would watch him fishing through binoculars to see what he did.

Bell's success in fishing imitative patterns was widely followed, and copies of his flies began to be tied commercially by Veals of Old Market Street, Bristol. Gradually the idea of using what one writer in the *Fishing Gazette* called 'imitation bait' began to spread. Many of Bell's flies are now traditional patterns. They include the Blagdon Buzzer, the Grenadier, and the Amber Nymph. Some of his flies are in the museum of the Flyfishers' Club in London.

Beetles Courtney Williams, Leonard West and Francis Francis have all said that the fly fisherman does not pay enough attention to beetles. One knows why. There are too many beetles, several hundred different families, land-bred and water-bred, and no doubt all have been or can be eaten by the trout, though not the water-skater, which seems immune.

Beetles fished either on or below the surface certainly do take trout, and if one considers a beetle carefully, face to face, there are certain common characteristics which, apart from size, are not too difficult to fit into a common pattern. Dr Terry of Bath, and Eric Horsfall Turner, a former Town Clerk of Scarborough, have both done this successfully and produced fairly similar patterns, though Horsfall Turner's was more yellow at the rear.

Putting the Terry-Horsfall Turner patterns together, (but mostly Terry because his pattern is slightly easier), you get something like this:

Tail: a short stub of orange or of mixed orange and yellow floss
Body: rounded yellow floss over which is tied green peacock herl, twisted with the yellow tying silk for strength

Jack Heddon

Hackle: a couple of turns, fairly long, of medium-red cock
Hook: from size 18 up to about 10

The beetle can be finished wet or dry but if it is regularly fished dry more hackle may be needed to help flotation. As with most other imitation bait patterns, lead wire can be added as an underbody for stillwater fishing.

Berners, Dame Juliana A lady generally believed to be the author or editor of the first English textbook on fishing, including fly fishing – *The Treatyse of Fysshynge Wyth an Angle*, published in 1496 from St Albans Abbey. Her name has been spelt in various ways but she is accepted as being what one historian called an illustrious female of noble birth who was prioress of the nunnery of Sopwell, near St Albans.

One did not need to be a misogynist to have slight doubts about the Dame but it was not until an amateur historian and fly fisherman, Jack Heddon, began probing into the Westminster Abbey records in the 1970s that doubt matured.

He found that Westminster Abbey's own researchers, looking for the site of Caxton's Press, found that it was close to a large house called St Albans. William Caxton, the first English printer, set up his press near the Abbey in 1476. The St Albans house filled most of the present grass-covered area to the east of the Chapter House where we now have the statue of King George V.

Heddon was able to point out that the colophon (publisher's imprint) on *The Treatyse – apud villa sancti Albani* – meant 'near St Albans house' and not the City or Abbey of St Albans. In other words *The Treatyse* was published from the large house called St Albans which adjoined Caxton's Press.

In some ways it is a pity to have lost the Dame. She has been with us for so many years. Heddon's evidence, however, seems to put the matter beyond doubt, though one problem solved does create another: if the Dame didn't write the Treatyse, who did? **Source:** Jack Heddon, private ms, 1983.

Bibio An Irish lough fly, first tied by Major Charles Roberts of the Burrishoole fishery, Newport, Co. Mayo in the late 1950s. The story goes that when asked to give it a name, as the fly was having some success, he said that he would call it the Bibio as he had seen the word somewhere and had taken a fancy to it. No doubt he later remembered that the word came from Bibio Johannes, the St Mark's fly. The dressing of the Bibio is the same as a Black Palmer but with an orange wool band in the centre of the black wool body. The orange shows through the black hackle palmered from head to tail. The Bibio is widely used on English reservoirs.

Black Gnat A convenient description of several hundred varieties of small black flies. They mostly belong to the order Diptera, which includes the housefly, but often not, and are midge or reed smuts. The simplest dressing for a Black Gnat is almost certainly Roger Woolley's:

Body: black quill or black silk
Hackle: black cock
Hook: 16, 18 or 20

If one feels there should be wings, as some do, then two small pale blue or off-white hackle points can be added, splayed out on either side of the body, but kept short. This is, some think, more effective than putting the wings along the back, as Halford did.

Entomologists and anglers do not see eye to eye on black gnats and nor do some of the best fly fishers either:

> The species which inhabits the Test is called *bibio johannis*, and appears, as its name implies, at midsummer, on St John's Day. It has a larger cousin, the hawthorn fly, *bibio marci*, which comes out at the end of April, and is at its height during the second or third week of May. It is not, I think, common on the Test; but it is the common black gnat of Devonshire, where the trout take it greedily and refuse anything else, and the black gnat season is the best for heavy baskets. I have done well with it on the Otter. (J.W. Hills, *A Summer on the Test*, Bles, 1924, 3rd edn. 1940)

'Black Palmer' Pseudonym of the author (now unknown) of *Scottish Loch Fishing*, 1882, one of the first books to emphasise the effectiveness of fishing Scottish lochs with a team of wet flies. The flies were, in general, fairly large patterns; March Brown, Mallard and Claret, Teal and Silver, tied to gut, fished on the drift with long greenheart rods – the type of fishing popular among Scottish angling clubs in competitions.

Black Spider A most useful, if not the most useful, of upstream wet flies; and a favourite of W.C. Stewart, the Edinburgh lawyer, who wrote about fishing on the Scottish Borders in his book, *The Practical Angler* (1857), in which he emphasised the importance of fishing the wet fly upstream. This was one of his favourite flies, lightly dressed, with a mobile hackle:

Body: brown silk
Hackle: greeny-black feather from a starling's neck
Hook: 14–16

Black Spiders do well in fast water, riffles, and eddies, in fact the kind of water you often get on the Tweed and tributaries.

Black Lure One of the very earliest reservoir lures which has been altered and added to by many fly dressers over half a century or more. Some of the changes have made it look prettier or more distinguished but none have made much improvement to it so far as catching fish are concerned. This was Willie Cox's dressing at Blagdon some 50 years ago which must be getting back fairly close to the original:

Body: black wool, fairly thick
Rib: silver tinsel
Wings: two, sometimes four, black cock saddle hackles, extending well past the bend of the hook and curving outwards so that when the lure is retrieved the hackles move slightly together, giving the impression of life
Hackle: black cock
Hook: long shank 6 or 8

In most cases the overall length of the fly is almost twice that of the hook.

Black and Peacock Spider A wonderful pattern for imitative fishing, particularly on stillwaters, the Black and Peacock has been a favourite now for nearly half a century. The surprising thing about this fly is that it came into being by accident. One day, in the 1930s T.C. Ivens was fishing a winged Alder artificial on a reservoir without success. He looked at it, wondering what was wrong, thought it was rather over-dressed, and cut off the wings. Almost at once the wingless Alder began to take trout. There was no need to alter the body dressing, only the name, so it became what a wingless Alder looks like – a black and peacock fly:

Body: bronze peacock herl
Head hackle: relatively long soft-fibred black hen, two turns only
Hook: 12 and 14 are the most usual but larger sometimes

Reservoir fishermen sometimes use lead wire or lead foil under the dressing to make it sink more quickly but this must be a matter of taste. The unleaded fly is often taken while sinking slowly through the water without other movement. It is one of Ivens' deceiver patterns and possibly the most popular.

It is incidentally of some interest that wings cut off a Butcher as well as an Alder will improve its effectiveness, according to an article by Robin Lemon in *West Country Fly Fishing*, edited by Anne Voss Bark (Batsford, 1983).

Black Pennell Another invaluable stillwater wet fly, one of a series designed some hundred years ago by H. Cholmondeley Pennell for lake and sea trout fishing. In the thicker and larger sizes the Pennells are very useful for the dap.

Body: black floss silk
Rib: silver tinsel
Tail: golden pheasant tippet
Hackle: black cock, rather long in the hackle. For wet-fly fishing dress sparsely, for the dap thickly
Hook: a matter of choice, the most usual being 10 or 8 standard sizes

The Pennell can be dressed in a great variety of matching colours, yellow body, yellow hackle; green body, green hackle; brown body, brown hackle; but the black is the most widely used.

Blae and Black A pretty and useful little fly, originally an Irish pattern, widely used for lake trout, with a number of variations; Blae and Silver, Blae and Gold, and so on, but as with the Pennell the black is the most popular:

Body: black seals' fur or black wool
Hackle: black hen but if only cock fibres are available then tie the cock hackle, fairly short, as a beard hackle
Wings: matched slips of coot lying low on the body
Tail: golden pheasant tippet
Hook: 12–14 for lake trout, larger for migratory trout

A silver tinsel rib may be added. The Blae and Silver has an all-silver body with blue dun hackle but the coot wings remain.

Blagdon Lake This reservoir, of some 440 acres, was stocked and opened for trout fishing in 1904. In the first few years the weight of the trout caught averaged between 4 to 5lb, a record never equalled by any other reservoir since. The reason, apart from Blagdon being a very fertile water, was that there was practically no fishing pressure, tickets being issued in the first few years only to directors of the Bristol Waterworks and their friends.

Typical of the results achieved in those early days is contained in a cutting from *The Field*, of 6 May, 1905, provided through the kindness of Fred Buller, which recorded that two fishermen, Mr M.R.L. White and Mr R.C. Hardy Corfe, fishing the March Brown at Blagdon, took 20 fish with a total weight of 90½lb. The average weight of the trout would be just over 4½lb. The largest fish taken weighed 8lb 4oz.

Blagdon has inspired much literature, including books and articles by H.T. Sheringham and Plunket Greene, but of further importance is that it was there that the first imitative lake patterns were tied, by Dr H.A. Bell during the 1920s and 1930s.

Blagdon Boil A turmoil of surface water caused by big trout attacking shoals of small fry. Brian Clarke gave a vivid description of a boil in his introduction to *West Country Fly Fishing*, edited by Anne Voss Bark (Batsford, 1983). The phenomenon is most likely to occur at Blagdon in August when the sticklebacks are breeding. The big trout come in and herd them into the shallows, especially at dusk when the water 'boils' with attacking trout and leaping sticklebacks.

Blagdon Buzzer An artificial fly designed some 60 years ago by Dr H.A. Bell to imitate the large black midge pupae:

Body: fine black wool tapered from a thin point by the bend of the hook to a larger body by the thorax, ending with a slight hump behind the eye of the hook
Rib: four or five turns of fine flat silver tinsel
Head: a tiny fluff of white wool or silk just behind the eye of the hook over the back of the hump of the thorax

Bell's dressing is very delicate and fine (*see* colour photograph 11). It might be as well to add that the true 'buzzers' are the winged midges which, when flying over the lake in myriad numbers, create a buzzing sound caused by the rapid movements of their wings. The Blagdon Buzzer artificial represents the midge pupa and is fished sink and draw fairly close to the surface, sometimes almost motionless in the surface film.

Blue Charm A traditional fully-dressed salmon fly, dating back to the mid-1800s, which is still popular for low-water fishing, especially in small sizes:

Body: black floss or wool ribbed with three or four turns of fine flat silver tinsel
Tail: golden pheasant crest, up-turning to meet the wing
Wings: two matching strips of dark mallard flanked as cheeks by thinner strips of light mallard or teal
Hackle: blue-dyed hen tied at the throat as a beard hackle

Blue Dun An artificial fly that suggests various olive duns, the original dressing by Walton's friend, Charles Cotton, in 1676. Cotton's dubbing for his Blue Dun were the combings of the blue under-fur from the neck of a black greyhound. Those who do not have access to black greyhounds will find the following dressing a not unreasonable substitute:

Body: yellow silk dubbed with mole or dark blue rabbit fur
Wings: starling or coot slips
Hackle: pale or medium blue cock
Hook: 14–18

In darker shades it might well do for an iron blue.

Blue Quill *See* Blue Upright.

Blue Upright Originally a Devon pattern, the Blue Upright has a twin brother, the Blue Quill. This dressing is by Austin of Tiverton:

Body: undyed peacock herl, stripped and taken from the eye feather of a peacock's tail
Hackle: steely blue gamecock wound on at the head or from head to shoulder
Whisks: several strands of the same hackle
Hook: 14–16

The quill body is probably the most useful, but if no quill is available dark rabbit fur or rabbit mixed with mole fur can be used as dubbings. The Blue Upright is generally used when olives are about. If the hackle is a little darker it can well stand in for B.W.O. or an iron blue. A very versatile fly.

Blue-Winged Olive Known for short as the B.W.O., the natural blue-winged olive (*Ephemerella ignita*) is a largish olive which floats downstream with its rather larger than usual wings cocked a little forward – with a little practice, not all that difficult to recognise. On the chalk streams they seem to hatch mostly at spinner time, in the evening, but in many spate rivers they are up during the day.

There are problems about the B.W.O.; everyone has tied lifelike artificials yet for some reason the trout may only take them occasionally and at some times not at all. Many fishermen have given up exact imitation and simply offer a Beacon Beige, Red Quill, Pheasant Tail, or Blue Upright when the B.W.O. are hatching.

For purists there are good dressings to be had from Halford, West, and others. One of the more attractive is David Jacques':

Body: yellow ostrich herl covered with olive coloured plastic, well-stretched
Wings: two pairs from the wing feathers of a coot
Tying silk: hot orange
Hook: 14

Jacques had grounds for believing that Skues' faith in the value of an Orange Quill during the hatch of B.W.O. cannot be sustained, and is only of value when the spent is on the water – a belief which seems to be confirmed by Goddard's underwater photography in *The Trout and The Fly*, Benn (1980). These underwater photographs of the spent show a distinct orange tone which might well match up with the Orange Quill.

Interestingly enough, the experimental pattern of the B.W.O. tied by Dr J.C. Mottram, probably around the year 1910 or earlier, was a forerunner of the principle incorporated by Peter Deane in his Shadow Mayfly in 1950. These odd-looking shadow flies can be effective. This is Mottram's dressing:

Body: none
Hackles: grey cock hackled from head to tail
Whisks: grey cock
Wings: two grey hackle points set upright
Hook: 14 or 16

Borgie The River Borgie is a mere seven miles long, running into Torrisdale Bay on the north coast of Caithness, however those seven miles provide some fine fly fishing. Spinning and worming are forbidden. Strutt and Parker let rods and the Borgie Lodge Hotel at Skerray provides accommodation. There are three main beats, with two rods on a beat, reached by a forestry road which runs almost the whole length of the river. New pools have been made in recent years and a hatchery built. Like all Highland salmon rivers it needs the right height of water to fish well.

Bourne Remember this line in the famous speech by Hamlet?

. . . The undiscovered country from whose bourn
No traveller returns . . .

Bourn or bourne means frontier, in most cases a frontier river. *Bartholemew's Gazeteer* lists 19 bournes from Bourne End to Bournemouth, but the only one that matters to a fly fisherman is Plunket Green's Bourne, a miniature chalk stream tributary of the Test immortalised in *Where The Bright Waters Meet*, Harry Plunkett Green (Philip Allan, 1924).

It is possible to get a rod from time to time on this water near Hurstbourne Priors. Enquire locally. It is not stocked, or was not until recently, and provides some of the most delicate and difficult fishing imaginable. In memory of Plunket Greene, fish a winged iron blue, size 16.

There is another Bourne, a small tributary of the Salisbury Avon, now inclined to dry up in the upper reaches in a hot summer because of abstraction, therefore, known as a winterbourne.

Bowlker, Richard and Charles These were the two best known columnists and angling writers of the mid-and late-1700s, joint authors of *The Art of Angling* (1747), the first edition written by Richard, the second by his son Charles. They were extraordinarily skilled fly fishers and fly dressers. This is Bowlker on the mayfly (*E. danica*):

Comes down the water about the twentieth of May, is of short duration, not lasting above nine to ten days. He is a large and beautiful fly, which both fish and birds are very fond of . . .

When these flies are in perfection, the fish refuse all other sorts and take these only. His wings are made of the feather of the grey drake, or rather the grey feathers of a wild mallard dyed yellow; the body is made of the yellow wool of a ram or wether; his body is ribbed with a dark brown, for which no feather does so well as the hackle of a bittern; it likewise makes the legs very artificially; his head is of a dark brown, made of a peacock's harle, and his tail with the hair of a fitchew's [polecat's] tail, the hook number 6.

It is of interest that the head of the fly was copied by the Bowlkers – one had the impression that Halford was the first fly dresser to do this – and that the angler was instructed always to fish the mayfly upstream:

[they] ought to be thrown about half a yard above the head of the fish, as they all swim gradually down the water . . .

The Bowlkers gave pretty accurate patterns of the mayfly nymph, dun and spinner, which are similar to many in use today. Heddon regards the Bowlkers' work as one of the great landmarks of angling literature, containing the foundation of modern fly dressing.

It must be remembered that Bowlker used a horsehair line and with this advocated throwing against or under the wind in preference to with it, which was the more usual method. His flies included the Blue Dun, the Palmer Worm which he thought was an imitation of a hairy caterpillar, and for salmon fishing a dragonfly pattern.

Bridges, Antony Now out of print, *Bridges' Modern Salmon Fishing* (Black, 1939, reprinted 1947), was an invaluable reference book which dealt with methods of fly, bait and spinning for salmon; with chapters on tackle and casting, and useful tables on the calculation of fish weights from body measurements and comparisons of the Pennell and Redditch hook sizes. Bridges' advice on strategy and tactics is as useful now as it ever was and in many ways a good deal more valuable and clear than in several later books on the salmon.

Bridgett, R.C. A Scottish schoolmaster, angling correspondent of *The Glasgow Herald*, author of several fishing books, including *Loch Fishing in Theory and Practice* (1924), and three others, *Dry Fly Fishing*, *By Loch and Stream*, and *Tight Lines*, which are published, undated, by Herbert Jenkins. All useful books but slightly schoolmasterish prose:

My chief purpose is to make known the virtues of the dry fly to Scottish anglers and others, whose great privilege it is to fish streams of cheerful flow; to show them how to take trout with the fly both from the sparkling currents and the placid pools, not only in spring, but also in the height of summer, not under cover of darkness but in the happier sunlight.

Brook Trout (*Salvelinus fontinalis*) The American brook trout, technically a member of the char family, is occasionally imported into Britain for lake or reservoir fishing, and is sometimes crossed with brown and rainbow trout, but does not as yet seem to be of major interest.

Brown Trout The brown trout of the Test, the silver sea trout of Devon, the gillaroo of Ireland, the sewin of Wales, belong to the same species, the brown trout (*Salmo trutta*). Although suspected as far back as 1860 it was not until the 1960s that scientists finally agreed that the differences in appearances were imposed by habit and environment.

S. trutta is native to Europe, parts of western Russia, Turkey, and North Africa, and has been established artificially from about 1863 onwards in many other countries, including New Zealand, Australia, North and South America, India and large parts of Africa. **Sources:** *The Trout*, W.E. Frost and M.E. Brown, Collins, *The New Naturalist Series*, 1967.

Brora A small Highland spate river on the east coast of Sutherland which has a reasonable run of salmon at times. It has good fly water, mostly private, but enquiries at the estate office may produce a rod. Small flies are best, mostly on a sink tip line.

Buchan, John A great fly fisherman, John Buchan wrote one of the best of all poaching stories, *John Macnab*, as well as many romantic adventure stories featuring Richard Hannay: *The Thirty Nine Steps*, *Greenmantle*, *The Three Hostages*, and others. He was for many years an MP and, as Lord Tweedsmuir, Governor-General of Canada.

Bucknell, Geoffrey Blagdon, Chew and other reservoirs feature in Geoffrey Bucknall's *Fly Fishing Tactics on Still Water* (Muller, 1966). He deals with boat and bank fishing, buzzers, sedge flies and olives, floating and sunk line tactics, and though the rods he recommended are now out of date the tactics are not.

Bumbles A Derbyshire pattern of trout fly, made use of by Halford, revived and redesigned by the Irish judge T.C. Kingsmill Moore, in his book, *A Man May Fish* (Jenkins, 1960) and in the new and enlarged edition, with a foreword by Hugh Falkus, published by Colin Smythe, in 1979.

The Bumbles, [wrote Kingsmill Moore], are general patterns for loch fishing which suggest surface life without any attempt at imitation. They must be translucent, have a certain amount of gleam, gentle contrasts, and must suggest the movement of insects caught in the surface film or blown by the wind. On Irish lochs they are generally fished on the drift.

A Man May Fish has been praised as one of the best books ever written about Irish fishing. Kingsmill Moore's dressing of the most popular bumble patterns, the Golden Olive is:

Body: golden olive seals' fur, ribbed fine oval gold tinsel
Tail: upturned golden pheasant crest
Body hackles: two cock hackles, one dyed golden olive, the other dun or medium red, palmered together down the body from head to tail, held in place by the gold rib
Shoulder hackle: a long flicker of blue jay

The Golden Olive was supposed to have a hint of green in it, a mimosa colour dipped in green chartreuse, so that if the golden olive hackle does not give that impression the dun or red hackle might be exchanged for one dyed light green. The Flyfishers' Club in London has a collection of the original dressings.

Butcher An admirable wet fly for lake fishing and downstream river fishing which was designed at least 150 years ago. Courtney Williams wrote:

The Butcher is said to have been invented by a Mr Jewhurst of Tunbridge Wells, Kent, in association with a Mr Moon, a butcher of that town. Originally known as 'Moon's Fly' it received its present name about 1838, probably on account of its connection with the 'purveyor of meat' mentioned above and possibly also because of its colouring, the red tag suggesting raw beef and the wings the traditional blue apron of a butcher.

George M. Kelson (1895) also mentioned a Mr Jewhurst in connection with the Butcher. On the other hand might it not have been Mr Dewhurst?

Whatever the origin it is a remarkably effective fly, even more so, according to Robin Lemon (*West Country Fly Fishing*, edited by Anne Voss Bark, Batsford), as a stillwater fly if the wings are taken off, as with T.C. Ivens and the alder. The standard dressing:

Body: flat silver tinsel sometimes ribbed with fine silver wire
Tail: originally red ibis, now more often red or scarlet floss
Beard hackle: black hen or cock
Wings: two matching slips of the blue-black feathers from a mallard drake's wing, excluding those with white tips
Hook: for delicate work on clear-water lakes down to 14 but up to 10 or 8 for night sea trout fishing
Variations: the Bloody Butcher has the same dressing but a scarlet hackle. The Kingfisher Butcher a gold body, orange hackle and fibres from a kingfishers' wing as a tail.

Buzzer Another name for a *Chironomid*, a long-legged gnat-like insect with a humped thorax, a long abdomen, and wings that are often slightly shorter than the body. The angler's name for them is derived either from their habit of buzzing around over the water surface or possibly because in a large swarm they do make a faint buzzing sound. (*See* Midge on page 136.)

Drag

I have often been accused in my method of greased line fishing for salmon of letting the fly drift downstream motionless, having got rid of all drag; but when you can see the fly you will see that every little eddy it floats down through gives the fly little twists and movement, just the same as some live insect would do, and that is one of the reasons why I wish to avoid what you call drag, and although the fly may be passing across the stream and downstream at the same time it behaves in a very natural way and there is no tension on the line.

A.H.E. Wood of Cairnton, in a letter published in *The Floating Line*, Anthony Crossley, Methuen, 1939

It all depends what you mean by drag.

Antony Bridges, *Modern Salmon Fishing*, A and C Black, 1939

C

Caddis The larva of the caddis or sedge fly, the best known of some 200 species being those that live in small tubes on the river bed which they construct from grains of sand, wood, plants or other tiny pieces of detritus. When the larva is fully developed it seals up the case and turns into a pupa which remains in the cocoon and inactive for some time, perhaps weeks, perhaps months, depending on conditions and on the species. When ready, it bites open the case and rises through the water to hatch, either from the surface or from a stick or rush on which it climbs until ready to change.

Trout feed on the pupae rising to the surface, on the freshly-emerged fly, and on the female flies while returning to the water to lay their eggs. **Sources include:** J.R. Harris, Martin Mosely, John Goddard and David Jacques.

Caenis Lake fishermen will sometimes find dozens of tiny white flies settling on their coats and hats towards sunset. They are known by a number of names, i.e. Caenis, White Midge, Anglers' Curse or White Broadwings. They belong to the Caenis species and are the smallest of all the ephemeropteran flies. Their wings are broad and very white, they have long tails and a stumpy body. They hatch in enormous numbers. Goddard's Last Hope is a useful fly when the curse is on the water but the hatch is often so numerous that one artificial in the midst of millions of the natural insect does not always stand much chance. Some anglers give up, and when trout are cruising round the lake souping up caenis, will fish a large lure.

Camel Holidaymakers at the little picturesque port of Padstow in North Cornwall who enjoy watching the fishing boats come into the stone-walled harbour may not know that this is the estuary of the River Camel, a small river with a good run of sea trout and some salmon. Tickets to fish the Camel for trout and sea trout can be had from fishing associations at Wadebridge, Liskeard and Bodmin. Ask at tackle shops. Fishing is mostly worm or spinner as the river is heavily bushed.

Caperer One of many sedges with hairy roof-shaped wings which are so similar to each other that unless you are an entomologist you may not be able to decide whether this is a caperer, a cinnamon sedge, or half a dozen others of a very large family of flies. The natural fly is reddish or cinnamon in colour and widespread and one reason why it is so popular is that the name is easily remembered. William Lunn's Caperer is a very good artificial:

Abdomen: strands from a dark turkey tail twisted on crimson tying silk
Mid-abdomen: two swan feathers, dyed yellow, to form a yellow band halfway along the body
Thorax: more strands of dark turkey as on the abdomen
Wings: coot or landrail substitute dyed chocolate brown and tied roof-shape close to the body
Hackle: red and black cock tied in front of the wings
Hook: 12 or 14 are usual, larger if bigger sedges are moving

The best, certainly the most evocative, advice about fishing the caperer is given by J.W. Hills in *A Summer on the Test* (1924):

On days when the river is as burnished metal, when the thinnest gut looks like a blind-cord, when you reduce your flies smaller and smaller but still the insolent trout disregard your almost invisible badger smuts and houghton rubies; why then, reel in and knot on your biggest caperer. Do not be afraid. Never mind that not one of the real insects is to be seen; never mind that the trout are obviously taking spinners; never mind that so heavy a fly falls with a sickening thump on the polished stillness of the water; never mind that to your eye as you stoop and blink anxiously along the glittering surface this great fly seems as unpalatable as an autumn leaf or the feather of a cock turkey; never mind all that, for you may be sure it will not have floated far before a trout will have gulped it, if there be a trout within reach. And then, oh my brother, oh my erring brother, do not behave as I always do and strike too soon.

Carey A small Devon stream, a tributary of the Tamar, with wild brown trout of between $\frac{1}{4}$–$\frac{1}{2}$lb that give excellent upstream fishing. There are occasional deep pools, good shallow runs and riffles, and nice picnic places in spring on banks lined with wild daffodils. All the Devon flies do well, and a dry Coachman, Blue Upright and Pheasant Tail are among the best. The Arundell Arms at Lifton has water.

Carter Platts, W. For many years angling editor of *The Yorkshire Post*, and author of *Modern Trout Fishing* (A and C Black, 1938). Platts had strong views:

To the liberal-minded angler there can be no more objection to fishing the maggot as a hook bait, than to the same use of a worm. It is the prodigal use of ground bait, to which the maggot fisher is often addicted, that is the bone of bitter contention between him and the fly fisher. From the ethical point of view alone, ground-baiting for trout is abhorrent to the soul of the fly fisher; he places it on the same level as throwing down a handful of corn to attract a covey of partridges and then blazing into the brown.

Cassley The Sutherland river made famous by Edward Grey (Viscount Grey of Fallodon) who fished the Rosehall beat for many years around the end of the nineteenth century and left a vivid account of what it was like in the classic, *Fly Fishing* (Dent, 1899, revised edition, 1930). Beats on Grey's water can be obtained through the Achness House Hotel, Rosehall.

Casting

I would say it is more difficult to make a decent cast than a century against the Australians. (C.B. Fry.) *See* opposite.

Catch and Release

These fish are too valuable to be caught only once. (*Lee Wulff*)

Catch and release, a principle pioneered by Lee Wulff in the 1930s, became necessary on many American rivers during the following 20 or 30 years to avoid the stock of wild fish being wiped out. Fly fishing in America is virtually free fishing in a large number of areas. All that is needed is a state licence to fish which costs something between ten to 25 dollars for a whole season. In most cases there were no restrictions on the size of fish that could be taken and no catch limits. Consequently, an unlimited number of fishermen were taking

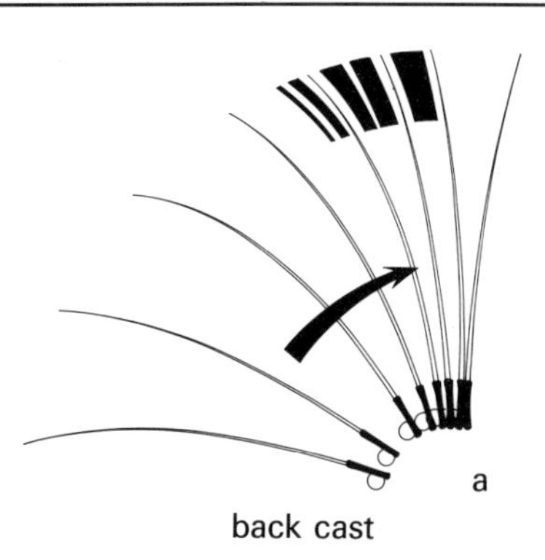

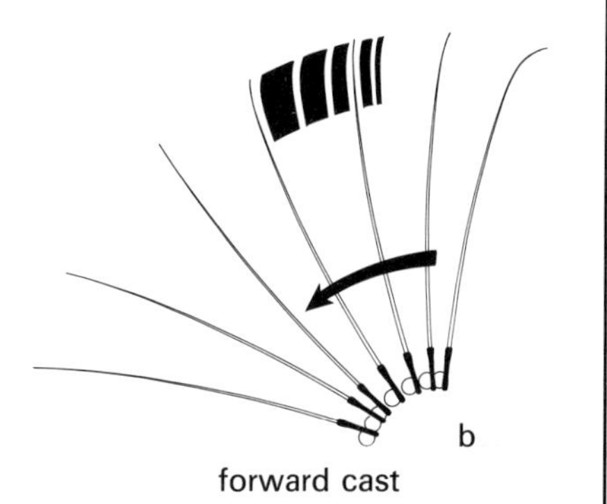

Casting. The task of the fisherman is to activate the spring of the rod and it is the rod, not the fisherman, which casts the fly.

Figure A shows the rod lifting the line off the water for the overhead cast and the dark areas show where the maximum power is applied. *Figure B* shows the forward cast. The rod is moved forward with the increase in power in the darkened area where the final power stroke or 'flick' of the rod is applied.

Casting faults are: too much wrist action, application of power stroke too soon or too late, jerky movements, reaching forward on the forward cast in an attempt to 'throw' the fly, gripping the rod too fiercely.

Line velocity can be improved by the use of the free hand hauling on the line either on the back cast alone – the single haul – or on both back and forward casts – the double haul

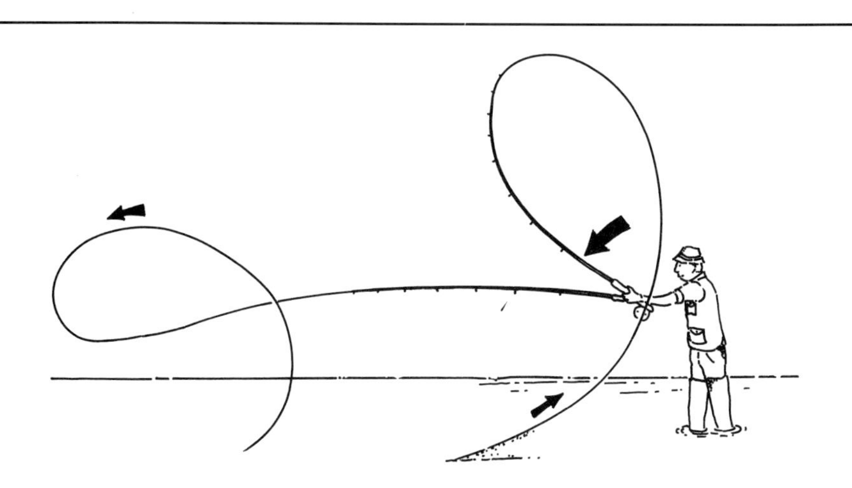

The roll cast

The Roll Cast In a sense a natural flip of the line which has many uses, being part of the action of a Spey cast (see p. 185). This shows the overhead roll cast in which the loop of line is brought behind the angler and then a power stroke of the rod sends it rolling out again. Not easy to show on paper and needs practice and a good teacher preferably a fully qualified professional.

home as many trout as they could carry, for sale or for the freezer. No river could stand that kind of pressure for long.

The various chapters (branches) of a conservation society, Trout Unlimited, brought pressure to bear on the state authorities who then declared a number of rivers or sections of rivers to be no-kill areas. This meant barbless hooks had to be used and all trout caught had to be immediately released.

The restrictions were successful. Adequate stocks of wild fish were restored. Many anglers now practise catch and release from habit, or on principle, whether or not they are fishing a no-kill area. It is said that on public water on a famous river, such as the Beaverkill in the Catskills, trout may well have been caught and released 14 or 15 times. They become more difficult to deceive. Fishermen pride themselves on taking the most difficult and wary fish.

Some exponents of catch and release net their fish or pick them out of the water by hand before releasing them but the most favoured method is to use barbless hooks and release them under water without the trout being handled at all.

No-handling is becoming more popular as scientific studies suggested that handling and netting both caused damage which might either shorten the fish's life or inhibit growth. Catch and release has been practised on one or two British fisheries and abandoned because of the damage caused to trout by handling.

Chess A small trout stream rising near Chesham in Buckinghamshire and flowing into the Colne near Rickmansworth. It was reported at one time that rainbow trout were breeding on the Chess but this does not seem in 1984 to have been confirmed: if they do breed they do not appear to be a self-maintained population.

Latimer Park Lakes, a well-run and well-stocked fishery has both lake and river fishing.

Chetham, James A seventeenth-century fisherman who came from Smedley near Manchester. Author of *An Angler's Vade Mecum* (1681) which owes a good deal to Cotton and Barker but produced some interesting patterns of flies for spate rivers (stoney rivers he called them), he was the first angling writer, so far as is known, who used a starling's quill feather for winging – an improvement on the mallard used by Barker and Cotton. He was meticulous in giving his dressings:

Little Blue Dun. Made of the Down of a Mouse for Body and Head, dub'd with sad Ash-coloured silk; Wings of the sad-coloured Feather of a Sheepstare's Quill.
Note, that the Feather got from the Quills or Pens of Sheepstares Wings, Throstle Wings, Fieldfare Wings, are generally better (the first 2 especially) to use for Dub-fly Wings than those got from a wild Mallard or Drake.

Sheepstare is the old name for a starling. Sad means dark-coloured.

Chetham also had a good dressing of the Black Gnat, probably derived from Cotton and Barker:

Black Midge or Gnat: Made of the Down of a Mole, Dub'd with Black Silk, Wings of the light grey feather of a Sheepstare's Quill.

The dressing is a basic one and has survived to this day. G.E.M. Skues has something like it. Halford certainly had similar dressings to many of Chetham's whose Blue Dun is an improvement on Cotton's, though all these old writers used dubbing which nowadays we would find difficulty in getting – such as hair from black greyhounds and old foxes. This is one of Chetham's:

Blue Dun. Made of the Down of a Water-Mouse and the Blewish dun of an Old Fox mixt together, Dub'd with sad Ash-coloured Silk; Wings of the Feather of a Sheepstare Quill.

Chetham in all his patterns was most concerned to imitate the natural insect as closely as possible, and in the second edition of his book (1689) made a point of saying that 'the fly is always to be on the very surface or top of the water'. **Source:** Chetham quotation from Jack Heddon's *A Brief History of The Floating Fly*, ms., 1982.

Chew The River Chew in North Somerset near Pensford is coloured and slow flowing but holds quite a reasonable stock of wild brown trout which are frequently wormed but will certainly take a nymph put to a bulging fish under the willows. Several fishing clubs have water and a good place is Bond's Bridge at Chew Magna.

Chew Valley Lake One of the 'big three' reservoirs (with Grafham and Rutland), Chew Valley Lake, 10 miles south of Bristol, covers 1200 acres and was opened in 1957. On the bank of the lake, at Woodford Lodge, there are tackle and changing rooms. Chew has car parks for the crowds that arrive for the opening of the season and there are power boats for fishing the drift. The total average catch for a season is around 20,000 fish and most anglers use fairly large minnow-type lures. There is a sailing club and a nature reserve.

Chironomid *See* Midge on page 136.

Cholomondeley-Pennell An Inspector of Sea Fisheries in the 1870s for a number of years, Cholomondeley–Pennell was a great all-round fisherman and his publications include *The Modern Practical Angler*, *The Sporting Fish of Great Britain*, and *Modern Improvements of Fishing Tackle and Fish Hooks*. He also edited the Badminton Library book, *Fishing*. Today he is probably best remembered for the Pennell series of trout flies.

Church, Bob A Midland tackle dealer who was among the pioneers of deep lure fishing on reservoirs in the 1960s onwards. Colin Dyson ghosted Church's book, *Reservoir Trout Fishing*, first published by Cassell in 1977, reprinted in 1978. The book was so popular A and C Black produced a second edition in 1983.

Brian Clarke

Clark, (James) Brian A professional journalist, later an industrial communications specialist, Clark has been absorbed all his life by what he once wrote of as 'the loveliness of light and water and trees and birds, and the separated, drowned-music mystery of fishes.' A prolific writer on angling and other subjects, and a regular broadcaster and photographer. Author of *The Pursuit of Stillwater Trout* (1975) which, helped to rehabilitate the art of imitative fishing on lakes. In 1980, with John Goddard, he published *The Trout and the Fly*, a detailed study of the trout which was described by Richard Walker as 'likely to prove to be the most important contribution to the literature of trout fishing this century.' Both books ran to several printings and translations. Clarke is angling correspondent of *The Sunday Times* and has contributed to a number of fly-fishing anthologies.

Coachman A most useful general pattern fly which takes fish on rivers and lakes, fished wet or dry, for most of the season. What it represents is uncertain, possibly a beetle or one of the dipterans.

The origin of the Coachman is obscure. It is often attributed to Tom Bosworth, coachman to the Prince Regent and the young Queen Victoria, and as the Prince Regent and his father were said to be interested in fly fishing it could be so; however, *Salter's Angling Guide* (1814) says:

> There is a fly used very much at Watford in Herts called Harding's Fly or the Coachman's; the merits of such flies experience will teach us how to appreciate.

The river would probably be the Colne which must then have been a fine trout stream, but whether Mr Harding or Mr Bosworth first tied the Coachman, or whether both tied a Coachman, remains unresolved. The standard pattern is:

Body: green peacock herl twisted in with the tying silk
Wings: two slips of white feather, swan or goose, upright for the dry fly, sloping back for the wet
Hackle: medium red cock
Hook: sizes vary according to how the fly is to be fished, from size 16 for a dry fly on a clear stream to 8 or 6, sometimes weighted, for stillwater and sea trout wet fly fishing

The white wing has great advantage for it can easily be seen, by the fish when fished wet, by the angler when fished dry. The Coachman, with variations, appears on many rivers world wide. In America, there is a Royal Coachman with a purple body, gold twist and a fluff of peacock herl at the tail.

Coch-Y-Bondhu A trout fly that imitates a Welsh beetle. Courtney Williams gives this dressing as standard:

Body: two or three strands of copper-coloured peacock herl twisted together with the tying silk for strength with two turns of flat gold tinsel as a tag
Hackle: Coch-Y-Bondhu, that is to say a cock feather with a black centre and a red list (red border)
Hook: 14–12

The Cochy is a good general beetle pattern and is not far off from others, such as Dr Terry's and Horsfall Turner's.

Collyer, David J. A regular column on fly-dressing in *Trout Fisherman* magazine gave David Collyer a reputation as one of the most inventive fly-dressers of the 1970s and 1980s. He is the author of *Fly-Dressing I* and *Fly-Dressing II*, both published by David and Charles, which give the details of the tying of a considerable number of patterns from chalk-stream dry flies to salmon and tubes and traditional feather wings.

Colquhoun, John Author of *The Moor and the Loch* (1840) which gives two fly patterns for lake fishing which quite possibly were forerunners of the Mallard and Claret and the Teal and Red. The first had a dark mallard wing and a brown mohair body, the second a teal wing with a claret mohair.

Connemara Black An import from Ireland which has been widely adopted as a reservoir and sea trout fly and deservedly so. With the wing level with the body and not cocked, the fly gives the impression of many larvae and pupae for lake fishing, either from the bank or fishing the drift. For stillwater fishermen, the Connemara is one of the best of the traditional general wet fly patterns:

Body: black wool or floss ribbed with fine oval silver tinsel
Wings: bronze mallard tied close to the body
Whisks: very small golden pheasant crest, up-turning to the wing
Hackle: black cock, dressed beard, with a tip of blue feather fibres in front, both dressed sparse; in the original dressing the blue feather was blue jay
Hook sizes: 14–10 for lake trout, larger for sea trout

Conon There is a Conon in Skye but the main salmon river of that name is in Ross and Cromarty, coming down from Loch Luichart over the great cascades of the Falls of Conon and on out into the Cromarty Firth. The Fairburn Estate has water and so have Cononbridge Hotel and Strathgarve Lodge Hotel.

Conversion Tables *See* page 237.

Conway Now spelt on the maps in true Welsh style as the Conwy, this is one of the best Welsh salmon rivers, with a famous fishing hotel the Gwydyr, at Betws-y-coed, Gwynedd, which has some 15 miles of good water.

Corixa A stillwater beetle, varying in size, often known as a water boatman or a lesser water boatman, but not to be confused with those gyrating surface insects which are water skaters. The corixidae have oar-like back legs which they use to shoot up to the surface fast for a drop of air and back again in their weed bed, jiggling about a good deal both ways. Some entomologist-anglers say trout do not eat corixa, some say they do. It may depend on the species or on the trout. The Chomper flies designed by Richard Walker may suggest corixa. Goddard and many others have devised patterns. This one is fairly standard:

Body: white floss silk, nicely rounded, over fine lead wire
Rib: fine silver wire
Wing cases: a bunch of dark mallard fibres tied fore and aft
Beard: hackle: a few fibres of grouse
Hook: 10–12

Costa The third and less well-known of the Yorkshire chalk streams – the other two being the Driffield and the Foston becks – this is a well-loved little river, quite narrow, which provides some excellent trout fishing.

Its origins are at Keld Head, Pickering, in North Yorkshire, and due to careful maintenance of the Pickering Club is once again regaining some of its former glory. The Costa, was always a favourite of that great angling writer, Eric Horsfall Turner, who in the years prior to his death could be found on most days stalking the butter-yellow-bellied trout of this little chalk stream. Such was his love of this water that plans are afoot to provide a bankside memorial to his memory. (H. Donald Overfield, 1984.)

Cotton, Charles (1630–1687) Translator, poet, fisherman, country squire, friend of Izaak Walton, author of the second part of *The Compleat Angler* in the fifth edition (1676). One of the best books about Cotton is *Charles Cotton and his River*, Gerald G.P. Heywood, Sherratt and Hughes (1928). Heywood's research into the Peak District, the River Dove, Charles Cotton's house at Beresford Dale and the Fishing House is unrivalled.

Cotton is believed to have studied at Cambridge. In 1658 he inherited the estates of Beresford and Bentley on the Staffordshire and Derbyshire borders. He learned his fly fishing as a boy, when he fished the Dove as it ran through the grounds of Beresford Hall, his father's house. But it was not until he was over 40 that he wrote the famous addition to Walton's *Compleat Angler*.

The dressings of 65 flies are given by Cotton. Many of them, with some

Charles Cotton – from a painting by permission of the National Portrait Gallery, London

variations, are in use today. He recommended casting a fly across the river or else up or down, according to the wind. The rod was a flexible 17ft with a tapered horsehair line some 3ft longer. Cotton's list of flies and instructions for dressings are given by Laurie.

Curse For the Angler's Curse, *see* Caenis, *also* Smut.

Cutcliffe, H.C. A surgeon whose home was at South Molton, Devon. While on active service as a doctor in India Cutcliffe wrote a book about fishing the Mole and the Bray in Devon. His book, *Trout Fishing in Rapid Streams* (1863) is notable for the elaborate details which he gives on fly-tying in the Devon style. He advocated the use of hackle flies fished upstream either on or just below the surface of the water. **Sources:** Laurie's *A Reference Book of English Trout Flies*, Pelham Books, 1967; Anne Voss Bark's *West Country Fly Fishing*, Batsford, 1983.

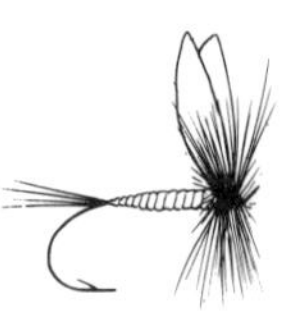

The Dry Fly

In all the long history of fly fishing there has been no change so great as the introduction of dry fly fishing. Until it came we fished much as our ancestors did in the 17th Century. Rods had been improved, certainly, but were in principle unaltered; the use of gut instead of hair had added a convenience; the invention of the reel modified the way of playing a fish; but the dry fly was more than all put together. It altered both the practice and the temperament of the angler. It called different qualities into request . . .

Its charm lies partly in the fact that all moves in the game are visible. Nothing is hid. When the fly comes over him you see him prepare to take it – or treat it with stolid indifference. You see him rise and take. The whole drama is played out before your eyes.

. . . Casting, too, has its fascination. Whenever the fish may be rising, your fly sails over him, hardly touching the water, wings up, floating like a cork, following every crinkle of the slow current. You gain an extraordinary sense of power. Your rod and line, right down to the fly, are part of yourself, moved by your nerves and answering to your brain.

John Waller Hills, *A History of Fly Fishing for Trout*, Philip Allen and Co., 1921

The change of upstream fishing was – and still is for every beginner – the real dividing line in trout fishing, the revolutionary event to overshadow all others.

Datus C. Proper, *What The Trout Said*, Alfred A. Knopf, New York, 1982

Daddy Longlegs The crane fly, a terrestrial, is avidly taken by trout when blown onto the water during August. Sometimes the trout will attempt to drown the bigger struggling flies before eating them, which means a strike on the second rise or when the fly line moves. There are a number of Daddy patterns, one of the main ones is Richard Walker's:

Body: veniard plastic mayfly
Wings: light ginger hackle points, tied spent (badger as an alternative)
Legs: six long strands of black horsehair or nylon knotted and tied to lie backwards along the body
Hackle: a collar of light red cock, six turns
Hook: up eye 10 or 12

The Parachute Daddy by Peter Deane is an interesting illusion fly:

Body: white nylon floss with the end projecting upwards behind the eye
Hackle: dark brown cock with fibres from $\frac{1}{2}$in. to $\frac{3}{4}$in. long (13mm–18mm approximately) tied parachute style round the projecting end of the white floss, leaving a flare of white floss visible overall.
Tail: half a dozen fibres of dark brown cock, tied rather long
Hook: 10 or 12 longshank

The upstanding white floss over the hackle gives this fly good visibility at a distance. Walker and Deane's patterns can be fished inert in or on the surface, occasionally twitched, sometimes moved on a long draw, like a wake fly.

Damselfly A smaller cousin of the dragonfly, the damselfly is more popular with lake fishermen because when plenty are about the trout feed well on the nymph, and the artificial nymph is smaller and more easily handled than imitations of the big dragon nymph. Most of the adult damsels are a vivid blue but the nymphs are darker, almost olive-green, sometimes slightly yellow.

Trout leap at the egg-laying adults but the nymph is the favourite. One of the best designs is Peter Lapsley's:

Hook: 8–10 longshank
Tying silk: brown, buff or yellow
Underbody: 10 to 14 turns of fine wire under the thorax (optional)
Tail: three cock pheasant tail feather fibre points, tied short
Abdomen: pale green seals' fur ribbed with fine oval gold tinsel
Thorax: pale green seals' fur
Wing cases: brown feather fibre
Legs: one turn of grey partridge, clipped short on the top by the wing case

An interesting point about the damselfly nymph is that it may well give an impression of a free-swimming sedge pupa in addition to what it is intended to represent, as can be seen in the illustrations drawn from life by C.F. Walker in his *Lake Flies and Their Imitation*. Standard patterns of the damselfly are not infrequently taken when there are sedge hatching but not a damsel in sight. The damsel, therefore, might well be in business as a general pattern of underwater insects, representing at least two of the most popular ones.

The natural nymph swims with a pronounced wriggle but the fact that the artificial cannot suggest this movement does not seem to put the trout off.

Peter Lapsley points out that one can easily distinguish between a dragonfly and a damselfly. The damselfly folds its wings over its body when at rest, the dragonfly leaves them wide open and flat, at right angles to the body.

Dapping Fishing the dap on Irish and Scottish stillwaters (loch in Scotland, lough in Ireland) is a highly effective way of taking salmon and trout. On the big Irish loughs the dap is highly prized during the mayfly season. The Irish traditionally use two live mayflies impaled on a hook, but in recent years the habit is being slowly abandoned in favour of large bushy palmer tied on a 6 or 8 longshank hook.

The dap is always fished on the drift, generally by two anglers rowed by a ghillie who selects the drift and keeps to it, sometimes fishing himself if the others encourage him to do so. The rod should be about 15ft long. To the ordinary reel-line some 10 yards of nylon monofilament is attached and at the end of this about six to eight yards of light floss. A nylon leader of about three or four feet long is attached to the end of the floss line (the blow line) with a palmer fly at the point.

The boat drifts with the wind and the flies are dapped in front of the boat at the end of the blow line. The trick is to try and keep the fly bouncing about close to the wave-tops without sinking it, at the same time moving the fly from side to side by gentle movements of the rod.

It is, in effect, fishing a dry fly slightly above the water surface, making the fish jump for it.

In Scotland it is a deadly way of taking sea trout on lochs such as Maree and Hope. It is the practice for one of the boat party to fish the dap and the other to fish wet fly. If the trout rising to the dap misses it the wet fly fisher covers the place at once with his wet fly in the hope that the trout is still looking for what it missed. At Altnaharra on Loch Hope they swear by the Willie Ross.

A fine description of the dap on Loch Maree comes from Geoffrey Snutch:

Dapping, like warfare, consists of long periods of inactivity with brief moments of intense excitement. I recall one long day without a single rise to the fly, and then a 6½ pounder and a 5½ pounder, and another lost in the last 45 minutes before the ghillie's 'going home time' at 5 p.m. Long light rods are ideal, with 200yds of nylon monofil, on a salmon reel, and a 'blow line' best made of grey nylon knitting wool.

Flies are varied in size according to wave height, but generally are very large and fluffy, up to a teacup size, and are dressed on fine wire salmon hooks. Essentially they must dance very lightly over the surface before the breeze and remain completely dry. A sodden fly raises no trout. Dressings consist mainly of very large hackles palmered down the shank of the hook, tapering to the bend. Combinations of natural hackle colours are used such badger and grizzles, but a popular fly is the Maree Favourite, composed of alternate dyed blue and black hackles. Possibly the best killer is an all-black fly, in a selection of sizes, and sporting a small but distinct red tail tied at the bend.

Apart from keeping the fly dry and on the wave, other essentials to dapping success are intense concentration and a very slow strike. A few seconds loss of attention, or an involuntary pull on seeing the trout rise to the fly, will pile up the missed offers. Anyone who thinks dapping consists of dozing in the boat has not done any.

Dark Watchet A trout fly of the northern streams, invaluable on rivers like the Wharfe in Yorkshire. It may suggest a nymph or a drowned iron blue, for it is almost invariably fished wet, upstream. The Dark Watchet is a puzzling fly for the fly-dresser because there are several patterns, some more hackled than winged, similar to the Bloas. This may be a compromise:

Body: two or three turns of bright scarlet silk showing at the tail, the rest dubbed lightly with mole's fur
Wings: dark coot or blackbird, lying well back
Hackle and whisks: dark blue cock
Head: scarlet silk
Hook: 14 or 16

It is of interest that on rivers like the Wharfe the flies – iron blues and olives – invariably hatch quickly and rarely ride the stream as the flies do on the chalk streams. The dry fly is therefore of much less importance. If the trout are seen rising they may well be taking nymph which, on these stony rivers, move fast. A Dark Watchet cast just above the rise and pulled in fast will generally provoke a take if the fish is still in position. Otherwise the Watchet can be fished inert on the drift just below the surface.

Dart Among the loveliest of Devon rivers, the Dart is one of many streams that rise among the great peat beds of Dartmoor. In the upper reaches it begins by being two streams, the East and West Dart, which provide delicate and exciting fly fishing as they wind their way through pools and rapids, high granite boulders, bright swathes of cotton grass and heather; gradually falling from the bleak heights of the moor towards Dartmeet, where they join and become the true Dart.

The two upper rivers, Duchy of Cornwall water, provide some of the cheapest wild brown trout fishing in England. Permits to fish the water at only a few pounds a year can be had from inns like the Forest Inn at Hexworthy and the Arundell Arms at Lifton and at some village shops and post offices.

The wild brown trout rise well to a dry fly fished in the pockets of water between the rocks, in the long glides in the curl of water under the banks. In the early season there are good hatches of March Brown and Large Dark Olive, followed later by the Olive Upright, the Blue-winged Olive and the August Dun. Popular artificials include the Hare's Ear, Pheasant Tail and Coachman. There are good articles on fishing the Dart by Mike Weaver and Charles Bingham in *West Country Fly Fishing*, edited by Anne Voss Bark (Batsford, 1983). David Barr writes:

Below Dartmeet the Dart reveals its true potential as a real salmon river, though in times of low water there are not many pools that remain fly-fishable. There is exciting fishing down to Newbridge, but the best of the Dart is to be found through Holne Chase down to Buckfastleigh, where pool is followed by pool, each one capable of holding salmon and sea trout. The Chase Pool at Holne Chase is a classic salmon pool with a low water taking-place close to its head and another lower down that is equally effective in six inches of floodwater. As has happened to nearly every river, the spring run for which the Dart was once renowned has diminished, but with rain in March and April there should still be fine fish to be caught. Between the weir at Totnes and Buckfastleigh, the local association controls most of the fishing. Above Buckfastleigh the water is almost entirely fly only – rightly so, because at the right level there is no more perfect fly water.

Davy, Sir Humphrey (1778–1829) As well as being a chemist, physicist, President of The Royal Society in 1820 and inventor of the miners' safety lamp, Penzance-born Davy was a devoted and lifelong fly fisherman who wrote happily of fishing the Colne and the Wandle, among other rivers. His description of a mayfly hatch on the Colne is frequently quoted as an example of fishing the floating fly.

Now I shall throw the drake a foot above him. It floats down and he has taken it.

Davy's mayfly dressing – he tied his own – was almost as good as anything we have today

Wings: mallard feathers dyed yellow
Body: monkeys' fur dyed yellow
Legs: olive mohair

He wrote a book on fishing, *Salmonia*, which showed a remarkable knowledge of insect life, well in advance of his time. It was written as a conversation between several fishermen rather on the lines of Walton's book but, unfortunately without Walton's charm. It is, however, still worth reading.

For my health I thank God and my ancestors; and though I do not expect like our arch patriarch Walton to number ninety years and upwards, yet I hope, as long as I can enjoy in a vernal day the warmth and light of the sunbeams, still to haunt the streams – following the example of our late venerable friend, the President of the Royal Academy, Benjamin West, in company with whom, when he was an octogenarian, I have thrown the fly, caught trout, and enjoyed a delightful day angling and social amusement, in the shady green meadows by the bright clear streams of the Wandle.

Deane, Peter Formerly in business in London, Peter Deane was commissioned into the Somerset Light Infantry early in 1940 and served in the Far East. While on leave he contracted polio and was invalided out of the army. He then set up a fly-tying business in Devon and soon established a reputation for quality and invention. His great successes include the Shadow Mayfly, Parachute Daddy Longlegs and the Beacon Beige. In spite of being confined to a wheelchair he is able to fish many rivers and is also a keen ornithologist.

Dee The Aberdeenshire Dee, about 80 miles long, rises in the Cairngorms and flows into the sea at Aberdeen on Scotland's east coast. It is one of the most attractive of salmon rivers and a great favourite of the Royal Family – their holiday home is on its banks at Balmoral. The river is notable for its spring fishing and, on this, good advice is given by John Ashley-Cooper in *A Salmon Fisher's Odyssey* (Witherby, 1982):

The river provides the most attractive fly water and it seems a shame to use anything else in it. Most people would say that small fly fishing with a floating line (as popularised by Mr. A.H.E. Wood of Cairnton in the 1920s) is the most attractive method. Though no one would deny its merits I am not sure that I altogether agree. I do find that fishing a medium-sized fly on a floating line with a sinking tip is a most enjoyable and effective method at a time when many fishermen are falling back on bait. If the water is cold I am only too glad to use a sunk line with a biggish fly . . . Few people realise how deadly a sunk fly can be in the hands of a skilled performer.

Bell Ingram of Edinburgh and Strutt and Parker of London are agents for some of the best beats but one has to wait a long time. Just above Balmoral are the Invercauld Estate waters which are very productive and are let on a weekly basis by the estate office at Braemar. The Invercauld Arms Hotel also has water for guests. The Scottish Tourist Board and Grampian Regional Council publish fishing guides; and *New Angles on Salmon Fishing* (Philip Green, Allen and Unwin, 1984) has invaluable advice on the Dee.

Dee (Welsh) A mixed fishery but there is a good salmon run at times and permits can be obtained from Bangor-on-Dee Angling Association. Most of the best water is private but the Golden Pheasant Hotel at Llwynmawr can arrange rods.

Derwent (Yorkshire) Sometimes this limestone stream gives the appearance of a chalk stream. Its trout are free-rising. There is some excellent fly fishing near Scarborough on the Derwent Angling Club water. Tickets for this long stretch of about eight miles can be obtained from tackle dealers or by hotel residents from the Hackness Grange Hotel at Hackness where they can also enjoy feeding tame rainbows in the hotel lake. Nymph fishing on the Derwent is restricted and most trout are taken on the dry fly – Greenwell, Blue Quill and Pheasant Tail.

Deveron A good salmon and sea trout river some 50 miles long in north-east Scotland which enters the sea at Banff. Bell Ingram of Edinburgh are agents for some of the best of the private fishing but beats are not easily come by. Tickets for association water can be obtained from tackle dealers at Huntley. John Ashley-Cooper records that the biggest Deveron fish weighed 61lb, caught in October, 1924, by Mrs Morrison on the Wood O'Shaws pool on the Mount Blairy water, taken on a 1½ inch fly – the biggest fish ever caught on a fly in Britain. He writes that the fish was not weighed until the day after it was caught, so its true weight might have rivalled Miss Ballantyne's 64-pounder from the Tay. **Source:** John Ashley-Cooper, *A Salmon Fisher's Odyssey*, Witherby, 1982.

Devon Lakes The best stillwater fishing in Devon is at Stafford Moor, near Winkleigh, in North Devon. It is a private fishery which issues day tickets, has a tackle shop and a fishing lodge. The trout are noted for their high quality. Reservoir fishing includes Fernworthy, near Chagford, and two adjoining lakes, Kennick and Tottiford, north of Newton Abbot. The usual large lures all take fish but small imitative patterns, especially small black flies, are likely to be more effective at times, especially on clear water lakes like Kennick.

Don Aberdeenshire is noted for its rivers and the Don is one of the most attractive, though it suffered badly from pollution and disease in the 1960s and 1970s. The Grant Arms Hotel at Moneymusk has good salmon water. The trout fishing can be excellent and some big fish are taken as the Don is a limestone stream and very fertile. Take March Brown, Dark Olives and Iron Blues with you, but the best fly for the Don trout is said to be Baigent's Brown, a large variant.

Dovedale Famous for its association with Charles Cotton and Izaak Walton, the River Dove at Dovedale, a National Trust beauty spot, is now the haunt of picnickers, paddlers and campers which makes fishing difficult and at holiday times impossible without a long walk upstream. Above and below Dovedale there is some excellent private syndicate fishing. Visiting Americans on a Walton-Cotton pilgrimage stay at the Izaak Walton Hotel at Dovedale which can provide fishing. There is an Izaak Walton museum at Shallowford Cottage in Stafford.

The Dove is a limestone stream with a good head of wild brown trout of ½lb to 1lb with a few larger fish from time to time. It has a good growth of weed and some nice hatches of olives, especially the blue-winged olive, and sedges. The river is fairly shallow and the fish take fright quickly and are inclined to desert those areas frequented by the holiday crowds.

Dovey (Dyfi) The sea trout (sewin in Wales) start to run the Dovey, as the English still think of it in spite of the Ordinance Survey, by June. There are salmon but the Dovey is really a sea trout river. As in Scotland, no Sunday fishing, and as in most of Wales a good deal of worming. Permits for association water can be had from most hotels and tackle shops but one should be careful about crowds on the pools during the height of the run. Night, early morning and late evening are best. Local flies with unlikely names are popular and it is best to try local patterns first. The best areas are around Machynlleth, Llanbrynmair and Dinas Mawddwy where the Brigands Inn has water.

Driffield Beck A beautiful chalk stream in east Yorkshire, which provides some of the best, though highly preserved, fly fishing that can be found anywhere in England. Donald Overfield says it is equal to the Test:

> The twin feeders of the Driffield Stream have their sources at the Kirkburn and the Elmswell springs due north of the market town of Driffield. They then flow southwards to join together at Poundsworth, the site of the Driffield Angling Club's superb headquarters and head-keepers house, from where they flow directly south through water meadows eventually joining the tidal river Hull.
>
> The Driffield Anglers' Club formed in 1833 is the second oldest flyfishing club in the country, the oldest being the Houghton on the River Test. The Club controls approximately twelve miles of pure chalkstream from the twin springs to the village of Wansford, from which point the stream is owned by the Golden Hill Club and then the West Beck Preservation Society. Midway down the Driffield Anglers' water the stream has a natural barrier in the form of a mill race and above the race the fishing is brown trout only, while below the barrier the water contains brown trout, stocked

rainbows and tremendous shoals of grayling. No day tickets issued and the water is closely controlled.

Driffield Dun An excellent Yorkshire fly; always fished upstream, similar in many ways to Border spiders:

Body: lead-coloured fur, mole or mole mixed with rabbit, ribbed with yellow silk, dressed sparse
Hackle: four or five turns of dun cock hackle, ginger or honey dun will do
Whisks: a few fibres of the same
Hook: 14–16

Drift Netting It is claimed that R.M. Fleming of Culdaff in County Donegal originated the use of a drift or hang net in the open sea for catching salmon more than 100 years ago, and it was in 1870 that the first open sea drift net licence was issued in Ireland in the area now under the jurisdiction of the Foyle Fisheries Commission.

Gerald Hadoke writes:

Today the open sea drift nets of Ireland capture over 80 per cent of the total national catch of salmon in the Republic. The drift net or floating gill net usually has a mesh size of 10–12 inches in the round – i.e. around the mesh – and this permits salmon of 3–10lbs weight to be caught. Each net is about 30–50 meshes deep and is tied to a head rope buoyed with corks. The net is shot across the tide and is attached to the boat while fishing. The length of drift nets vary according to local regulations. In the Northumbrian area they do not exceed 600 yards and are usually fished within the 6 mile limit from the shore: Irish drift nets are usually one mile in length and fished out to the 12 mile limit. The introduction of monofilament twines, which are nearly invisible to salmon in the sea, has permitted drift nets to be operated in daylight hours in addition to the former traditional night-time period.

The Atlantic Salmon Trust considers that drift netting is a good method of catching salmon, but, because of its nature it is an indiscriminate form of capture and tends to be wasteful, and therefore, should be phased out. Drift netting is operated in areas where salmon returning to their home rivers are accustomed to mix before migrating towards their own particular river. Thus scientists are unable to allocate the drift net catch to the individual rivers of origin, hampering management decisions.

That drift netting is a damaging form of exploitation which is both wasteful and harmful to the salmon resource has been clearly established by the International Council for the Exploration of the Seas Working Group on North Atlantic Salmon. Scientists have shown that during drift netting operations off Greenland salmon can be lost through predation or by dropping out of the net when the latter is being hauled in. In addition, salmon which escape the drift nets by breaking through them become severely damaged and are likely to die before reaching their home rivers. The numbers of fish lost to fishermen are difficult to quantify, but scientists have made estimates in their reports to I.C.E.S. suggesting that a figure approaching 25% of the total Greenlandic catch of salmon is appropriate. It has been reported from Norway, where a large drift net fishery has been allowed to develop, that 80–85% of salmon caught in the rivers were badly damaged by drift nets. Perhaps more importantly from an economic point of view, it has been reported that gill nets made of Ulstron (multi-filament) caused rupture of the blood vessels in the muscles. This factor could jeopardise the successful smoking of salmon caught by this method, as the breaking of blood vessels would cause 'staining' of the smoked sides.

Dry-Fly Fishing

You can angle for him at all times with a lying or running ground line, except in leaping time, and then with an artificial fly. *The Treatyse of Fyssinghe Wyth an Angle*, (1496).

The term 'dry fly' came into general use towards the end of the nineteenth century to distinguish a particular method of fly fishing on the chalk streams advocated and pioneered by Francis Francis, G.S. Marryatt, F.M. Halford, and others. The essence of the method was that the fly itself should be constructed in such a way that it floated longer than previous fly designs, even when it sank it could be dried by false casting, and should fall on the water in an upright position with wings cocked. The flies were designed to imitate as closely as possible the flies on the water and were cast upstream to trout taking the natural insect and allowed to float down over the rising fish without drag.

The effectiveness of the new flies, called split-wing floaters, and the accuracy and delicacy of their presentation with silk lines, long leaders and split-cane rods, was remarkable. The fishing journals of the time were full of reports of heavy catches by 'the new method of the dry fly'. One great advantage on the chalk streams was that a sizeable fish could be singled out and deliberately fished for when it was taking duns floating on the surface, something that meant it was now possible to avoid taking undersized fish. Indeed, the advantages of the method were so many and the making of artificial flies that matched the natural in every possible way was so absorbing that many clubs and syndicates decided that only the dry fly should be fished on their waters. One man, F.M. Halford, was mainly responsible for the exclusion and banishment of the wet fly and for the establishment of the dry, and it was not for many years that the upstream wet fly was revived on some southern chalk streams as a result of the advocacy of G.E.M. Skues.

Today, after something like three-quarters of a century of argument, sometimes bitter and recriminatory, the position of dry versus wet has reached an aimiable compromise, worked out by agreement among the various clubs and syndicates. Some still insist on dry fly only. Some allow the Skues's upstream wet fly patterns of nymphs to be classified under the term 'dry fly' – a form of sophistry which gets rid of the problem in a remarkable fashion. On such waters the weighted Sawyer nymphs are not allowed. Other clubs and syndicates insist on the dry fly until July 1, after which nymphs, weighted and unweighted, are allowed, but only of a certain size. Most southern chalk streams ban the use of mayfly nymphs at any time.

The charm of fishing the dry fly seems boundless. So many have sung its praises. One of the great dry-fly fishermen of the mid- and latter half of this century, Dermot Wilson, says that to see a trout rise and take a dry fly is the most exhilarating and intoxicating experience:

One moment there's the fly. The next moment there it isn't. The thrill is electric. And dry fly fishing is a good deal easier than it is often made out to be. The only skill you have to master is to cast well. If you cast clumsily and splash your fly down you will frighten the trout and if you cast wide of the mark you will probably waste precious minutes since rising trout seldom move far to take a fly.

One aspect of the dry fly which appeals to intelligent people (like you and me) is that nearly every trout has to be tackled with a well-thought-out campaign in mind. This is not a hit and miss affair, something that is over in as short a time as taking a pot shot at a pheasant. Catching a trout on a dry fly usually involves a logical sequence of activity, each step leading to the next and so prolonging the excitement perhaps for an hour or more.

First of all you have to spot the rising fish, then to decide on its diet. Is it, for instance, taking duns or spinners. If there are only a few duns coming down it may be either. Then the rise form gives the best clue. If the trout's neb appears on the surface, or if there is a large rise form, then that will indicate duns. A quiet sip will suggest spinners. Then you have to decide whether your fly matches the natural fly closely enough. 'Enough' is the critical word. The 'exact imitation' days of the Halford era are long past.

Then, having got so far, you have to stalk the fish. How close can you get without being seen? Is there good cover? What about your fly getting hung up behind – and last but not least – will the set of the current allow your fly a good drift over the trout without drag? Only when all these problems have been solved can you make your first cast – it should be a measuring cast, falling short of the fish, so as to judge distance. The next cast can be the crucial one, the covering cast, letting the fly settle delicately on the water just a foot or so above the fish. Then, if the river god is on your side . . .

But the sequence is not yet complete. If the trout takes, you must strike or rather tighten correctly, though what *correctly* is, is a little difficult to say. I generally tighten just as soon as I see my fish rise, but always deliberately and never with a snatch, and I do not seem to miss more fish than the next man.

This, then, is the systematic chain of observation and action which never ceases to be enthralling. This is, as we say, fishing the rise. Now we come to fishing the water.

On many rain-fed rivers you will come across periods when no fish are rising yet the fact is that a number of hungry trout are waiting just below the surface hoping for food to come their way. This is when you cast your fly to places where you think these trout will be.

Fishing the water is seldom successful on chalk streams since the well-fed chalk stream trout need a fair amount of fly to tempt them to the surface. On rain-fed streams, where trout have a leaner time of it, they are far more likely to keep a lookout for a stray fly or an insect dropping off the bushes. One looks for places where a wide expanse of water converges into a narrow run, the turn of eddies, and sheltered places below overhanging trees and bushes.

The pace of the water is important. Trout do not like the conveyor-belt of food over their heads to be too slow nor do they like the stream to be so fast they use up too much energy to stay where they want to stay. My own pet place for picking up a trout is where the current narrows under a bank, especially if the bank has trees or bushes on it.

Many people do tend to think of the chalk stream as the be-all and end-all of the dry fly but up and down the country are hundreds of rain fed rivers and brooks on which the dry fly is supremely enjoyable and highly successful.

One frequent problem of the chalk streams, is that you often get repeated refusals from a rising fish. What do you do? Keep on casting? Try another fly? Move on to the next fish? My own belief is that you should stick to that fish, for there is nothing more satisfying than eventually to deceive it.

Your fly may be dragging, but so slightly you cannot see it. Watch tiny bits of debris coming down near it. They may take a slightly different course. Then change your fly – for he has seen it before – and try presenting it from a different angle. If this fails study your trout carefully. Even if duns can be seen coming down he may, nevertheless, be taking spinner, or perhaps black gnats, which are very difficult to spot on the water.

The trout may be taking flies on one side of him instead of from overhead. In some cases they may be partially blind in one eye. If all fails try a dramatic change in the size of fly. If you have been using 14s and 16s, try a 20 or a 22 – the pattern is not too important – and then drop a 12 on his head. It sometimes works wonders.

But when all is said and done, good casting and good presentation of the fly are far more important than choice of fly pattern or fly size. Gentle and accurate presentation is a joy in itself and almost the entire secret of competent dry-fly fishing.

Dry Flies The most popular dry fly patterns (*see* colour photograph 11) are the Blue Winged Olive, the Blue Upright, Lunn's Particular, Tups, Kite's Imperial, Sherry Spinner, Iron Blue Dun, Ginger Quill and Wickham's Fancy. The 33 patterns recommended by Halford are rarely carried these days. Dry-fly fishermen may often have large numbers of flies with them, especially if they tie their own, but probably use not more than half a dozen or so. Some chalk stream fishermen use more or less one pattern all the year round, a Greenwell, a Kite's Imperial or a Pheasant Tail, and they seem reasonably successful. They are inclined sometimes to miss the fun of changing a fly, which even if not necessary is certainly good for morale and self-confidence. Dermot Wilson's choice is:

My own favourite half-dozen for the chalk streams begin with two from Peter Deane – his Beacon Beige (size 14) and Terry's Terror (16). The others are the Iron Blue (16), Lunn's Particular (16), Houghton Ruby (18), Black Gnat (20). But then I would beg permission to add the Hawthorn in May, a good Sedge for the evening rise, and of course the Mayfly during its season.

Sources include: *Fishing the Dry Fly*, Dermot Wilson (Black, 2nd edn., 1983); John Waller Hills, *A Summer on the Test* (Bles, 1924); *A Modern Dry Fly Code*, Vincent Marinaro (Putnam, New York, 1950); *Famous Flies and Their Originators*, Donald Overfield (Black, 1972); *The Origins of Angling*, John McDonald (Doubledays, New York, 1963); *Reflections on A River*, Howard Marshall (Witherby, 1967); Courtney William's, *Dictionary of Trout Flies* (Black, 4th edn., 1967) and the works of Dunne, Halford, Moseley and Skues.

Dry Fly Origins

It seems only sensible to assume that if our ancestors imitated a winged fly then they fished it or attempted to fish it where winged flies were to be found – on top of the water. (Jack Heddon, ms, 1982)

Many claims have been made about the origin of dry-fly fishing. An academic point, it has, nevertheless, the quality of being able to spark controversy almost every time it is discussed. Why this should be so is a little difficult to explain. Perhaps it is because the dry fly, certainly in the 1920s and 1930s, acquired a snob value which it has been trying hard to lose ever since. It was then thought of as a cachet of the chalk streams and, therefore, exclusive to rich landowners and their friends. Perhaps this is so, but one suspects there is much more to it than that. There is a mystery about the dry fly. Effective, in some ways obvious, yet no one knows where it came from or how it happened.

Fly fishermen who are also historians have made efforts to resolve the problem, notably John McDonald in America, and in our own country John Waller Hills. The latest, after some 20 years or more of study, is Jack Heddon, a fly fisher and a business man in London who became fascinated by the subject and spent much of his spare time going through the original documents, finding some that throw new light on the problem. Jack Heddon says:

> For many years I had been puzzled by the apparent contradiction posed by the southern chalk stream school of fly fishermen evolving their method of dry-fly fishing for trout, on the one hand and, on the other, the indisputable fact that floating flies have been fished . . . if not from time immemorial . . . certainly since the sixteenth century.
>
> With hindsight I can see that the problem resulted from the lack of a clear understanding of exactly what constituted 'dry-fly fishing', aggravated by a lack of knowledge of the history of fly-fishing by so many of the great angling scribes of the nineteenth and early twentieth centuries. F.M. Halford appears to have been the first person to attempt a definition of dry-fly fishing . . . this he did in his first book, *Floating Flies and How to Dress Them*, first published in 1886:
>
> 'To define dry-fly fishing, I should describe it as presenting to the rising fish the best possible imitation of the insect on which he is feeding in its natural position. To analyse this further, it is necessary, firstly to find a fish feeding on the winged insect; secondly, to present to him a good imitation of this insect, both as to size and colour; thirdly, to present it to him in its natural position, or floating on the surface of the water with its wings up, or what we technically term, "cocked"; fourthly, to put the fly lightly on the water, so that it floats accurately over him without drag; and, fifthly, to take care that all these conditions have been fulfilled before the fish has seen the Angler or the reflection of his rod.'
>
> In his next book, *Dry-Fly Fishing in Theory and Practice* (1889), Halford more or less repeated the above definition and also wrote of 'the dry or floating fly'. His contribution to the 'Country Life' two volume *Fishing*, published in 1904, began: "A floating or dry fly is one fished on the surface, . . ." A similar definition was given by J.J. Hardy in his 'Hints on the Art of Angling' which were printed in every Hardy Brother's *Angler's Guide* from about 1907 until 1964 and which were obviously very widely read. J.J. Hardy defined: ". . . the art of dry-fly fishing is to present a fly that floats, . . . and floats perfectly, . . . to the notice of a rising fish in such a manner that it is mistaken for the natural *ephemera* which is hatching out, and in the result is accepted as such by the fish."
>
> What Halford, Hardy, and many others failed to realise was that *there was absolutely nothing new in any of these points*. Let us look at Halford's five requirements; firstly the rising fish. In *Salmonia; or Days of Fly Fishing* (1828), Sir Humphrey Davy describes a days fishing at Denham on 18 May, 1810. After watching a large trout take five May-flies in a minute he said to his companions "Now I shall throw the drake a foot above him. It floats down,

and he has taken it." Secondly, the best possible imitation of the fly on the water; this has surely been a requirement since the fifteenth century and the *Treatyse of Fysshynge Wyth an Angle*. Certainly Robert Venables, writing in 1662, instructed that the artificial should be made "as like the natural fly as possibly you can" and not only added that the fly-dresser should "for his better imitation let him lay the natural fly before him" but also that he should wet his dubbing when matching for colour. For Halford's third point, floating the fly in a cocked position, we can turn to *The Fly Fisher's Guide* (1816), by George Bainbridge and his instructions for fishing the artificial 'Gray Drake' which conclude: "This fly should be thrown directly over the fish, and so managed, if possible, that the wings may not touch the water." Putting the fly lightly on the water again dates back to the earliest days of fly-fishing; Richard Bowlker, writing c. 1746, said "The Greatest skill is to make your Line fall as lightly as possible on the water, . . . When you see a Fish rise at the natural Fly, the best way is to throw a Yard above him, . . . and let your Fly move gently towards him, by which means you will show it him more naturally." Around 1810 George Scotcher, writing of the Black Gnat, said that he used a single hair, ". . . which falls excessively light and will lie on the water". As for Halford's fifth point, keeping out of sight, surely this was the reason behind Cotton's oft quoted dictum "fine and far off"; or to quote Scotcher again "be very cautious in approaching the water, for if you are once seen, all chance of success is over . . . The shadow of yourself or rod destroys all sport."

I find it most interesting that in the first edition of *Dry-Fly Fishing in Theory and Practice* Halford was still open-minded enough to write:

". . . I for one am a strong advocate for floating a cocked fly over a likely place, even if no movement of a feeding fish has been seen there . . . There is no doubt, too, that an angler catching sight of a trout or grayling lying near the surface or in position for feeding can often tempt him with a good imitation of the fly on the water floated accurately over him at the first cast."

These statements were considerably modified in later editions of the work.

Charles Kingsley, author of *Chalk Stream Studies* (1858), was no dry-fly purist; indeed, as G.E.M. Skues pointed out in an article in *Salmon and Trout Magazine*, December, 1933, Kingsley entirely ignored the dry-fly. His rules for chalk-stream fishing were simple and are as valid today as they were in 1858: ". . . always fish up-stream; keep out of sight of the fish; use the shortest possible line and finally, when you have hooked a fish, fight him kneeling down, hold him hard, give no line and always pull him down stream". Skues was right about one thing, Kingsley made no mention of dry-fly fishing, indeed he didn't mind if his flies floated or sank:

"Now . . . put your Green-drake on; and throw . . . wherever you see a fish rise. Do not work your flies in the least, but let them float down over the fish, or sink if they will; he is more likely to take them under the water than on top. And mind this rule: be patient with your fish; and do not fancy that because he does not rise to you the first or the tenth time, therefore he will not rise at all."

The only difference between Kingsley and Halford was the latter's insistence on fishing with a floating fly, and there was nothing new about the floating fly. Indeed it would have been illogical for fly-fishing to have evolved with anything else, and certainly as early as 1590 flies were being made with cork bodies "to angle with aloft on the water". Throughout the literature of angling, from 1590 until the present day, there is a continuous record of fishing with a floating fly.

Wet-fly fishing for trout developed between the middle of the eighteenth and the early years of the nineteenth century. There is a reference to fishing with a sunk-fly in *The Experienc'd Angler* (1661), by Robert Venables; Chetham, Howlett and Best were but three of the many authors to copy Venables and it was not until *The North Country Angler* of 1786 that anything new was written on the subject – the anonymous author suggesting that as most flies are bred in the water and rise to the surface to hatch they are "an easy prey to the lazy trouts, who feed on them under the surface." (Surely we have found the 'father' of nymph fishing?). By about 1830/1840 the sunk-fly had become dominant on many rivers and two distinct schools developed; one fishing down-stream with large, well sunk, attractor type flies such as the Butcher, Silver March Brown and Alexandra; the other fished up-stream with small flies, generally lightly hackled with one or two turns of a soft game-bird feather at the head, such as the Partridge and Orange and Snipe and Purple.

It may well have been on the limestone streams of Derbyshire that anglers first noticed the effectiveness of an unused, dry fly, the first time it was cast over a rising fish. In his book *On Fly Tying* (1879), James Ogden claimed to have introduced his floating flies "some forty years ago," which would have put the date at 1839. He described how he came upon the idea as follows:

"I have always made it my rule never to leave a good rising fish while he was feeding. I have tried every dodge, and often every fly in my book. By changing my end fly (not intending to do so) I have occasionally made a cast with a dry fly. . . . I found while my fly was still on the surface, without a ripple, it has tempted the fish to seize it, after I have been throwing a sunk fly over him in vain, scores of times. These observations were the cause of my introducing floating flies."

The earliest mention in angling literature of deliberately fishing with a dry, unused, fly is in the first edition of G.R.P. Pulman's *Vade-Mecum of Fly Fishing for Trout*, published in 1841. As this is a fairly scarce book I will quote the relevant passage in full:

"Now it is impossible to make a soaked artificial fly swim upon the water as the natural ones do, so that, when cast by the angler to a fish thus occupied feeding on surface flies it must escape his notice, engaged as he is with "things above", by sinking in the water beneath him. This is plain, because if the wet and heavy fly be exchanged for a dry and light one, and passed in artistic style over the feeding fish, it will, partly from the simple circumstances of its buoyancy, be taken, in nine cases out of ten, as greedily as the living insect itself. We admit, however, that to ensure this, imitation of the predominant species, at least as regards colour and size, is required; . . ."

The second edition of 1846 was only slightly altered, but the third edition of 1851 was considerably enlarged and the above passage expanded to include a reference to false casting:

"Let a *dry* fly be substituted for the wet one, the line switched a few times through the air to throw off its superabundant moisture, a judicious cast made just above the rising fish, and the fly allowed to float towards and over them, . . . This dry fly, we must remark, should be an imitation of the natural fly on which the fish are feeding . . ."

At first sight this looks like dry-fly fishing as we know it; however, a few lines further on Pulman continues:

"We mention this as an illustration of the importance of imitating action, and must not be understood to recommend the constantly substituting of a dry fly for a wet one, over every rising fish."

The final chapter of the 1851 edition includes the following instructions under the heading "General Remarks . . ."

"Whatever the season, you should never omit taking advantage of a windy day, when the surface of the water is ruffled, to fish the deep parts of the river, . . . These you should fish slowly and carefully, upwards or downwards as the wind may render more convenient, . . . Perhaps we need hardly state that the angler should endeavour at all times to fish with the wind blowing from behind him . . .".

Obviously Pulman was still a long way from dry-fly fishing as we know it, but the germ of the idea was there, a floating fly which imitated the insect upon which rising trout were feeding. However, his false casting was *to dry the line, not the fly*, and he lacked a rod powerful enough to cast up-stream irrespective of wind direction or to dry a fly by false casting.

Here I think I should make clear what I consider to be the difference between fishing with a floating-fly and "dry-fly fishing". Fishing with a floating-fly has been practised since at least the sixteenth century and is merely fishing with a fly which floats on the surface of the water; dry-fly fishing is with an artificial fly which has been constructed to fall onto the water in a "cocked" position and to be dried by false casting in the air.

By the middle of the nineteenth century the idea of casting a "dry-fly" over rising trout was spreading. In the *Field* of 17 December, 1853, there was a most interesting article entitled "Notes of the Month by the Hampshire Flyfisher" in which, after discussing the question of casting up or down-stream, the writer said: "but on the other hand, so far as fly-fishing is concerned, fishing up the stream, unless you are trying the Carshalton dodge and fishing with a dry fly, is very awkward." A very important correspondence was published in the *Field* in 1906, regarding the use of the dry-fly at Winchester College. A letter in the issue of 7 April, from an old

Wykehamist who had fished the College water on the Itchen between 1844 and 1848 included:

"There was no such thing as dry-fly fishing known in those days, though we had found out that there was some virtue in a dry fly. We did start by looking round to see if a rise was visible, and if so we did make a point of putting the fly while still unwetted over it. It did now and then succeed . . . On changing the fly one also gave the fresh fly a similar chance when dry . . . it never dawned on our minds that the fly could be kept dry by waving the rod to and fro in the air . . ."

In the *Field* of 24 March, 1906, another old Wykehamist who had "fished nearly every day of both seasons" (1862 and 1863) said that he never saw anything used but the dry-fly. Another letter in the same issue was from "Gammel Man", who entered the College in 1866, and wrote "Certainly in 1866 no one thought of employing any other method than the dry fly." If only the dry-fly was fished, it is certain that the fly was dried by false casting.

In an article entitled "Gossip about the Hampshire Streams," printed in the *Field* of 12 December 1857, Francis Francis wrote:

". . . however fine you may fish, even the motion of your fly and line will at times startle the fish. Accordingly I recommend the angler frquently to try a dry fly – e.g., suppose the angler sees a rising fish, let him allow his casting-line and fly to dry for a minute previous to making a cast; then, calculate his distance, throw carefully and lightly, letting his fly alight a sufficient distance above the fish . . ."

It is most interesting that Francis, certainly one of the greatest anglers of his age, made no mention of false casting even as late as 1857. This suggests that "the Carshalton dodge" of 1853 was merely tying-on an unwetted fly and hardly related to dry-fly fishing as we know the craft.

Probably the earliest suggestion in angling literature of false casting to dry both fly and line was made by William Shipley and Edward Fitzgibbon in *A True Treatise on The Art of Fly-Fishing*. . . (1838), and related to fishing on the River Dove.

"Let your flies float gently down the water, . . . We distinctly recommend frequent casting. A fish generally takes the fly immediately it has touched the water – provided always it be delicately and lightly flung – and the quick repetition of casting whisks the water out of your flies and line, and consequently keeps them drier and lighter than if they were left to float a longer time in the water."

Several years later the Rev. James Martin's *The Angler's Guide* (1854) contained a very similar statement to that made by Shipley and Fitzgibbon:

"Never throw your fly on the water in a wet state, for if you do it will sink the moment it gets there, which is not well. To prevent this, whisk it once or twice through the air before you let it fall on the water . . ."

However, as the reverend gentleman devoted only seven pages to fly fishing out of a total of one hundred and ninety one, and as he made no mention of up-stream fishing or casting to rising fish, I suggest that he had merely copied the suggestion from other writers.

In the years between 1857 and 1867 Francis Francis discovered the advantages of false casting, for in his greatest angling work, *A Book on Angling*, he described dry-fly fishing in detail:

". . . it is of course imperatively necessary to fish with a dry fly, and between every cast the angler will have to make several false casts, or casts in which the fly does not touch the water, to shake the wet from the fly and to get it as dry as possible."

In *An Angler's Autobiography* (1903), F.M. Halford describes dry-fly fishing as he found it on the River Wandle in 1868:

"The local anglers at once impressed upon us the necessity of 'fishing-dry'. We gradually worked out approximately the number of false casts required to free the fly from moisture and were soon converted to the doctrine of waiting for a rising trout . . ."

He also said that the flies generally used were dressed on number 16 or 17 Limerick hooks, with double-rolled upright wings of starling and that, being dressed with far less hackle or other material to represent the legs than in modern patterns, they were proportionally more difficult to float.

Thus we can say that the dry-fly probably emerged between the years 1857 and 1862, and was fairly well established by the end of the 1860s. But it was still very much a sub-imago; at least four mechanical developments were essential before one could say that the perfect insect had arrived; the eyed hook, the double split-winged "floater", hexagonal split-cane rods and the heavy plaited silk line with its oil-dressing.

I have already expressed the opinion that the essential difference between fishing with a floating-fly and dry-fly fishing is that in the latter case the fly has not only been specially constructed to float, but also to be dried by false casting. The final link in this development was the modern eyed-hook. By no means a new invention, the eyed-hook was illustrated as early as 1760 in the first Hawkins edition of *The Complete Angler*; it was strongly recommended by Hewett Wheatley in *The Rod and Line* (1849), and patented by J. Warner and Sons of Redditch in February, 1866. However, these were all either straight ring-eyed or needle-eyed hooks and failed to interest the majority of fly-fishermen. Wheatley described himself as "Senior Angler" and said eyed-hooks were "somewhat of a pet, though not exactly the child of my old age; rather the mistress of our youth and the friend of riper years." Certainly one of the most important inventions in the entire history of angling, the final development of the eyed trout-fly hook was mainly the work of H.S. Hall.

The first detailed description of dry-fly fishing for trout was given by Hall in two articles which were printed in the *Fishing Gazette* in March 1883. In the second of these he explained how, after spending time and trouble in tying very neat and delicate imitations of the natural insects, the constant false-casting necessary to dry the fly frequently cracked the gut at the head of the fly, making it untrustworthy.

"Many a time have I known a stubborn fish resist all my efforts until the gut has 'necked off', and then, of course, he would rise to the fly boldly, and keep it . . ."

He then told how the idea of using eyed-hooks for dry fly fishing came from his acquaintance with Mr W.H. Aldam and his book *A Quaint Treatise on Flies and Fly Making* (generally issued in 1876, a few copies being issued in 1875). Aldam supplied Hall with some eyed-hooks in 1878; these were japanned Limericks and proved unsatisfactory. Later in the same year Hall contacted Hutchinson and Son of Kendal and in February 1879 received the first samples of what were later to become "Hall's Snecky Limerick Bend Eyed Hooks." Hitherto hooks had been made with either straight "ring-eyes" or "needle-eyes", Hall evolved the first turned-up eye. Much of his early development work had been done with a Mr George Bankart; however, whereas Hall was concerned with producing very small hooks for dry-flies, Bankart was mainly interested in the larger sizes for loch and sea-trout flies. In January 1885 W. Woodfield & Sons of Redditch were advertising "Mr Hall's Improved Eyed Hooks" and in March of the same year H. Cholmondeley-Pennell introduced the first turned-down eyed hooks, for which he unsuccessfully tried to register a British patent. The impact created by eyed-hooks was such that F.M. Halford's first book, *Floating Flies* . . . (1886), began:

[On eyed-hooks.] "Before many years are past the old-fashioned fly, dressed on a hook attached to a length of gut, will be practically obsolete, the advantages of the eyed-hook being so manifest . . . ." Halford was certainly right; whilst the respective merits of turned-up and turned-down eyes are still debated no-one questions the advantages of the eyed-hook.

Where and when the first split-winged floating flies were tied will long remain a matter for speculation, but it is certain that the first dry-flies were imitations of the more common may-flies, *Ephemera danica* and *Ephemera vulgata*. As we have already seen Sir Humphrey Davy in 1810 and George Bainbridge in 1816 both fished floating may-flies. Francis Francis contributed an article headed "Gossip about the Hampshire Streams" to the *Field* of 12th December, 1857, in which he praised the floating flies of Mr Pottle, a Winchester fishing-tackle dealer; and said that if "the wings are not *too heavy* or violently unnatural, the hook will when thus quiescent bring the fly into its natural position, and will be almost hidden under the body." G.E.M. Skues has said that when he fished the Old Barge in 1875 and 1876 "The fishing . . . was then entirely dry-fly work – though the flies fell generally on their sides and were not built to cock . . . ." Elsewhere he said that the flies sold by John Hammond in those days were "dressed then of necessity on gut, and generally with both wings made from the same slip of feather" and differed scarcely at all from the ordinary wet flies used on rough rivers such as the Tweed. "In those days many chalk-stream anglers were still fishing down stream . . . and the tackle dealers, such as John Hammond, had to cater for these down-stream anglers as well as for the up-stream dry-fly men, and no doubt sold similar flies to both." Hammond was very much a central figure in the evolution of dry-fly fishing on chalk-streams. When G.S. Marryat returned to Winchester from Australia in 1870 Hammond taught him to fish, probably on the Old Barge. About 1874 H.S. Hall found his way to Winchester "and took a ticket on John Hammond's length . . . Hammond showed me over the water – the 'Old Barge' stream and mill-pond below the town." Marryat, described by Viscount Grey as "the greatest angler I have ever met", was the *eminence grise* of the new dry-fly school and encouraged Hall in the development of the eyed hook; later he selected Halford to be scribe and recorder of the dry-fly. In the *Fly-Fishers' Journal* No. 47, Autumn 1923, Skues reproduced some letters from Marryat to Hall, dated November and December 1882, which made it quite clear that Marryat invented the method of winging "double dressed floaters" described by Halford in *Floating Flies*. Dr T. Sanctuary, a friend of both Marryat and Hall, has said that Marryat learnt much of his fly-dressing, including the double dressed floater, from Mrs Cox, a professional fly-dresser who lived in Winchester. Skues had said that the first double dressed split-winged floaters that he had seen were tied by Mrs Cox and displayed at the Fisheries Exhibition of 1883. Certainly by early 1884 Mrs G.T. Cox of Parchment Street, Winchester, was advertising "Flies tied on eyed hooks." I think it most probable that Marryat learnt the basic principles of fly-dressing from Mrs Cox and later taught her some of the new methods he and Hall had evolved between 1879 and 1882 for the new eyed-hooks.

Two more developments were necessary to complete the evolution of chalk-stream dry-fly fishing – the hexagonal split-cane rod, capable of drying a fly by false casting and of throwing a fly up-stream in almost any wind condition, and the heavy oiled-silk line required to 'work' the rod.

History tells us that the Chinese were the first to use bamboo cane rent into strips then glued and bound to obtain the full strength of cane without the diameter occasioned by the hollow centre; this they did some three thousand years ago, but only for water-carriers to hang their pails upon. Where and when split-cane was first used for fishing rods is obscure.

From W. Wright's *Fishes and Fishing* (1858), it is clear that "glued-up bamboo fly-rods" were being made in London about the year 1805. These were almost certainly triangular, as were the rods made by Thomas Aldred and exhibited at the New York "World's Fair" of 1851; these rods were also advertised in *The Angler's Guide* (1854), by the Rev. James Martin. In 1855 William Blacker wrote of his "beautiful rent and glued-up bamboo cane fly-rods . . . rent and glued-up in three pieces." In 1873 Farlow's advertised "quadrangular glued-up bamboo rods." Mr Deller of the London tackle-makers Eton and Deller was making hexagonal split-cane rods for Halford, Marryat and their friends in 1880.

The stiffer split-cane rods required much heavier lines than the mixture of silk and hair which had been adequate for the greenheart hitherto generally used. Much of the credit for the development of high quality oil-dressed silk lines must be given to Halford; working at first with Mr Deller and then, after his death, with Mr H.P. Hawksley, a surgical instrument maker, he produced the double-tapered oiled-silk lines which Skues said were "of a beauty and finish never since surpassed and only perhaps equalled later on by . . . the late Walter Durfee Coggeshall."

These lines were a fairly late development; in January 1884 H.S. Hall wrote to the *Fishing Gazette* and asked if a paraffin dressing could be applied to a mixed silk and hair line for fly-fishing. However, Hall did not switch from greenheart to split-cane until the 1885 season. In *Floating Flies* (1886), Halford said of fly-lines "there is plenty of room for improvement in the quality of silk used, in the mode of plaiting, and the composition of the dressing," and recommended that lines be rubbed with red-deer fat. This suggests that the final developments in line dressing came after the manuscript of *Floating Flies* and before the publication of *Dry-Fly Fishing* in 1889. Reviewing the second edition of *Dry-Fly Fishing* in the *Fishing Gazette* of 7 September, 1889, R.B. Marston wrote; "it is almost hopeless to expect that lines made exactly as here described will ever be obtainable in the trade . . ." Lines were obviously the last major item to be developed.

As we have seen, the sub-imago of dry-fly fishing emerged between 1857 and 1862; when did the imago arrive? The nearest I can suggest is 1857 or '88. Where is much easier to place; Marryat, Francis, Hall, Halford, Carlisle, Senior, Skues and Viscount Grey all fished on the waters leased by John Hammond on the River Itchen in the Winchester area; these included the College water, Winnal, St. Cross and the Old Barge and Mill Pond. If any one of these waters was the home of the dry-fly it was the Old Barge, and the central figure throughout was Hammond. Was Hammond the inventor of chalk-stream dry-fly fishing?

Duck Fly A trout fly of Irish descent which suggests a midge. Why it is called duck, is not known for certain but it has been suggested that ducklings, before they are strong enough to dive for weed, eat small black flies, probably midge pupae, floating on the surface.

The most usual dressing is the Black Duck Fly. This is J.R. Harris':

Body: black floss silk thickened near the shoulder
Wings: two dun or cream cock hackle points tied sloping backwards
Hackle: a few turns of rusty black cock tied in front of the wings
Hook: 12–16

The Olive Duck Fly (large olive midge) is of similar design with a pale-green or apple-green body ribbed with thin gold wire.

Dunkeld A fly for all seasons, for salmon as well as trout, originally tied at Dunkeld on the Tay, now frequently used in stillwater fishing:

Body: gold tinsel, sometimes ribbed with gold wire as well
Tag: golden pheasant crest, upturned to meet the wing
Wing: dark mallard
Cheeks: jungle cock
Hackle: beard hackle of hot-orange feather fibres
Hook: almost any size but small stickleback size for lake trout; for salmon not much larger than a 6 because mallard fibre is short and one must try to get a reasonable balance between the mallard wing and the golden crest coming up to meet it.

Dunne, J.W. An aeronautics engineer who designed one of the first aircraft used by the Royal Flying Corps during the First World War, Dunne was also a mathematician and philosopher and his book *An Experiment With Time*, which dealt with the subject of precognition, was a best seller of the 1930s. Dunne was a passionate and inventive fly fisherman and his book, *Sunshine and the Dry Fly* (Black, 1924, 2nd edn. 1950) introduced white painted hooks with a dubbing of rayon floss (cellulite) which when oiled became translucent. The wings were made from silks blended to mathematical formulae. The flies were successful but never became popular because of the difficulty of obtaining the right materials for tying them. Quite apart from his invention, the book remains fascinating to read for his enthusiasms and interpretation of the pleasures of fishing:

> Fly fishing stands almost in a class of its own. For the lore of nature which a fly fisherman may enlist to his advantage covers an area a hundred times greater and a thousand fold richer than are those which lie open to, for example, the votaries of bait and minnow. And indeed it may almost be said that in no sport in the world, with the possible exception of big game shooting, does knowledge, as opposed to mere physical dexterity, prove so fascinating in acquirement, or reap so delightfully satisfactory reward.

Durnford A sporting clergyman, the Rev. Richard Durnford fished the upper Test and the Anton from 1809 to 1819. His Fishing Diary first published in 1911 gives some fascinating vignettes of sporting life in Regency days.

Points of View

Sir Henry Wootton would say that angling was a rest to his mind, a cheerer of his spirits, a diverter of sadness, a calmer of unquiet thoughts, a moderator of passions, a procurer of contentedness, and that it begat habits of peace and patience in those that professed and practised it.

Izaak Walton, *The Compleat Angler*, London, 1653

Fly fishing may be a very pleasant amusement; but angling or float fishing I can only compare to a stick and a string with a worm at one end and a fool at the other.

A saying attributed to Dr Johnson in *Hawker's Instructions to Sportsmen*, London, 1859

Eden There are four Eden rivers but the best known is the one that rises on Black Fell Moss and flows by Appleby, Kirkby Stephen and Carlisle into the Solway Firth, and a fine river it is with a good run of sea trout and salmon at times as well as some good stocks of wild brown trout. The sea trout run from June onwards. The salmon can be sparse. Bracken Bank Lodge at Lazenby has water.

Two other Cumbrian rivers, the Ehen and Calder have good runs of sea trout and the Sella Park Hotel at Calderbridge has water. Several Cumbrian angling associations have water, some with day tickets, but as on the Border Esk there is a good deal of local bait fishing.

Arthur Ransome fished the Eden and paid tribute to a great Eden fisherman, William Nelson, in *Rod and Line* (first published 1929, Oxford Paperback, 1980). Nelson fished the river between Wild Boar Fell and Armathwaite and by the rapid glide under the Castle Rock at Appleby. William Nelson was also a good grayling fisherman:

> He was a great hand at creeper-fishing, for which he had invented some ingenious artificial insects, and few could best him in the use of the minnow.

Ransome said that Nelson's book, *Fishing in Eden*, will be read by Eden fishermen as long as the river runs but unfortunately did not give the name of the publisher or the date – it must have been in the 1920s or before – and copies do not seem to be available today.

Edmonds and Lee Harfield H. Edmonds and Norman N. Lee were close friends and fishing companions and together published a book privately at Bradford in 1916 with the long but precise title of *Brook and River Trouting, A Manual of North Country Methods*. This is possibly the greatest book on North Country fishing ever written, certainly among the top two or three. Copies are rare.

Edmonds and Lee presented a deluxe edition to the Flyfishers' Club library in London which contains samples of the actual silks and materials used in the dressings of North Country flies and of flies themselves, all beautifully tied and framed. The 36 flies include the Waterhen Bloa, Snipe and Purple, Partridge and Orange, and winged and hackled tyings of the Dark Watchet. It is noticeable how small and delicate these flies are, most of them tied on very small – 16 and 18 – hooks.

Edmunds and Lee's emphasised the method of fishing upstream with a short line, casting frequently to a rise or to likely places, by no means a matter of chuck and chance it:

> . . . though the dry fly purist may shrug his shoulders at the remark, it is not too much to say that if he were transferred from the pellucid waters of the Chalk stream to some rapid broken river of the North, and were to endeavour to fish the wet fly, it would be some considerable time before he achieved any great success. Whereas the man who had thoroughly mastered the art of fishing the wet fly upstream would be able quickly to adapt himself to the conditions and surroundings of the home of the dry fly.

Ebble A small chalk stream that rises near Tisbury in Wiltshire and flows into the Hampshire Avon below Salisbury, providing very delicate and fine fishing:

A nice little brook, often weedy and sometimes overhung, and like most of the little chalk streams exclusive, with long waiting lists to get a rod. Enquiries around Odstock and Coombe Bissett might produce something.

Esk (Border) Comparatively short yet one of the most prolific sea trout rivers in Britain. The Esk and its tributaries form part of the border of the west coast between England and Scotland before the main Esk enters the Solway Firth north of Carlisle. At one time the Border Esk was spoilt by extensive worming, especially legering, but there are now some controls over bait fishing in certain places, nevertheless visitors should find out in advance if the rods they are offered are on fly-only waters. In the late 1970s, about 5,000 sea trout were taken each season, some of them up to 10lb. Flies are standard Teal Blue and Silver (the Falkus Medicine) Peter Ross, Black Pennell and Mallard and Claret. There are one or two local patterns, one of the Whaup and Yellow, tied with a yellow silk body and a curlew (whaup) wing. In low-water conditions, very small flies are used, down to 12s and 14s. Most of the fishing takes place at night but the smaller sea trout (herling) can often be taken during the day on a small dry fly or a 14 or 16 wet fly. The Esk and Liddle fishing association has water to let at Canonbie.

Esk (Cumbrian) This is Hugh Falkus's river, a clear moorland stream that rises near Scawfell and flows into the sea at Ravenglass. In recent years the river is said to have suffered from increased acidity. The sea trout, when there, run large. The Pennington Arms at Ravenglass may be able to arrange fishing.

Esk (North and South) Two delightful salmon rivers, the North Esk and South Esk are on the east coast of Scotland, coming into the sea at or near Montrose. Dalhousie and Gannochy Estates and Brechin, Montrose and Kirriemuir angling clubs are able to provide fishing. The spring and autumn runs of both salmon and sea trout are best. Salmon suffer from intensive netting. John Ashley-Cooper considers that the best beats on the North Esk lie immediately below Morphie dyke on the lowest two miles of the river above the tide and gives good advice about the fishing. **Source:** John Ashley-Cooper, *A Salmon Fisher's Odyssey*, Witherby, 1982.

Esk (Yorkshire) A splendid river, quite short, not more than 30 miles long, which has seen better days. It runs into the sea at Whitby on the Yorkshire coast and the best of the fly fishing was from Glaisdale to Ruswarp. David Barr writes:

A little miracle was wrought by enterprising local fishermen when they stocked the river with salmon eggs and within three years, in 1872, they greeted the first returning salmon. With the breach or improvement of various dams, the Yorkshire Esk gradually turned into a prolific spate river from which large catches of salmon, sea trout and bull trout were made – 885 in 1895 over 1000 in 1924. Many times this number were taken in nets at sea. It is a modern fishing tragedy that this attractive river, flowing through unspoilt moorland gorges and deep valleys, has deteriorated so much [in 1984] that it can scarcely be rated any longer as a quality sea trout and salmon river. There are many causes – a persistently dry weather being the most important, for in low water conditions the estuary fish have been mercilessly netted and poached. The various responsible authorities do not appear to have done much to help. One can only hope that a low tide in the affairs of this lovely river has been reached.

Essex Lakes It is never easy to get good fly fishing near London, especially north-east London, but there are two good Essex reservoirs: Ardleigh, near Colchester, and Hanningfield near Chelmsford. Both have bank and boat fishing and are stocked with brown and rainbow trout.

Exe Rising on Exmoor, the river Exe turns south, runs past Dulverton and Tiverton in Devon, and into the sea at Exmouth. There is a good run of salmon but, surprisingly enough for a Devon river, very few sea trout.

The salmon disease, UDN, which hit the river badly in the 1960s and 1970s seems to have diminished to a considerable extent. Private water is often open to the public (see *West Country Fly Fishing*, edited by Anne Voss Bark, Batsford, 1983) and the Carnarvon Arms Hotel has some fine salmon water on the Exe as well as good trout water on the Barle and Haddeo. The Fisherman's Cot Hotel at Bickleigh also provides salmon rods and the South West Water office at Exeter has some salmon water just above the town.

The Exe has a number of small tributaries which provide good wild trout fishing. Fishing hotels include the Tarr Steps and, at Simonsbath, the Exmoor Forest.

The Culm, one of the Exe tributaries, is a particularly delightful clear water stream for which permits can be obtained from the tackle shop next to the post office at Uffculme.

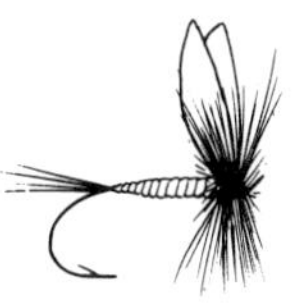

Fishing Upstream

Fishing the sunk fly is as exacting and entrancing an art as fishing the dry: in fact I am not sure that fishing it upstream when you cannot see your fish is not the highest art of all.

John Waller Hills, *A Summer on the Test*, 1924

Most people imagine that the small moorland-fed rivers of Exmoor and Dartmoor are generally fished wet fly downstream but this is not so today and the main records that survive of Victorian fishermen suggest that fishing upstream was preferred whenever possible.

From *West Country Fly Fishing*, an anthology edited by Anne Voss Bark, Batsford, 1983

Wade a shallow fast stream, if the bottom be hard and if you cast your fly up and against the Stream, the Trout that lies upon the fin in such strong Currents, and discerns you not, being behind him, presently takes your bait.

John Wolrlidge, *Systema Agriculturae*, 1669

Falkus, Hugh Actor, naturalist, film director, Spitfire pilot during the Battle of Britain, Hugh Falkus's wildlife films have received international acclaim and reached audiences worldwide. For ten years he made programmes about animal behaviour with the Nobel prizewinner, Professor Niko Tinbergen. Their study of animal communications, *Signals for Survival*, won the two major awards for documentary films, the Italia Prize and the American Blue Riband.

His books include *Freshwater Fishing*, with Fred Buller (Macdonald and James, 1975), *Sea Trout Fishing* (Witherby 1971, 2nd edn 1975) and *Salmon Fishing* (Witherby, 1984). All three are elaborate productions, lavishly illustrated with photographs and line drawings, and have the Falkus hallmark – the closest attention to the most minute detail, how to tie knots, how to cast, the tackle to use, the best rods, the strength of nylon, the best flies, strategy, tactics – all the many things a beginner needs to have explained.

Farson, Negley A foreign correspondent of the *Chicago Daily News* in the 1920s and 1930s, Negley Farson travelled the world for his newspaper but always took his fly rod with him. The publication of his fishing adventures in *Going Fishing* (Country Life Publications, 1942) was highly praised and was one of the few fishing books this century that came into the best-seller lists. Farson in his introduction wrote:

> This is just a story of some rods and the places they take you to. It begins with surf casting on the New Jersey cost, when I was thirteen, and carries on to such scenes as fly fishing the headwaters of the Kuban in the upper Caucasus, and casting for rainbow trout in the rivers of southern Chile with a volcano erupting every ten minutes in plain view. There is not a record or even a very big fish in it; and some of the finest things fishing has given me I have found beside the streams of the West Country in England.

Farson had a cottage in North Devon for some years and fished the Barle and the upper Exe.

In America, Arnold Gingrich said that *Going Fishing* contained some of the grandest reading in all angling literature. It was warmly greeted over here by many writers and fishermen, including H.E. Bates, Colin Willcock and Jack Hargreaves. The book was reprinted several times and a beautiful edition produced by Clive Holloway Books in 1981. In a foreword to this, Hugh Falkus wrote:

> I first read *Going Fishing* in 1943 when, as a prisoner of war, I was serving a term of solitary confinement following an escape attempt, and a friendly guard smuggled the book into my cell. For a couple of months it was my only literature, so I can claim to have read it pretty thoroughly! But Negley Farson proved more than a solace, he was a revelation. Of all the fishing books I had read, his was the best. It still is.

Field, The First published in January, 1853, *The Field* to begin with was a more general weekly newspaper, covering Parliament and London social life as well as country sports. The original idea for *The Field*, known as the *Country Gentleman's Newspaper*, came from R.S. Surtees, creator of Jorrocks. The idea was developed by the owners of *Punch*, and *Punch*'s Editor, Mark Lemon, became the first Editor of *The Field* with Surtees as the principal hunting

Hugh Falkus

correspondent. Over the years the political and social reports in *The Field* declined and successive editors concentrated more and more on hunting, shooting, fishing and farming.

One of the first writers on fishing was Francis Francis in the late 1850s, and others who followed him included among others, William Senior, F.M. Halford, G.E.M. Skues, John Bickerdyke (the pen-name of C.H. Cook), H.T. Sheringham, H.D. Turing. William Senior who was for many years the angling correspondent before becoming Editor, encouraged Halford and Marryat to write of their experiences with the floating fly at Ramsbury on the Kennet and later on the Itchen and Test.

The Field has led many campaigns on country matters, fighting for clean rivers, against corruption and misleading advertisements about fishing lets, and was one of the first papers to take the lead in investigating reports about the Loch Ness Monster – made difficult at one moment by a practical joker who, among other things, used a hippopotamus's foot to make strange footmarks in the muddy shore. *The Field* was not deceived.

In recent years *The Field* has been notable for distinguished essays on fishing by Dabchick, the pen-name of Wilson Stephens, who was Editor from 1951 to 1977. His successor, Derek Bingham, also a fisherman, was an industrial correspondent before joining *The Field* in 1968. He resigned in 1984 and was succeeded by Stephen Courtauld.

Findhorn A fast spate river in Moray and Nairn, not all that far from Speyside, with some spectacular rapids and falls at Dulsie Bridge. The Cawdor Estate office at Cawdor has good beats on the middle river where fishing can be very good indeed in the right height of water. Even in low water there will be fish ready to take in the throat of the pools if one puts a small dark fly over them and lets it play. The Cawdor water includes the famous Quilichan pool which is reached by an open bucket bridge.

On the upper river, fishing is available from the Freeburn Hotel at Tomatin.

Fish Farming Some 6,000 tons of trout were bred by United Kingdom fish farmers in 1981–82. The total includes retail sales for the table as well as live trout for stocking. It may be that the total tonnage is an under-estimate for it may not cover the returns of all the hatcheries. During the same period something like 1,000 tons of salmon were raised in salt-water fish farms off the Scottish coast, a major factor in causing a reduction in the market value of wild fish.

The interests of fish farmers are represented by the Intensive Livestock Division of the National Farmers' Union in London.

Fly Dressings The standard reference work on fly patterns for trout fishing is Courtney Williams' *A Dictionary of Trout Flies* (A and C Black, 5th edn, 1978), which gives the dressings of some 500 trout flies for rivers and stillwaters.

For lake and reservoir fishermen, the dressings of some 40 of the most popular flies are contained in *Stillwater Flies: How and When to Fish Them* (Benn, 1982), edited by John Goddard, with contributions from Syd Brock, Bob Carnill, Bob Church, John Ketley and Dick Walker. Line drawings by Ted Andrews show how the flies are tied.

The basic skills of how to dress flies are shown stage by stage in colour photographs in *Fly Tying Techniques* by Jacqueline Wakeford (Benn, 1980). The book goes into great detail: how to wax thread, put a hook in the vice, tie a whip finish (called the wrap knot) and shows the various stages in tying dry flies, wet flies, streamers, parachute flies, even cork-bodied and upside-down flies. The photographic sequences were taken by Miss Wakeford's husband, David Hawker. A correspondent writes:

> There was a sudden outburst of inventiveness among the design of reservoir lures from about the mid-1960s onwards, much of it based on American influence, the Nobbler patterns of the 1980s derive from American lead-head jig. Many American lures were directly imported without any alteration in the dressings, such as the Muddler Minnow and the Popper Bug.
>
> Artificial flies for river trout were inclined to move away from direct imitation towards impressionism, such as the Shadow Mayflies designed by Peter Deane. Halford's list of 33 dry flies for the chalk streams declined in influence, many skilled dry fly men using a mere one or two patterns – a Lunn's for the spinners and a Beacon Beige for the duns.
>
> Salmon flies were considerably simplified with the growing popularity of hairwings

on singles, doubles, trebles and tubes. The influence of Esmond Drury trebles appeared to increase, that of Waddington to decline. The Munro Killer and the Torridge Special, two black hairwings, illustrated the trend towards simplicity.

Fly Patterns The most popular fly patterns vary from year to year but on rivers they tend to be fairly constant, possibly one pattern becoming a little more fashionable than another, most likely because of more frequent mentions in river reports one year, but then falling back to a previous level in a year or so's time. So far as can be ascertained, only two new patterns have made the best-selling lists in the last 30 years or so – Kite's Imperial and Deane's Beacon Beige. Reservoir flies and lures change far more rapidly. Some of the most popular patterns of the 1950s are now rarely seen.

The best-selling salmon flies are now hairwing tubes. The fully dressed feather-winged doubles and singles are still in demand though the dressings are generally much more simple than they were when first published, largely because so many of the exotic feathers used in the dressings are no longer obtainable.

The following list of best-selling flies was prepared by Farlows of Pall Mall in 1980:

Dry Flies: winged or hackled. Blue Winged Olive, Blue Upright, Lunn's Particular, Tups, Kite's Imperial, Sherry Spinner, Iron Blue Dun, Ginger Quill, Wickham's Fancy. Sizes 14–16.
Wet Flies: Butcher, Black Pennell, Dunkeld, Invicta, Mallard and Claret, Greenwell, Black Zulu. Sizes 14–6.
Nymphs: Black Buzzer, Corixa, Sawyer Pheasant Tail, Sedge Pupa and Palmer Nymph. Sizes 14–10.
Sedges: G.H. Sedge, Silver Sedge, Cinnamon Sedge, Murragh, Green Peter, Dark Brown Sedge, Alder. Sizes 12–10.
Mayfly: Grey Wulff, Deane's Shadow Mayfly, Lunn's Spent Gnat – and, included in this section, the Daddy Longlegs. Sizes generally longshank 10 or 8 on fine wire hooks.
Reservoir Lures: Muddler Minnow, Sweeney Todd, Whisky Fly, Appetiser, Black Chenille, Black Lure, Ace of Spades, Baby Doll. Sizes 10–6, often longshank.
Salmon Fly Tubes: a big demand for heavy tubes for early and late fishing in colours of yellow and orange (often known as the Garry, Garry Dog or Yellow Dog) black and yellow, and all-black. Sizes ½in.–2½in.
For summer fishing the tubes are lighter and smaller and include dressings that suggest more traditional patterns – Stoat's Tail, Hairy Mary, Thunder and Lightning. Sizes ½in.–1in.
Salmon Fly Singles: fully dressed, Yellow Torrish, Jock Scott, Thunder and Lightning, Silver Doctor, Black Doctor. Sizes 10–5/0.
Salmon Fly Doubles: hair winged, Stoat's Tail, Hairy Mary, Shrimp, General Practitioner, Munro Killer. Sizes 4–10.
Salmon Fly Trebles: Esmond Drury hairwings.

Popular flies are discussed and illustrated in colour in *Trout and Salmon Flies* by Douglas Sutherland and Jack Chance, with contributions from Major the

Hon. John Ashley-Cooper, Hugh Falkus, Geoffrey Bucknell, John Goddard, Wilson Stephens, Derek Pattinson and Colonel Joseph D. Bates Jr.

Flyfishers' Club A social club for fly fishermen based at 24A Old Burlington Street, London, W.1. The club was founded in 1884 'for the social intercourse of gentlemen interested in the art of fly fishing'. Many famous fly fishermen have been members in past years, including Skues and Halford, and the present membership includes many well-known names in the fishing world. The club library, containing some 2,500 fishing books, is the most comprehensive in Europe. During the year there are many social events, lunches, rummage sales and an annual dinner. Membership applications need sponsors. The club Secretary (1984) is Commander Norman Fuller, R.N. (Retd).

Foston Beck Like the Driffield Beck, another of the great Yorkshire chalk streams:

> Foston has its origin in the chalk springs of the Yorkshire Wolds that surface in the area of the village of Kilham and then flow directly south. The stream widens into fishable proportion at Bracy Bridge, at which point it is reminiscent of the Itchen, from where it flows down through the tiny village of Lowthorpe its speed of progress slowing as it approached the village of Foston, some six miles in all. The water is controlled by the Foston Angling Club. Day tickets are not issued. (Donald Overfield)

Fore and Aft Fly A type of fly dressing, still sometimes used in which there is a larger hackle at the tail than at the head, with the body dubbed in between the two. This tilts the fly forward on the water which is said to give it an appearance more similar to the position of the natural fly when riding the stream. David Jacques used the fore and aft dressing for his mayfly pattern.

Fowey A good Cornish sea trout river with a long and picturesque estuary leading to the sea at the port of Fowey (pronounced Foy). Some big sea trout come in quite early, in March or April. The National Trust at Lanhydrock is a good place to enquire about day permits on association water, but beware holiday weekends and bait fishermen. Like most Cornish rivers, the Fowey is well bushed and in many places a fly is almost impossible.

Francis Francis (1822–1886) Angling Editor of *The Field* from 1854 onwards for over 40 years, Francis Francis was born Francis Morgan, the son of a naval officer, at Seaton, in Devon, but changed his surname to Francis in accordance with a stipulation in a relative's will under which he inherited property. He published many articles and books on fishing, was one of the first to advocate the use of the dry fly, and was a great campaigner in the columns of *The Field* about the bad behaviour of Englishmen fishing the Norwegian rivers. He called them 'British snobs' and said that sometimes they behaved 'disgracefully'. His best known publication *A Book on Angling*, was published in 1885 and ran into six editions.

Frome This lovely river rises in the hills above Dorchester where it is a chalk stream with excellent trout fishing. Its several tributaries merge and flow through Dorchester, thence eastwasds through former water meadows, and therefore at times through two or more channels. Aylmer Tryon writes:

Below Wool the river deepens as it winds its serpentine way to Wareham, named after an ancient weir and salmon trap which virtually destroyed the entire salmon run until litigation at the end of the 19th century at last allowed rods to fish for salmon with some hope of success. The Frome flows into the sea at Poole Harbour, a short distance below Wareham, near the mouth of its sister river, the Piddle, which is similar in most respects but even smaller.

At the beginning of this century the salmon fishing improved very rapidly and the river became famous for the size of its spring fish which averaged over 20lbs. Sadly, like many other runs, this spring run has greatly diminished in numbers if not in size. A possible or even probable reason is that the majority of the parr smolt after one year in the river and therefore spend an additional year in the sea and thus are more likely to be caught at sea by drift nets, legal and illegal, or on long lines. The summer run of fish has increased but by then the almost insoluble weed problems makes their capture often impossible.

The Frome fly fishing for salmon is difficult and often discouraging because most fish lie in the deep bends under the banks which often overhang, so the majority of fish are caught on baits and until a few years ago on prawns. However, in recent years the Wessex Water Authority restricted the netting while the Frome and Piddle Association introduced a voluntary ban on prawns in the spring months with the object of restoring the spring run, and this is showing signs of at least having some effect.

Fly fishing in the Frome in March when the season opens is perhaps more likely to succeed with large weighted tube flies fished deep and slowly. Personally I prefer the old-fashioned and beautiful 5/0 flies such as Torrish and Thunder and Lightning which are slightly less dangerous to my ears. But as the water warms in May and June then at times on a windy day Shrimp flies and Hairy Marys, sizes 6 or 8, fished fast and stripped up under the near bank with an inshore bend may well produce an enormous rise or even a huge fish which in such a small river seems to have added proportions – often with disastrous results. For the trout on the upper chalk streams, and indeed wherever they may be, there is a good grannom hatch in March and early April; in some years plenty of mayfly in late May and early June: in July a good rise of BWO; and in summer evenings sedges are popular with fish and fishermen. There are some large grayling on some beats.

The mayfly time is especially exciting since there is always the chance of an early large sea trout and I have seen salmon taking the mayfly on several occasions. I once hooked a salmon of about 15lbs which broke me, rose a large sea trout three times; and caught a brown trout of 3½lbs all in one never-to-be-forgotten day. Many fishermen would have been more successful but how many rivers would provide such a treble chance?

The record Frome salmon weighed 42½lbs, caught in 1929. The record, and indeed the British record sea trout, weighed 22½lb and was taken in 1946 on a prawn. Two of over 15lbs were taken on the fly in 1981, whilst in the following year a pike was killed by electric fishing which weighed 27lbs and was found to contain a 5lb grilse! Some very large brown trout have been caught, whilst a sturgeon of 120lbs, now in Dorchester Museum, was landed by somewhat doubtful means. Altogether the Frome is a river of fish to dream about.

Most of the Frome is estate water. The Dorchester Fishing Club sometimes has day permits for trout but not for the mayfly period. The Woolbridge Manor Hotel, near Wareham, has rods. Advance booking is necessary.

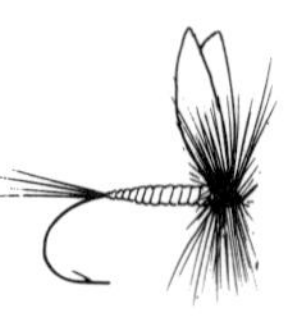

The Kelt

This fish was what rod and line fishermen called a well-mended kelt, because it had the silvery appearance of a fish new from the sea although it was thin. They said a kelt mended itself, that it changed from river-brown, the tarnish and dislustre of stagnation, to an argentine anticipation of ocean; and how it mended itself, they declared, whether or not it fed during or after its perlustration, was a mystery, like the primal sea change of smolts while yet in the river. The bright deposit was an armour against corrosion, a temper for brine-weighted water, and it was made from an excretion of the body, a waste product, a kind of solder sweated on each scale. Thus the kelt, exhausted salmon, was reborn; its sharp teeth and bright scales were a death-desperate hope of resurrection.

Henry Williamson, *Salar the Salmon*, Faber Edition, 1972

Garry Dog Created by James Wright of Sprouston in the mid-1800s, the Garry Dog was probably the first hairwing salmon fly ever dressed; certainly it is likely to be so in the absence of claims about the Hairy Mary, also an early hairwing. Wright took the hair for the Garry Dog from the Minister's dog, Garry, though we do not know what kind of dog or what colour hair. The dog is buried in the footpath between Sprouston and the Butterwash. The grave had a headstone at one time but this was stolen in the 1970s and is believed to be somewhere in Gateshead on Tyne. **Source:** Donald Overfield, *Famous Flies and Their Originators* (A and C Black, 1972), Irvine Hall, Jean Partington.

The original dressing probably had brown or yellow hair from a working dog, possibly a labrador or spaniel, and with some fibres of contrasting colour. Overfield gives this dressing:

Tag: yellow or gold floss or silver tinsel
Tail: golden pheasant crest and ibis
Body: black floss
Rib: oval silver
Hackle: blue gallina
Wings: yellow bear's fur or bucktail; a few red fibres at the base
Head: black varnish

That would be a dressing for single hooks, for doubles it has been much simplified, and there is little doubt that James Wright would not recognise the dressing now common for tube flies. The Garry Dog tube is similar to another but much later pattern, the Willie Gunn. The body is of black wool ribbed with flat silver tinsel; the hair wings a mix of yellow and red dyed squirrel, or similar flexible fibres.

Gnats *See* Midges.

Gobage French for a trout's rise, meaning 'mouthing', from which derives the slang 'Shut your gob'.

Gilbert, H.A. An invaluable reference book for the Wye, *The Tale of a Wye Fisherman* (H.A. Gilbert, Methuen, 1928) contains a picture of the biggest rod-caught Wye salmon, weighing 59½lb, together with the records of five other Wye fish over 50lb. It also has Miss Doreen Davey's account of how she caught a 59lb springer at Cowpond in 1923:

At about 5.30 p.m. having lost all hope and fully expecting another blank day I hooked a fish on a small minnow I had put on for a change. The fish swam about and did more or less what he liked . . .
At about 7 o'clock he got quite cross and we could see how big he was, and my father's chauffeur, John Hellis, lit a fire on the bank so we could see to gaff him. Other people came up and brought candles . . .

The end came with almost dramatic suddeness. The fish was steered in and in a mix-up of splash and spray the faithful John Hellis with the gaff, and Charlie Donald with his hands as much round the tail of the fish as he could get them, managed to haul him out of the water. The fish was landed at 7.55 p.m. after being hooked at 5.40 p.m. . . .

I have had dozens of nice letters of congratulation from friends and from complete strangers. Among the strangers some have sent poetry and one proposes that I should marry him. However, this is another 'catch' and I am not rising.

John Goddard

Ginger Quill A variation of the Orange Quill and the Red Quill which is said to be most useful when spinners are on the water. The dressing is similar, a peacock body and ginger cock hackle and whisks – the quill can be left undyed but most fishermen prefer it dyed to match the hackle.

Goddard, John A leading authority on fly fishing entomology and a distinguished underwater and macro photographer, Goddard was born in London in 1923 and began fishing in the Thames while still at school. He served as a paratrooper in World War Two and afterwards, as head of the family tackle firm of E.F. Goddard and Co., became interested and then absorbed in fly fishing.

In company with his friend Cliff Henry and encouraged by David Jacques, he began a new classification of flies, and their matching artificials which he was able to photograph from life, in many cases for the first time. The result, *Trout Fly Recognition* (Black, 1966) was recognised at once as a major work, comparable to those of Ronalds, Harris and Halford. Three years later came the companion volume, *Trout Flies of Stillwater.*

Collaboration with Brian Clarke and the use of Goddard's new and highly sophisticated underwater cameras resulted in *The Trout and The Fly* (Benn, 1980), which brought about a considerable advance in our knowledge of the underwater world.

The camera, hidden beneath the surface of the stream, captured for the first time the appearance of the natural fly and its matching artificial, the flare of wings approaching the trout's window, how floating nylon looks from below, the flash of a line, the brilliant glow of a spinner's wings in the sunset, and many other trout's eye views which had involved hundreds of hours of research and filming.

Goddard's latest experiments, concerning trout vision, begun in 1980, are still continuing (1984).

Gold Ribbed Hare's Ear Sometimes called Hare's Ear, or GRHE; a chalk stream variant of a much older trout fly known in the West Country as a Hare's Fleck. The Fleck has a body dubbing of hare's fur, dun hackle and whisks, and starling wings, the dubbing kept in place by gold wire, and is a useful pattern when olive duns are hatching. The chalk stream pattern is sometimes tied without wings or hackle to suggest an emerging nymph, and is fished in the surface film. In America and a number of other countries rabbit fur is frequently substituted for hare's fur and has become a standard emerger pattern. There are no standard patterns of the GRHE these days as there are so many variations in the dressing. This is a common and effective emerger:

Body: medium-coloured hair from a hare's ear – taken from the base of the ear – or dun-coloured rabbit's fur
Whisks: a few short fur fibres
Rib: fine gold wire or thin gold tinsel
Thorax: thicker dubbing of fur, covered over the back with dark feather fibres from a hen or cock pheasant to suggest the wing cases
Legs: strands of fur picked out with the dubbing needle
Hooks: 14, 15 or 16 to suggest the emerging olive, larger to suggest various stillwater insects. A damsel fly larvae will need an 8 longshank, weighted

Grafham Water This big Midland storage reservoir, of 1,670 acres, provides anglers with about 30,000 trout every season. Deep fishing from boats is practised as well as long casting lures on sinking lines from the bank, but there is a good deal of light fishing with floating lines, flies close to the surface, especially during a fall of hawthorn or a heavy hatch of the big black midge.

Grafham produces a fast growth rate of fish which are stocked regularly from the opening of the season until late summer, a total of about 40 or 50,000 rainbow and 5 or 6,000 brown. Bob Church, Dick Shrive, and other regulars, fishing from boats, experimented with deep sunk lures, lead lines and drift control rudders in the mid-1970s. Another pattern of fishing was developed by Arthur Cove of Wellingborough who fished a large pheasant tail nymph on 8 or 10 longshank hook on a floating line. Towards autumn, the trout feed avidly on coarse fish and on most evenings there is a good midge rise as well as a hatch of medium sedge.

Some of the methods of controlling drifting boats – rudders and leeboards – were banned at Grafham in the mid-1970s for safety reasons much to the annoyance of some of the regulars who had been highly successful in catching limit bags with the use of this equipment, together with echo sounders, lead lines, and large lures.

Restrictions on fishing methods were discussed at the London conference of the Salmon and Trout Association in 1974 when the fishery officer responsible for Grafham's development, Major Fleming-Jones said that while sympathising with the views of traditional fly fishers, nevertheless they had to be realists:

Public fisheries on our reservoirs exist for the enjoyment of the angling public generally, they must be attractive to a large number of anglers so that sufficient revenue is obtained to continue to stock with such a volume of trout that a worthwhile catch per angler-visit results.

Grand Masters Howard Marshall borrowed this phrase from chess to describe super flyfishers. They were, he said, often unknown to the world outside, were not inclined to boast and were unaccompanied by cameramen. But their talent became legendary in spite of themselves – men like Dr Bell of Blagdon, John Hamp and Frank Fortey of the Kennet, and some others:

Just as it is said of the successful gardener that he has green fingers, or of a great horseman that he has good hands, so there should be a label for the fishing wizard. There is a touch of wizardry in the sense that some supernatural percipience appears to play a part in their success. It is not a flamboyant quality, and I daresay it could be analysed in terms of visual coordination and muscle control. It is there, though, whatever it may be, and we can see it in the performance of men like Sir Donald Bradman, the cricketer, Jim Clarke, the racing driver; in Arnold Palmer, the golfer, and Joe Davis, for so long the uncrowned king of snooker; and Davis, possibly the greatest champion of all in terms of sheer control technique, was practically blind in one eye.

We do not hear much of the great practitioners of game fishing for it is an individualistic do-it-yourself pastime as compared with the great spectator sports like football, cricket and boxing. In spite of this there are certain men who have become widely known for their outstanding skill. There was G.S. Marryat, for example, generally recognised as the greatest dry-fly fisherman of all. There was G.E.M. Skues, also blind in one eye, the prophet of nymph fishing in the chalk streams. There were others – not many – who qualified for the title of master, and there are some alive today, which brings me to my point. Almost everywhere you go you will come across a man who is outstanding among local fishermen; a man who catches more trout in any condition of water than anyone else in the district. These are the unsung Bradmans and Palmers of the angling world, and I happily met one of them some years ago in the West Country.

I was wading and fishing dry fly for the lively little trout of the River Barle. The fish were obliging enough and would take my fly explosively, but somehow I could not hook them. I may have been too late or too quick on the strike but, whatever it was, my basket was empty, until I heard a voice behind me. I looked round and saw an elderly man who had waded into the river in his ordinary clothes to give me a helping hand. He asked if he might use my tackle and then, casting with beautiful rhythm, and ease, he proceeded to take fish after fish. 'You see', he said in due course, 'it is really quite easy but you must strike when you see them coming up halfway through the water on the way to take your fly, otherwise you will miss them every time.'

Now it was not only the precision of his placing of the fly and his striking which impressed me, but his water vision. I found that sometimes I caught the gleam of a fish turning on the fly, but often I saw nothing until the last moment of the take. He somehow saw through the not particularly clear water and timed his strike with the accuracy of a computer. Then, as he told me afterwards, he had been peering into that water for close on seventy years and he knew what to look for. There is something in that, of course, for water vision is of great importance and it can be improved by much hard practice. I am sure, though, that some men, for this particular purpose, have keener eyesight than others, and that all great fishers have the water vision of a heron.

I know a doctor on the Kennet*, no longer young, who can see the trout's mouth open and close upon a nymph four feet below the surface. It is no wonder that he catches many big fish in places where the less gifted angler would say there were no fish at all. I remember being told by the cricketer Duleepsinhji, nephew of the famous Ranjitsinhji, that there was no need for him to watch the slow bowler's hand in order to detect which way the ball would turn because he could see the ball spinning as it came to him through the air. Such eyesight is phenomenal, but great fly fishers have it in the same degree, and their performances are phenomenal also (Howard Marshall, *Reflections on a River*, Witherby, 1967)

Grannom (*Brachycentrus subnubilus*) Almost everything that needs to be said about this charming little sedge fly which appears on many rivers in the spring, sometimes in vast numbers, covering the bushes for miles, was contained in *Fisherman's Fly* by David Jacques (Black, 1965):

. . . how can I fail to feel affection for this gentle insect in whose delectable company I have passed so many hours? From its very birth I watched it, clumsily and awkwardly engage in tumbling games with its brothers and sisters; then, through its infancy and maturity, nestling in its case, harming no other living creature, but waiting patiently and trustingly for the victuals on which its life depends to be brought to its threshold; to its breath-taking metamorphosis from an aquatic animal to a fairy-like creature of the air and, finally, to its lonely death in obscurity . . .

Jacques bred grannom in his home and lived with them, watching their every move for hours at a time. They opened a new world for him and his comments, of which the above is but one, make fascinating reading. There have been many tyings of the grannom – it is the greentail fly of the fifteenth-century writers but this is probably the easiest if not the best:

Body: dark hare's ear dubbed on green tying silk with a tiny ball of light green wool at the tail
Wings: two slips from the wing feather of a hen pheasant, tied roof shape sloping well back close to the hook
Hackle: in front of the wings, rusty dun cock
Hook: 14

Courtney Williams gives many other dressings.

Gray, L.R.N. Lindsay Gray was better known under his pen-name, Lemon Gray, an outspoken fisherman who ran a private house, Devon Lodge, as a fishing hotel with water on the Torridge in the 1950s and 1960s. He recounted his experiences in *Torridge Fishery* (Nicholas Kaye, 1957). Maurice Wiggin, then fishing correspondent of *The Sunday Times*, wrote in a foreword:

. . . He [Gray] is a prickly outspoken privateer clean out of his age, the horror of bureaucrats, the scourge of committees. An exhausting, uncompromising, cruelly effective tutor, a first rate fly fisherman and fly dresser, a staunch friend . . .

Gray had a great deal to say about fishing and fishing hotels. When he had guests at Devon Lodge he did not like he would ask them to leave. When they asked why, he would say that if they stayed on he would have to tell them and as he was a kindly man he did not like to be rude.

* Probably the late Dr Cecil Terry of Bath.

Grayling Society The first annual general meeting of The Grayling Society was held at the Wendover Hotel, Salford, Lancashire, in February 1978, organised by Dr. R.B. Broughton, in response to a suggestion from Reg Righini, sponsored by fishermen from Nottinghamshire, Yorkshire, Lancashire and Perthshire. The society aims to promote a proper appreciation of the sporting qualities of the grayling, to collect and record information about it, and provide members with information and advice about grayling through a newsletter. The officers (1984) were: President, Mr N. Roose, Nottinghamshire; Chairman, Dr R.B. Broughton, Salford, Lancashire; Secretary and Editor of the newsletter is Mr D. Liversedge of Comrie, Perth. Dr Broughton writes:

> The annual meetings are always preceded by a symposium and are held in a different part of the country every year to give as many local anglers as possible a chance to take part. There are active local committees in northern England, Wales, and in southern England a reasonable proportion of members. We are in contact with other countries and fishermen in France and Italy are members.

Green, E. Garrow A frequent contributor to *The Fishing Gazette* between 1900–1930, Garrow Green wrote under the pen-name of Black Hackle about fishing in Ireland, where he had served as an army officer, and in Devon, where he lived. His book on Dartmoor fishing, *Trout Fishing in Brooks*, containing excellent advice, was published in the 1920s.

Green Peter An Irish fly, fished wet, which suggests a sedge. The dressing is similar to the Woodcock and Green, though without a tag. In Ireland the wing is often hen pheasant. A simple dressing becoming popular on English stillwaters.

Greenwell's Glory A famous trout fly tied by James Wright of Sprouston on Tweed to the design of Canon Greenwell of Durham in May, 1854. Wright named the fly at a celebration dinner probably at the nearby town of Kelso.

A little difficult to be certain what the Greenwell's Glory was intended to represent; probably one of the larger olives.

Body: yellow silk
Wing: inside feather of a blackbird's wing
Hackle: coch-y-bondhu
Hook: 14–16

The wings of the original are upright, not sloping, though the wet fly dressing now has sloping wings. The fly is mostly tied with whisks of the same colour as the hackle and a fine gold rib added, but neither were in the original dressing.

Grenadier An imitation bait for lake and reservoir fishing designed by Dr Bell of Blagdon in the 1920s and 1930s, the Grenadier suggests a small red larvae or midge. It was originally tied unweighted:

Body: red silk
Rib: fine gold tinsel
Head hackle: one or two turns of partridge, the fibres short
Hook: 14

Canon Greenwell of Durham – from a painting by permission of the Society of Antiquaries of London

Dr Bell always fished his patterns very slowly, allowing them to sink quite a way down, then bringing them in gradually. He generally had three flies on the same cast, the Grenadier in the middle or on the point.

Grey Duster A very useful general-purpose trout fly which probably suggests a dun but will take fish when sedge are on the water. Courtney Williams found it effective during a hatch of the big mayfly on both the Inny and the Test. The standard dressing does not seem to have whisks, but they can be added:

Body: light-coloured rabbit or hare's fur, slightly blue
Hackle: well-marked badger with black centre and white list
Tying silk: brown
Hook: usually 14 or 12

Grey, Edward (1862–1933) Sir Edward Grey, Viscount Grey of Fallodon, is best known to fishermen as the author of *Fly Fishing*, first published in 1899, followed by several editions and reprintings over the next 40 years. In the wider field of public affairs he was one of Britain's most distinguished statesmen and held the office of Foreign Secretary from 1905 to 1916. During

Viscount Grey of Falloden – photo courtesy of the B.B.C. Hulton Picture Library

that time he strove hard to avert the danger of war with Germany. Some have argued that if public opinion had been less neutralist and pacifist at that time he might have succeeded; however he failed to get support in the Cabinet for his proposal for a firm declaration that Britain would stand by France and Russia in arms against German aggression and some months later the inevitable happened. Grey, in the Cabinet room at Downing Street on the day war was declared, looked out of the windows to the lights of Horseguards and made the prophetic remark 'the lights of Europe are going out one by one'. During the next three years his greatest success lay in keeping up good relations with the United States. He resigned his office because of failing eyesight not long before the United States entered the war.

Grey was a sensitive and evocative writer on country matters and for some time had a small cottage on the Itchen. He fished the Rosehall water of the Cassley, the Lochy, Spean and Tweed. His advice on both salmon and trout fishing was admirable. The best edition of his book is the one which he revised in 1930, published by Dent, with line drawings by Daglish. Here is Grey's description of fishing in the Highlands:

The pure act of breathing at such times seems glorious. People talk of being a child of nature, and moments such as these are times when it is possible to feel so; to know the full joy of animal life – to desire nothing beyond. There are times when I have stood still for joy of it all, on my way through the wild freedom of a Highland moor, and felt the wind, and looked upon the mountains and water and light and sky, till I felt conscious only of the strength of a mighty current of life, which swept away all consciousness of self, and made me a part of all that I beheld. (Edward Grey, *Fly Fishing*, André Deutsch, 1974)

Grey Wulff *See* Mayfly.

Grouse and Green A useful wet fly for lake and river trout, better known in the north of England than the south. The grouse hackle can be long or short. If the colour of the body wool or floss is changed the fly then becomes grouse and orange or grouse and purple, etc. The green body is the most popular:

Body: apple green wool or floss
Rib: fine gold or silver wire
Tail: a few golden pheasant tippet fibres, quite short
Hackle: grouse breast or rump

Gut Fine gut casts (leaders) were made in fairly short lengths from silkworms, the lengths knotted together to create a taper. This is how the gut was obtained:

When the worm was about to spin it was placed in vinegar, split open, and the interior drawn out through holes in a metal screen. This was known as fine drawn gut and the terms 1x, 2x, and so on, described the size of the holes. Silkworm gut began to be used in place of horsehair at some time in the early 1700s. It was stronger than horsehair but had to be well softened in water before knots could be tied in it without the danger of splitting; hence gut dampers, rounded boxes with felt pads that could be soaked with water and the gut casts placed between them so that they would be ready for use when the angler reached the river. Gut casts were in common use until after the Second World War when they were replaced by nylon.

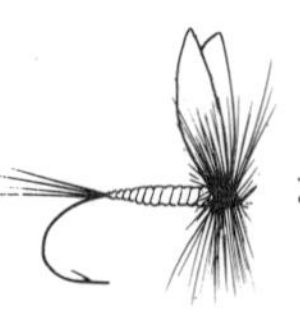

Recreation

No life, my honest Scholar, no life so happy and so pleasant, as the life of a well-governed angler; for when the lawyer is swallowed up with business, and the statesman is preventing or contriving plots, then we sit on cowslip banks, hear the birds sing, and possess ourselves in as much quietness as these silver streams, which we now see glide so quietly by us. Indeed, my good Scholar, we may say of angling, as Dr Boteler said of strawberries, 'Doubtless God could have made a better berry, but doubtless God never did': and so, if I might be judge, 'God did never make a more calm, quiet, innocent recreation, than angling'.

Izaak Walton, *The Compleat Angler*, 1676 edition

And angling too, that solitary vice,
Whatever Izaak Walton sings or says:
The quaint old cruel coxcomb in his gullet
Should have a hook and a small trout to pull it.

Lord Byron, *Don Juan*, Canto XII

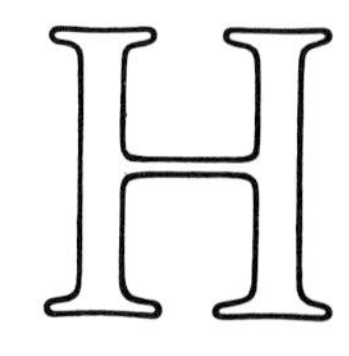

Hairy Mary A hairwing salmon fly, especially liked and well-used on many Scottish rivers. It is rarely seen on Speyside but is frequently in use on Tay and Tweed and has spread widely elsewhere, including many Norwegian rivers. It is difficult to say how far back it dates or who the Mary was who sacrificed some of her light brown hair for the original dressing:

Body: black floss
Rib: either oval silver or oval gold tinsel
Tag: plain flat silver tinsel
Tail: golden pheasant crest, up-turned towards the wing
Throat hackle: dyed blue hen tied beard style
Wings: light brown bucktail or squirrel dyed light brown
Hook sizes: up to 5/0, even 8/0 for Norwegian rivers, but mostly a fairly moderate 1/0 down to 2 or 4

Halford, Frederick M. (1844–1914) A great angler-entomologist who was highly praised during his life and frequently criticised afterwards, sometimes by those who had never read his works, F.M. Halford's achievements are admirably summarised by Donald Overfield in *Famous Flies and Their Originators* (Black, 1972).

Halford came from a wealthy Midlands family and began worm fishing as a boy in a pond near his home almost as soon as he could walk. The family moved to London, when he was seven, where he continued to fish in the Serpentine and the Thames, and also in the sea at Eastbourne.

In 1868, when Halford was 24, a friend offered him a day's trout fishing on the Wandle. The river which runs into the Thames at Wandsworth is now polluted and built over, but in those days was a clear chalk stream. Halford. knew little or nothing about fly fishing and followed the advice of the members of the syndicate on the Wandle to cast a dry fly upstream to the rising fish.

Fascinated, he gave up sea and coarse fishing to concentrate on the fly. In 1877 he became a member of the Houghton Club on the River Test which had about 17 miles of some of the best trout water in Hampshire.

In 1889, quite by chance, Halford met a retired army officer, G.S. Marryat, who had the reputation, according to Sir Edward Grey, of being 'the best trout fisherman in England'. Whether that was so or not, Marryat was able to give Halford good advice on flies and fly tying, they became friends, and the next year Halford took rooms at Bossington Mill on the Test with the intention of studying, with Marryat's help, the natural flies of the river and their matching artificials.

> . . . throughout our work [Halford wrote] we never departed from the determination we had mutually arrived at, to reduce to writing the results of any experiments, and consider them, carefully, together, and where possible verify them . . .

Nothing so comprehensive had been undertaken since the work of Ronalds which had resulted in the publication of *The Fly Fisher's Entomology* 44 years earlier, in 1836. This time there were two leisured and wealthy men – Marryat had a private income as well as his army pension – who could concentrate together on the study of the insect life about them and select, prepare or invent

F.M. Halford – photo courtesy of the Flyfishers' Club

the appropriate matching artificials. After six years intensive work came the result, Halford's *Floating Flies and How to Dress Them* (1886).

We do not know why Marryat refused to have his name given as the joint author, but there is little doubt that he had equal if not a major share in the preparation of the book. What was the reservation on Marryat's part? The two men were very different. Marryat was never a purist to the extent Halford was. Here, perhaps, were the first faint signs of a disagreement. It is impossible to say.

Whatever the reason, Halford was now set to become the leader of the dry fly movement which eventually triumphed over all others so far as the Hampshire streams were concerned. The main point about the dry fly was simply that it was the most efficient way of taking trout which were feeding on duns and spinners.

Halford's works now followed fairly rapidly: in 1889, *Dry Fly Fishing in Theory and Practice*; in 1895, *Making a Fishery*; in 1897, *Dry Fly Entomology*; in 1903 his life story, *An Angler's Autobiography*; in 1910 *The Modern Development of the Dry Fly*; and in 1913, *The Dry Fly Man's Handbook.*

Halford's influence can only be understood by comparing his work in the context of his time. Worm and minow were frequently in use on the chalk streams. During the big mayfly hatches, dapping the natural fly was the most favoured method. The artificial flies in use were more or less wet fly patterns that soon sank below the surface. There were no effective floatants.

Marryat and Halford redesigned fly patterns to make it easier for them to float. They used quill bodies which would not absorb water. They used stiffer hackles, making them more bushy, so the fly would stay afloat longer. They introduced double split wings so that the fly when properly cast would descend delicately down to the surface where it would ride cocked upright on the water. When such progress is taken into account, together with the emphasis on false casting to dry the fly, the changes that Halford and Marryat made raised fly fishing to a sophistication and efficiency previously unknown. Halford's instructions on how to fish the dry fly were precise:

Dry-fly fishing is presenting to the rising fish the best possible imitation of the insect on which he is feeding in its natural position. To analyse this further, it is necessary, firstly to find a fish feeding on the winged insect; secondly, to present to him a good imitation of this insect, both as to size and colour; thirdly, to present it to him in its natural position or floating on the surface of the water with its wings up, or what we technically term, 'cocked'; fourthly, to put the fly lightly on the water, so that it floats accurately over him without drag; and, fifthly, to take care that all these conditions have been fulfilled before the fish has seen the angler or the reflection of his rod.

Halford's mistake was to imagine that the dry fly had superceded all other methods of fly fishing, an understandable enthusiasm which ultimately led to egotism and intolerance, a lack of humour, and a rigid code from which no deviation was permissable. Great men – and he was a great man – have faults. The best assessment of Halford's influence was made only a few years after his death by one of his disciples, John Waller Hills:

Halford's place in the history of fly fishing is well marked. He is the historian of a far-reaching change, and as such it is probable that he will always be read . . . He established the dry fly as we know it, and there have not been many changes since he wrote. Tackle has been refined still further, rod, reels and lines are if possible more excellent, flies are more closely copied, and in particular the nymph and spent spinner are novelties. But the method of fishing is unchanged. You still have to find your trout rising, or willing to rise, and to cast accurately and delicately. Halford's directions are as good and as useful as on the day they were written.

If he is to be criticised it is because like most reformers he overstated his case. He considered that the dry fly had superseded for all time and in all places all other methods of fly fishing, and that those who thought otherwise were either ignorant or incompetent. He did not realise, and perhaps it was impossible that he should have realised that the coming of the floating fly did not mean that previous experience and previous knowledge were as worthless as though they had never been; but that it meant that from then onwards fly fishing was divided into two streams. These streams are separated but they run parallel and there are many cross channels in between them.

Looking back more than a generation to Halford's first book, and taking note of what has happened, two tendencies are apparent. The floating fly has spread far beyond its original territory. When he first wrote it was the common but not yet the universal practice in a limited area: the chalk streams of Hampshire, Berkshire, Wiltshire and Kent, the Wandle, the Hertfordshire and Buckinghamshire streams, and the limestone streams of Derbyshire. Speaking generally, and without reckoning such outlying areas such as Driffield Beck, Derbyshire was its northerly and Dorsetshire its westerly boundary. At his death, it had spread over all England, over Scotland, Ireland and parts of France, Germany, Scandinavia, America and New Zealand; in fact it was practised by some fishermen in most places where trout are to be found. It must not be imagined that wherever it went it conquered, for such was far from the case. But it won its way on rivers in which trout sometimes run large, such as Tweed or Don, and particularly on Irish rivers, of which the Suir is one. It has also come to be used more and more on lakes which hold big fish, such as Blagdon or Lough Arrow. And the new sport of fishing it for sea trout has been invented. Altogether, Halford, in the time between his first book and his death, saw its empire spread over a large part of the earth.

An unpublished story about Halford is worth recording. It was told one day over lunch in the Reform Club by Toby O'Brian, a Civil Servant, about his uncle, Tommy White (M.R.L. White) who was a great athlete and a great fly fisherman at Blagdon in the early days. White was invited by Halford to fish the Test with him at some time or another around the year 1910. Toby O'Brian continued:

Tommy was thrilled. There he was, fishing with the great man. Halford put on a delicious little fly and cast it perfectly. The trout took no notice: Tommy followed Halford and put up a bushy monster that has no relationship whatever to the flies on the water, cast it to the trout, and the trout took it at once. Tommy was not asked again.

Halford's Flies In some ways to think of Halford's flies is a misnomer, many listed by Halford were Marryat's and some were traditional, such as the Coachman. Halford's first list of 100 flies for the chalk streams was later reduced to a more manageable 33, though today it is doubtful if any good chalk stream fishermen uses more than a dozen.

The point about the Halford-Marryat dressings is that they were all designed specifically to float, and float well, in days when no good floatant was available. When one studies them – there is a collection in the Flyfishers' Club museum in London – it is at once clear how small and delicate they are, how well though lightly hackled, and how important were the dubbings, mostly quill, in aiding floatation.

About the best known, still in general use, are the Rough Olive, Medium Olive, Iron Blue, Blue Quill, Blue Dun, Red Quill, Red Spinner, Ginger Quill, Wickham, Blue-Winged Olive, Grannom, Alder, Black Gnat, Silver Sedges, and several different mayflies (Green Drakes) and mayfly spinners (Spent Gnats).

The story is well known why Halford deleted the Gold Ribbed Hare's Ear from his list. It was because he could not decide what natural fly the GRHE was supposed to represent.

Half Stone A Devon trout fly, fished wet or dry, almost always upstream:

Body: yellow silk with a pinch of mole fur on the shoulder by the hackle
Whisks: strands of blue cock
Hackle: four or five turns of blue cock
Hook: 12–14

Hampshire Lakes In 1981 there were some 60 private trout lakes fisheries in Hampshire, all of which provided trout fishing, some of very high quality, either on club, subscription or a day ticket basis. The first and most distinguished is the pioneer fishery at Two Lakes near Romsey, the first of its kind to be established, and probably the best stillwater trout fishery in England. There is no effort to breed large trout, though many ten-pound rainbows are caught every year, but to provide trout of high quality and strength at an average weight of well over 2lb. The Avington fishery on the Itchen is based on a different philosophy. Whereas Two Lakes is a subscription water, Avington is day ticket and likes to hold the British record for producing the largest trout, which it does. There are two other lake fisheries of high quality which must be mentioned, Rockbourne and Damerham, both near Fordingbridge, both day ticket water with limited access, both with very clear water where individual fish can be stalked and fished for.

Halladale A salmon river in Caithness flowing north into the sea at Melvich, a river of great charm winding through wild valleys in empty mountainous country, a spate river, as are all its neighbours in Caithness and Sutherland – Thurso, Helmsdale, Naver – all approached by twisting single-track roads where you are just as likely to meet deer as men:

> Mid-summer is the time to expect low-water and fishing will then be very dour, but a day or so's rain will make all the difference and fish will be on the move in no time. Small flies on a sink tip line are favoured except in spates when big heavy tubes and sinking lines are needed.

The Forsinard Hotel has beats on the Halladale and the Melvich Hotel at the mouth can also arrange fishing. Private water is let through agents. Sea trout fishing on many of the lochs is a great consolation if the rivers are out of condition.

Hare's Fleck Sometimes known as Hare's Flax, a very old and, probably, a West Country fly, not dissimilar to some other traditional flies, the Maxwell series. Why fleck or flax is difficult to say. Fleck means spotted, flaxy is light-coloured. Another possibility is that fleck may be derived from fletched, meaning feathered; in other words a hare-bodied fly feathered. Whatever the origin it is a good trout fly, an ancestor of the Gold Ribbed Hare's Ear.

Body: hare's fur, often ribbed with fine flat gold tinsel or thin wire
Hackle: rusty blue cock or sometimes a red gamecock
Whisks: three or four fibres of the same colour
Hook: 14–12

Quite apart from its home territory in Devon it has also done remarkably well on the Kennet when a supply of the Gold Ribbed Hair Ear ran short.

Harris, J.R. A lecturer in the zoology department of Trinity College, Dublin, J.R. Harris wrote *An Angler's Entomology* (Collins, New Naturalist Series, 1952). The book marked an important stage in the understanding and classification of trout food insects, some of which were seen in colour photographs in a book for the first time. Harris's work has been compared with the great step forward in knowledge made by Ronalds 116 years earlier as well as providing encouragement and pointing the way to the work of Goddard in the 1960s. Harris's book is of lasting value, not least for the clarity of the writing and the enthusiasm of a dedicated fisherman.

Hawthorn Fly (*Bibio marci*) A terrestial, hatching in late April and early May, often blown onto the water in large numbers during the week or so the hatch lasts. When trout are taking a fall of hawthorn they will often look at little else. The hawthorn fly, when flying, is recognised by its long trailing legs. This is a traditional dressing:

Body: black ostrich herl
Wings: pale starling
Hackle: black cock with two long strands of stripped black ostrich herl to suggest the legs
Hook: 12

If the fly is inclined to sink below the surface an ordinary black palmer floats perfectly and can be twitched now and then to suggest the struggling fly.

Helmsdale A short but prolific salmon river rising in the high lochs of Sutherland, entering the North Sea at Helmsdale. There is good control of letting and the river is fly-only. Ashley Cooper thinks highly of the Helmsdale which has an annual rod catch of some 2,000 to 2,500 fish.

The river suffered badly from disease in 1980 and since then the big two-winter summer fish have been noticeably scarce. The grilse (1980–82) have been good but very small. Possibly this is because they do not spend any time at sea or go any distance, returning after only a few months of sea feeding.

Henderson, John From just before the death of Queen Victoria until well after the Second World War, John Henderson fished almost every kind of lake, loch, lough and reservoir you can imagine in all parts of the United Kingdom. He died in the late 1970s aged 95 plus, a great fly fisherman, one of the longest-serving members of the Flyfishers' Club. He published some fly dressings privately and contributed the chapter on dry fly fishing on lakes to Halford's *Dry Fly Man's Handbook*, published in 1913.

One of Henderson's techniques of bank fishing on large lakes and reservoirs was to cast out a dry fly with the wind coming over his left shoulder and walk along the margin of the lake, keeping time with the fly as it floated with the wind.

One fisherman tells a charming story of John Henderson who he met in the 1950s fishing at Weir Wood in Surrey which was then a stocked trout fishery.

I saw this old man, rather sad-looking, sitting by the wall of the dam, rod in hand, doing nothing, and somehow I felt sorry for him and asked him how he was. He was quite cheerful and said he was waiting for the hatch and he thought there might be one soon. I realised he was going to fish dry and felt even more sorry for him because I'd never see the dry fly fished on a reservoir before and I didn't think it was much good. I told him a wet fly would do better and he smiled and said it might, but made no move to change. An hour or so later there was a rise and I saw him coming along the bank with a fish, a good one. That taught me a lesson.

J. Waller Hills – photo courtesy *The Illustrated London News* Picture Library

Henzell, H.P. Another book about the Scottish lochs but from a man who was devoted to the fly, Henzell's *The Art and Craft of Loch Fishing* (Philip Allan, 1937) is well named and contains illustrations of traditional wet and dry flies.

Hills, J. Waller (1867–1938) One of the most charming fishing books of all time was J.W. Hill's *A Summer on the Test* (Philip Allan, 1924) and one of the most informative *A History of Fly Fishing For Trout* (Philip Allan, 1921). He wrote other books, including an autobiography, *A Sportsman's Life*, but none of the others reached the level of the former two, though *River Keeper* came a close second.

John Waller Hills, the second son of Herbert A. Hills of Highhead Castle, Cumberland was educated at Eton and Balliol, qualified as a solicitor and was a director of a number of companies. He was first elected as a Conservative MP for Durham but lost his seat in 1922 and then re-entered Parliament as the member for Rippon in 1923 and remained its member until his death. At one time he was Financial Secretary to the Treasury. He was twice married and had a son, born in 1933.

Although nearly 50 at the time of the First World War he joined the Durham Light Infantry and in only two years rose to command a battalion. In 1916 he was falsely reported killed in action. He was, said *The Times*, a man of great character and courage.

A reprint of the second edition of 'A Summer on the Test' was published by André Deutsch, with a foreword by Anthony Atha, in 1983.

Hobbs, A.E. *See* Thames Trout

Holiday, F.W. Authentic glimpses of fishing in Wales are rare but some of the best are in F.W. Holiday's *River Fishing for Sea Trout* (Herbert Jenkins, 1960). Wales has many miles of association water open for visitors and though spinning and worming seem to dominate these lovely bright rivers if there is more use of the fly it is largely due to enthusiasts like Holiday. Some of his advice on night fishing with a slack line may raise the eyebrows of those who have learnt their fishing elsewhere but it seems to work well in Wales.

Hook Sizes The variation in hook sizes is considerable. The hooks used in America, for example, bear no resemblance to the Redditch scale sizes in use over here. An American size 24 hook is more likely to be closer to our own size 18 or 20. Our own New Scale or Pennell Scale of hook sizes in use up to the 1930s has now been replaced by the revived Redditch scale. This is an approximate comparison:

Redditch:	6/0	5/0	4/0	3/0	2/0	1/0	1	2	3	4	5
Pennell:	20	19	18	17	16	15	14	13	12	11	10
Redditch:	6	7	8	9	10	11	12	13	14	15	16
Pennell:	9	8	7	6	5	4	3	2	1	0	00
Redditch:	17	18									
Pennell:	000	0000									

Eyed hooks were in use in the earliest times and the British Museum has some examples. The first mention of eyed hooks in England is in Brooke's *Art of Angling* (1740). The modern eyed hook was developed by an engineer fisherman, H.S. Hall, in conjunction with G.S. Marryat, in the late 1800s.

Houghton Club For over 160 years members of the Houghton Club have fished some of the loveliest fly water in England on the Test above and below Stockbridge. The club's honorary secretary, P.K. George, writes:

The Houghton Club was established in June, 1822, with 12 founder members, representative of the church, the arts, and other professions. Then, as now, the club's headquarters were The Grosvenor Hotel in Stockbridge, though to ensure their evening fishing in those early days of slow travel members used to dine in a tent pitched on the river bank two miles below the town.

Initially, members relied on the grannom and mayfly for their sport. The floating fly had not been invented; dapping and fishing downstream with two flies were the order of the day. It was not until 1888 that the first fish is recorded as having been taken on the dry fly. Little fishing took place after early June. For the first 25 years or so grayling, introduced to the Test in 1818, competed with trout in popularity. The average weight of trout and grayling caught well into the 20th century ranged from 1¾lb to 2lb. For a number of years in the latter part of the 19th century club waters were stocked with bought-in fish; but in 1890, William Lunn, who came to Houghton in 1887, started a hatchery.

His arrival, coinciding with the advent of the dry fly, constituted a milestone in club history. A self-taught naturalist, he invented, amongst other flies, the Lunn's Particular and the Houghton Ruby. He was succeeded by his son Alf, in turn to be followed by

Mick Lunn, who runs the club fishing today (1986).

Consisting of 24 members, the club's waters are bounded to the north and south of Stockbridge by Leckford and Bossington estates. There are no written rules but anyone wishing to become a member must have fished at least once as a member's guest before his name may be entered in the candidate's book. No one living within 10 miles of Stockbridge may qualify for membership.

Fish, bred from club stock, both brown and rainbow, average a little over 2lb. Around 1,700 are taken annually.

Houghton Ruby A trout fly that imitates the spinner of the iron blue, created by W.J. Lunn, river keeper of the Houghton Club from 1887 to 1932.

Body: red hackle stalk showing crimson silk underbody
Tail: three rather long white hackle fibres, spread
Wings: two light blue hackle points at right angles to the hook shank
Hackle: bright red cock, clipped under, so that the fly lies low in the water
Hook: 16 or 18

Companion creation to the Houghton Ruby is Lunn's Particular which imitates the spinner of several of the olives.

Hughes-Parry, J. A well-known fisherman on the Welsh Dee for many years, Hughes-Parry is the author of *A Salmon Fisherman's Notebook* (Eyre and Spottiswoode, 1949) which A.G. Street described in the *News Chronicle* as 'the best book on salmon fishing I have ever read'. Hughes-Parry's book is admirably written and though he had a partiality to bait his advice on fly fishing is sound. His favourite flies were the Torrish and the Jock Scott, diminishing in size as the water temperature increased. Hughes-Parry, like all great salmon fishermen, had a humble approach:

The span of human life is too short to enable one to gain even the rudimentary knowledge necessary for the successful catching of salmon.

Hybrids Crossbreeding of trout and char, of rainbow and steelhead, rainbow and brook trout, have been common among fishery managers since the 1880s but although some interestingly marked fish have been produced with attractive names – sunbeam, tiger, cheetah, and so on – they do not seem to survive the experimental stage. Some hybridisation of fish takes place naturally at times.

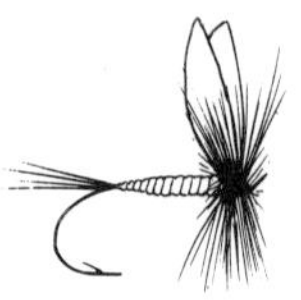

Concentration

It is often said that one of the virtues of trout fishing is that it gives you glimpses of wild animals and birds in their natural environment. The drumming of the snipe over the water meadows, or the eerie cry of the plover in spring, are supposed to compensate us for standing up to our knees in mud with our fly firmly fixed to a branch of a tree behind us just as we have found a rising fish. It may be so. The man of creative imagination may find his consolation in the flash of a kingfisher, but for most of us the fishing is the thing. I do not suppose that the stockbroker, escaping from the city at the weekend, drives eighty miles and dresses up in thigh boots and a fishing jacket, and a most peculiar waterproof hat, in order to hear the drumming of the snipe. He knows that fishing consists of a series of misadventures interspersed by occasional moments of glory, and that, to achieve the glory, he must concentrate on the matter in hand.

Howard Marshall, *Reflections On A River*, Witherby, 1967

International Fly Fishing Association National organisations from England, Scotland, Ireland and Wales belong to the IFFA which organises lake fly fishing competitions between teams from the four countries which are sponsored (1984) by the National Westminster Bank.

The competition rules are strict and the amateur status of those who take part is rigidly observed. No competitor or official can accept gifts of fishing tackle from any manufacturer or dealer, allow his angling status or success to be used for commercial purposes, or his name used by any tackle manufacturer or dealer. There are restrictions on accepting fees for articles or interviews.

The competitions are for lake fishermen fishing the drift on big waters such as the Rutland and Chew reservoirs in England, Trawsfyndd in Wales, Loch Leven in Scotland and Lough Conn in Ireland, among others. The winners hold various trophies for a year. There are no money prizes but help can be given with expenses.

Invicta An invaluable and versatile wet fly for lake trout and sea trout, designed originally by James Ogden of Cheltenham around 1845, the dressing subject to modifications since then:

Body: yellow fur ribbed gold twist
Body hackle: red cock palmered down the body and held in place by gold ribbing
Shoulder hackle: red cock with a beard hackle of blue jay in front
Wing: hen pheasant tail feather slips
Tail: golden pheasant crest

A pleasant variation is the Silver Invicta which dispenses with body fur and palmer hackle in favour of an all-silver body made in several ways, mostly plain silver tinsel, sometimes with a silver wire rib.

Iron Blue (*Baetis pumilus, B niger*) One of the smallest and darkest of the Baetis family of flies, the iron blue is found on most rivers of the British Isles. They are small, dark, inky-blue flies which, once identified, can generally be recognised again without difficulty.

Various wet fly patterns, the Infallible in Devon, the Dark Watchet in Yorkshire, suggest or are based upon the natural iron blue. A number of good patterns suggest the floating dun, of which this is one:

Body: peacock quill, dyed inky-blue, or mole's fur dubbed thinly, showing two or three turns of crimson tying silk at the tail
Whisks: white or pale blue cock
Hackle: dark blue or dark green cock
Wings: starling, dyed inky blue
Hook: 16

The spent fly is best suggested by W.J. Lunn's Houghton Ruby. Skues has a good dressing of the iron blue nymph.

A characteristic of the iron blue which endears it to fishermen is its apparent indifference to cold and rain. It will sometimes hatch on the most unlikely of days in March and April. The best hatch will be in mid-summer and though it may tail off a little there can be sudden flushes again in the autumn. Plunket

Greene in *Where The Bright Waters Meet* (1924) paid the best tribute ever to the iron blue, the winged fly, not the hackle:

It is not merely a Test fly, for I have caught a two-pound trout with it in a little Scottish burn, casting it dry on chance upstream into likely places. There used to be a superstition that the iron blue was a bad weather fly only useful in a thunderstorm but my experience is that it is the best of them all on glass-smooth water in bright sunshine. In fact it is often the only fly they will take in such conditions and it is certainly the only thing they will look at when they are smutting . . .

There may be some physical reason for it. They may be very fat or very tasty – why else should they [the trout] be so partial to mere hors d'oeuvres like the smuts? – or else they may look very luscious against the light; whatever it is the trout could not have a greater affection for it than I have.

It is, no doubt, imagination, but the iron blue always seems to me to be happier and keener and have better manners than all the rest. He is an aristocrat, a prince of the wing, far above the world of underwater hackles, as he sails down serene on the streams, oblivious to wind or rain or sun, above board in his every thought, and ready to work for you again and again till he disintegrates and falls to pieces from very exhaustion.

Itchen Quite a short river, only 32 miles long, flowing through Hampshire to the sea at Southampton Water, the Itchen is fed by a thousand or more springs that come from the chalk downs. The source is generally recognised to be at the head of one of the tributaries, the Tichborne Brook. There are two other main tributaries, the Candover Brook and the Arle, and the three of them join together within a matter of a few hundred yards to form the true River Itchen, just downstream of the town of Alresford. Ron Holloway writes:

If the Test is generally recognised as the king of the chalk streams then the Itchen must, indisputably, be the queen. Between Ovington and Winchester lie some of the famous beats where men like Lord Grey of Fallodon, Skues, and in later years, Dermot Wilson, pursued their love of dry fly fishing. These beats, with such evocative names as Ovington, Itchen Abbas, Lovington, Itchen Sroke, Chilland, Martyr Worthy, Easton, Abbotsworthy and Abbots Barton, are regarded as the cream of wild brown trout chalk stream fishing in the country, or perhaps the world.

The uniqueness of the Itchen, with its constant flows of pristine spring water at constant temperatures, are of interest these days to far more people than dry fly chalk stream enthusiasts. Because of its very nature, this river is ideal for fish farming and the pressures which the river has to sustain with several large fish farms only adds to the other pressures which the waters now have to bear. Only through wise ownership and management of these beats has the nature of the river been maintained at its present standard, although the balance is very precarious, necessitating constant vigilence on the part of the keepers and managers and owners.

The famed Skues water at Abbots Barton is becoming an island sanctuary increasingly pressurised by the city planners and the expansion of the city of Winchester. The city, through which the Itchen flows, maintains public waters through the city boundaries and allows public fishing and many good fish can still be caught in the weirs. It is encouraging to see the young fishers of Winchester casting a dry fly.

The middle Itchen, between Winchester and Eastleigh, although split in places in various streams, affords superb fishing, but to alleviate the demand on some of these waters, considerable stocking has to be done, mainly with brown trout though with mature rainbow in places. The lower Itchen, although holding considerable numbers of trout, is mainly known as a salmon and sea trout fishery, but with the decline of the Atlantic salmon over the past few years these fisheries are now looking more to the trout fishing for their sport.

Access to the waters of the Itchen is limited to the few waters which allow day ticket access, but mainly it is held by riparian owners and their tenants and various fishing clubs.

On the beats above Winchester, only two stock regularly and these are the two lower beats – Abbots Barton and Abbots Worthy. The remainder of the famous beats are still able to maintain a self-sustaining head of the traditional Itchen wild brown trout.

The insect life of the Itchen is still as plentiful as it has always been. Although the mayfly on the upper Itchen has always been sparse, the middle beats still have good hatches. The traditional natural flies of the upper Itchen are the olives – small, medium and large; the blue winged olive; iron blue and sedge. Along with a Lunn's Particular, an imitation of any of these would keep any angler satisfied. Sizes 16, 18, and 20s are the order of the day as the Itchen is a small fly river.

Pollution is an ever present major threat to any river, but no more so than here, with the proliferation of fish farms and intensive agriculture and the frightening aspect of chemical spillage from nearby newly-built motorways. However, the dedicated work of the few remaining full-time river keepers, along with understanding riparian owners, this unique river is still in good heart.

The Winchester tackle shop, The Rod Box, is sometimes able to provide rods on the Itchen but applications should preferably be made well in advance.

Iven, T.C. No one had more influence on the development of reservoir fishing techniques than T.C. Ivens with the publication in 1952 of his *Still Water Fly Fishing* (Deutsch) which has been republished a number of times.

Ivens and his friends fished the Midland reservoirs and developed new simplified types of fly and new techniques of fishing them. He divided fly patterns into two categories, the attractors and the deceivers. The attractors were lure-type flies like the Alexandra and his Jersey Herds. The deceivers were nymph or larvae-like patterns, not tied to imitate any one creature, but to suggest a number. One of the most important of these which has retained and even increased its popularity, for it is widely in use in the 1980s, is the Black and Peacock Spider.

Ivens was one of the first reservoir fishers to emphasise the importance of long casting which he demonstrated in a series of photographs. His deceiver flies, which he preferred to fish whenever possible, were fished very slowly so that their shape and movement coincided with those of the trout's usual food. The attractors were generally used in heavy water or when trout were sticklebacking, and were fished fast. Though there were exceptions, as there always are, in general he regarded dry-fly fishing as a waste of time. His aim was to put reservoir fishing on as scientific and simple a basis as possible and his book and his whole philosophy had an instant appeal to large numbers who were being attracted to reservoir fishing for the first time since the Second World War as well as those who had previously been fishing traditional wet flies without quite knowing why.

The Magic Circle

I would infinitely rather fish to the rise than to visible fish. I love looking into the light on the water, watching for the rise, and seeing my float down into the ring, and never knowing till it comes to him whether he will take it or not. This is the chief charm of the evening rise at Stockbridge. You fish to the ring, and the tense excitement of watching it enter the circle and waiting for the strike is, for me, far greater than seeing any fish, however big, come to your fly.

Harry Plunket Greene, *Where The Bright Waters Meet,* Philip Allen, 1924

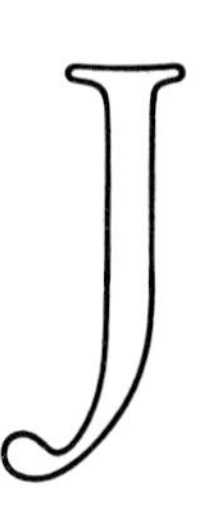

Jacques, David (1906–1983) A leading entomologist, angling editor for A and C Black, the publishers, contributor to many journals on fly life and fly fishing, David Jacques was awarded a fellowship of the Royal Entomological Society for his original ecological research.

His brilliant essay on the life of the grannom (*see* page 79) is contained in *Fisherman's Fly* (Black, 1965); in 1974 Black published his *Development of Modern Stillwater Fishing*. He also revised the third edition of Courtney Williams' *Dictionary of Trout Flies* and wrote a life of Viscount Grey. At the time of his death he was preparing a commentary of The Boke of St Albans. A collection of short stories and poems is to be published postumously. Among his many friends was John Goddard who he encouraged to write his first book, *Trout Fly Recognition*, to which Jacques devoted lavish care.

He was a good fisherman, on Test, Avon and at Two Lakes, as well as being a good entomologist, and would often break off in the middle of fishing, take out a lens and study some tiny insect, not minding in the least that he might be missing the only fish of the day. In an appreciation, John Hillaby wrote:

> Although my good friend David Jacques could not be described as an academic, he was in his own particular way at college all his life. He was for ever learning, exploring, getting down to the fundamentals of whatever stimulated his agile mind. He grasped the essentials of Hebrew, Yiddish, Latin and a fair amount of Greek and applied them to his impeccable English, a fact attested by his books on fishing . . . Should all this sound over-austere, many of us will remember a loving and learned man.

Jed Water A tributary of the Teviot, the little Jed has affinities with most of the Border trout streams whose names, not without too much imagination, sound like a chime of bells – Whiteadder and Blackadder, Till and Teviot, Ettrick, Gala and Leader Water.

Chalk stream fishermen who think that spate rivers are easy had better try a river like the Jed. It can be as clear or sometimes clearer than the Test. The trout do not wait if they see you. They are gone. The river is emptied for the next thirty yards.

The truth is that to fish any of these Border rivers especially in high summer and low water, demands the highest qualities of presentation and river craft; one false move, one splashy cast, and all will be lost.

Upstream is obviously the best, one accepts that now, the lessons that Stewart sought to teach have gone home, but there are times and places where across and down seem inevitable. There are no rigid rules to stay the hand either, so that one can fish according to the way of the stream.

Small flies of the spider type, size 16 and 18, do well in the surface film, a dry olive or an iron blue if there is a hatch, or else an 18 or 20 black gnat.

For Till and Teviot and Tweed, remember that the Greenwell Glory came from Sprouston. It is rewarding and satisfying to fish a Greenwell in its home waters.

Permits to fish the Jed can be obtained through enquiries at Jedburgh, probably at the Royal Hotel or the ironmongers, and the same is true of most of the Border rivers. The fishing associations welcome visitors and provide day tickets.

Jersey Herd An attractor pattern, a minnow fly for reservoir trout, designed by T.C. Ivens, named because the copper-coloured foil used for the body came from the top of a bottle of Jersey Herd milk:

Body: an underbody of wool formed in minnow shape, covered by copper-coloured tinsel or foil tied in at the tail and wound to the head
Back: about 12 strands of bronze peacock herl with the ends projecting as a tail beyond the bend of the hook, the ends of the herl by the eye wound round to make a head
Head hackle: two turns of bright orange hen
Hook: 8 or 6 longshank

Jock Scott The most elaborate of traditional salmon flies. A good modern dressing is by Veniard but even so some of the feathers may now be unobtainable:

Tag: silver tinsel and yellow floss
Tail: topping and Indian crow
Butt: black ostrich herl
Body: in two equal parts – No 1, yellow floss silk ribbed silver tinsel, butted with toucan and black ostrich herl. No 2, black floss silk ribbed silver tinsel with black hackle over
Throat: guinea fowl
Wings: two strips of dark mottled turkey tail, golden pheasant tail, bustard, grey mallard, peacock wing, blue and yellow swan, red macaw, brown mallard, and topping
Sides: jungle cock
Cheeks: blue chatterer
Horns: blue macaw
Head: black
Hook: almost any size from 5/0 down to 1 or 2

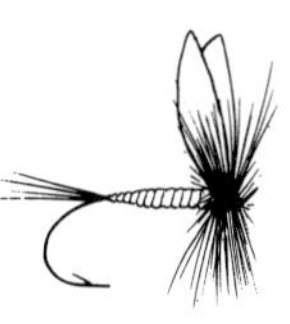

A Dropper For Salmon

With a cast of three flies, the tail fly fishes as would a fly fished singly. The centre fly comes nearer the surface and care must be taken to avoid having it make an undesirable underwater wake . . . It is the top dropper which brings the great results. Draw it across at right angles to the stream and it will rise fish that have refused a fly presented in the orthodox manner. If it misses the fly it will almost certainly rise again until it is caught or has touched the fly or cast or been disturbed for some other reason. I rose a grilse one day eleven times before I caught it and there were only a few seconds rest between each rise. Times without number I have fished down a stream with a cast of three flies just as I would with a single fly, and risen nothing until I was opposite the lie with shortened line bringing the dropper across it. This seldom fails to bring the chance of a fish in fair conditions.

When I say to bring the dropper across the stream I do not mean a mostly useless bobbing across. Bring the fly across so that it makes a steady wave – a V – against the current and vary the speed at which it is brought across on successive casts. By this 'wave' I mean the steady wave a quarter-submerged fly makes and not the undesirable drag an almost completely sunk fly makes, as when the fly is not tied on properly and hangs obliquely instead of straight. A dropper treated with dry fly solution is as unsatisfactory as allowing a drag on your fly when fishing a dry fly. An undesirable bubbly effect is produced. I prefer a large dropper fly – size six or even larger.

Charles McLaren, *Fishing For Salmon*, John Donald, Edinburgh, 1977

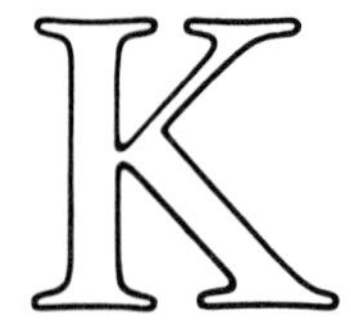

Kelson, George M. *See* Salmon Fishing page 183.

Kennet The River Kennet is one of southern England's loveliest chalk streams, rising in the Marlborough Downs, flowing in a great curve through Avebury and Marlborough and on to Hungerford. Just past Newbury it is joined by the lovely Lambourn to end somewhat unceremoniously under the shadow of the gasworks at Reading where it is swallowed by the Thames. Although Peter Rennie wrote only about a small part of the river he captured the spirit of the whole:

My knowledge of the Kennet is restricted to the stretch from Ramsbury upstream to Axford – rather less than two miles in which the river flows gently and the trout grow strong on a seemingly endless supply of fresh water shrimp, larvae and other delicacies. The water level scarcely ever varies save in the worst drought and even in so short a stretch the country through which it flows changes from iris-filled water meadows at one end which are kept neat by a flock of Jacobs sheep, to fly-tangling woods at the other where once I counted no fewer than thirty-four swans.

You might think that a river which varies so little would to the fisherman be equally predictable; but not the Kennet. There can be whole weeks when the only serious rise to be seen has turned out to be that deceptive ring left by a diving dabchick. And yet on a good day . . . there is a particular spot just past a maytree where the weed has grown coarse and thick and has made a narrow funnel in the stream. At the tail of the funnel there is a certain fish. Having previously marked the spot, my wife watched and waited for more than an hour; was it to be one of those days? Then just as I joined her the hatch started; swallows swept low over the water and dipped to take the first of the grey-sailed olives. Even a family of mallard busily hoovering the far bank joined in. The long string of olives floated down through the funnel into the lie and at last up came the back and with an audible slurp the first of many olives was lining the walls of that long-awaited trout.

My wife selected the identical fly; she dropped it in between the live olives directly in line with the fish not once but three or four times. And still he rose with that swirl which the French so aptly describe as 'une gobbage'. "Try another fly" I said helpfully. Half a box later, feeling quite spent herself, she tied on a spent olive whose dressing she had taken from *Trout and Salmon* and had made up in high hopes but had never previously used.

Another slurp and it was gone – the first mad dash downstream – then back straight towards her – desperate hand-lining – and away again. "Mind the weeds!" A few more sorties and he was coming towards the bank. Why do I remember this of many such fish? Well, he got away and I was acting ghillie and he must have weighed 3lb (they always do) and he was inches from my net. Why else would I remember?

When we first took rods at Ramsbury there was no chance of the thrill of a mayfly hatch. Two years ago we counted half a dozen or so and last year (1983) many morc. So, despite the fame of other stretches of the Kennet we are only now able to look forward to enjoying the same heart-lifting, hand-shaking trauma of a serious mayfly hatch in future years.

In the meantime and throughout the long winter, my wife prepares our stock of blue-winged olives, of pale wateries, of gnats and sedge and hatching sedge; and then, for use in July, tiny upstream nymphs which tempt those crafty Kennet trout. Other patterns which at the right time show considerable promise are Gold-ribbed Hare's Ear, Greenwell, Lunn's Particular, Beacon Beige and Orange Quill – in fact the pride of anyone's dry fly box.

There is a fascinating contrast between the gentle lethargy of the Kennet and the craft and speed of its trout. Strangely, a fast-running river like the Itchen contains fish which seem to apply their minds principally to the flow of the river and may simply drop or ease ahead when disturbed by the approaching fisherman, while on the Kennet they have time to watch the bank and an incautious approach will result in little but the flash and bow-wave of a fleeing fish.

Kennet: The Hungerford Water The main A4 trunk road – the Old Great West Road – crosses the Kennet at Hungerford. No one quite knows why it is called a hunger ford. Certainly there was a ford there but the hunger part may well be a corruption of Early English. It is an ancient town and the Hungerford town water has a unique history. The fishing rights of this part of the river, above and below the bridge, were given to the town by John O'Gaunt in the fourteenth century as a reward for sheltering his troops during a battle of the Wars of the Roses. After John O'Gaunt died in 1388 his heirs tried to regain the fishing in legal battles which lasted on and off for 200 years. Queen Elizabeth I, however, came down on the side of the town and in 1574 confirmed to Hungerford,

> . . . such liberties and profits and benefits as heretofore, time out of mind and remembrance of man they have used and enjoyed . . .

Since then the town fishing has had a continuous recorded history and is run by the Town and Manor of Hungerford Charity whose rules are set by the annual meeting of commoners, who have the free fishing rights, at the annual Hocktide Court.

Day rods are sometimes available on the Kennet. Enquiries should be made at the tackle shop, Roxton's, in the High Street. Rods on the Kennet can also be had from Barton Court, Kintbury; the Craven Estate, Hampstead Marshall; and the Denford Fisheries, Lower Denford.

Kenny's Killer A sea trout fly, named after Ken Burns of Gordonbush, Brora, very useful on fast clear Highland rivers and lochs. The dressing is in Tom Stewart's *Fifty Popular Flies* (Vol. 3, Benn, 1969):

Body: flat silver tinsel with round or oval tinsel or wire as ribbing
Tail: long upturned strands of golden pheasant tippet
Wing: long and sparse dyed black squirrel or glossy black hair from a retriever's tail, merging with the upturned tippet
Hook sizes: from 12 up to 6, generally long shank

Ketting's Duck Fly An unusual fly introduced to this country by a Dutch fishing journalist, Kees Ketting, in 1979, which had a remarkable success at Kimbridge on the Test. The odd thing about the fly is the hackle, which gives the impression of a grey mist.

Body: brown tying silk or nylon, tied thinly from the bend of the hook to the head
Hackle: a transparent-looking grey feather taken from the anus of the mallard duck, about four or five turns. The feathers have long fibres and when tied in these fibres are pulled forward over the eye of the hook and clipped at the ends so that they do not appear too long, as they suggest the wings
Hook: 14, 16 or 18

It could well be that the fly suggests a black gnat or a chironmoid but it is taken freely during the evening rise to spinner; whatever it may suggest there are times when it is highly effective. The only trouble is collecting anus feathers.

Kingsley, Charles The Rev. Charles Kingsley, author of *The Water Babies*, also wrote *Chalk Stream Studies*, an essay contained in Prose Idylls, Macmillan, 1884, frequently quoted at the time for his praise of the alder fly . . . "Oh, thou beloved member of the brute creation . . . would that I could give thee a soul if indeed thou hast not one already."

Kingsmill Moore, T.C. One of the best books about trout and sea trout in Ireland is Kingsmill Moore's *A Man May Fish*, first published in 1960, reprinted in a revised and expanded edition in 1979 (Colin Smythe Books) with a foreword by Hugh Falkus. Kingsmill Moore's own tyings of the Kingsmill and Bumble sea trout flies are in the Flyfishers' Club museum in London.

K.M., as he was always known to his friends, was born in Dublin in March, 1893 and died there in 1979 at the age of 85. He was at school at Marlborough, took a degree at Trinity College, Dublin, and served in the Royal Flying Corps in France during the First World War. On his return to Dublin he became a barrister and during the Irish Civil War (1922–23) was, for a short period, the war correspondent of *The Irish Times*. He was later elected to the Senate and played a considerable part in the rebuilding of Irish life after the bitterness of war. In 1947 he was appointed a judge of the High Court and in 1951 of the Supreme Court. He retired in 1965.

It was once said of him that quite apart from being a judge his real profession was fishing. His wife, Alexandra, a lifelong companion and herself a fisher, persuaded him to write *A Man May Fish* and he was pleased as well as surprised by its considerable success, both here and in America. The main character in the book, Jamsie, is a classic portrait of an Irish ghillie.

Kite, Oliver One of the great names of nymph fishing and inventor of the phrase known as the 'induced take', Major Oliver Kite wrote the standard work, *Nymph Fishing in Practice*, first published by Herbert Jenkins in 1963 and later reprinted by Hutchinson. A French edition, *Practique de la Pêche à la Nymphe*, translated by Paymond Rocher, was published by P.E.L. Paris, in 1981.

Oliver Kite was an army officer stationed at Bulford on Salisbury Plain who fished the service's water from 1955 onwards. He lived from 1958–68 in a cottage at Netheravon. Frank Sawyer, the keeper, taught him to fish the nymph and Kite went on to develop his own style which he named 'the induced take' method. In 1957, ill-health had caused his retirement from active service and he was given the job of writing the army infantry manuals, retiring from the army in 1965. For the last five years of his life he had his own successful programme, *Kite's Country*, on Southern Television.

Quite apart from nymph fishing, Kite was also a good dry-fly fisherman and one of the flies he designed, Kite's Imperial, was still in the best-selling lists in 1980. (For Kite's description of the technique of the induced take *see* Nymph

Oliver Kite – photo courtesy John Marchington

Fishing on page 142. Oliver Kite died, while fishing, in the summer of 1968. The weekly articles he had written for *The Shooting Times* were published, posthumously, by André Deutsch, in 1969, under the title of *A Fisherman's Diary*.

Those who fished with Ollie Kite, as he was always called, and those who saw him on television, were always drawn to his home-spun personality, soft voice and friendly charm. Major John Walker, former chairman of The Wiltshire Fishing Association, writes:

He had simple tastes. To augment his lunchtime sandwiches he would pluck wild watercress from the river's edge and drink his home-made wine. All this the public loved. He was a great letter-writer and after fishing one's water would include in his 'thank-you' letter a full description of his day, with the flies seen, weather conditions, and anything interesting or unusual that had happened, very often accompanied by a sketch map showing where fish had been caught or seen to move. He was very fond of fishing for grayling and in the winter months, when they are in their prime, accounted for vast numbers on the Avon and elsewhere.

He was constantly on the look out for sites for filming. One day motoring with him, he suddenly stopped the car. There was a cottage at Fullerton near where the Anton flows into the Test. It had a thatched roof and flint and stone walls with vines growing over them and was altogether delightful. "This is it!" he said. "Just what I am looking for!". The next time we met, he explained "I had been searching all over the south of England for a thatched cottage with flint and stone walls and vines, so I took the crew down there to film it for a special programme. Do you know, three days later I found a cottage exactly like it just a hundred yards from where I live!".

One thing is certain: with his writing, his television programme, and above all with his coaching of young people, Ollie Kite gave back to fishing a great deal more than he ever laid on the river bank.

Kite's Imperial Twenty years after it was first tied this fly is still in the best selling lists. It was designed in March, 1962, by Oliver Kite to suggest the large dark olives which were then hatching on the River Teifi, near Pont Lanio, in Wales:

Body: four undyed heron primary herls, slim in the abdomen, doubled and redoubled to make the thorax
Rib: fine gold wire
Whisks: grey brown or dun cock feather fibres
Hackle: honey-dun or pale ginger cock
Tying silk: purple
Hook: 14 or 16

The fly was called the Imperial because the gold rib and purple silk are the Imperial colours. In *Fisherman's Diary* (André Deutsch, 1969) Kite explained that he used the Imperial whenever any duns were on the water – olives, iron blues, or blue-winged olive – and that it seemed to work with them all.

Heron herl is now difficult to obtain as the heron is a protected bird. Grey goose, pigeon, or the saddle feathers from a grey cock could be used as a substitute.

Knots There is a considerable literature of knots – fishermen's, sailors', rock climbers' – even an international guild of knot tyers. Knot fashions come and go. For fishermen the Double Twist is coming back into favour, having been 'rediscovered' as the Grinner. The Blood is no longer quite so fashionable as it was. The popular Needle Knot is uniquely a game fisherman's knot: no one else seems to have thought of it.

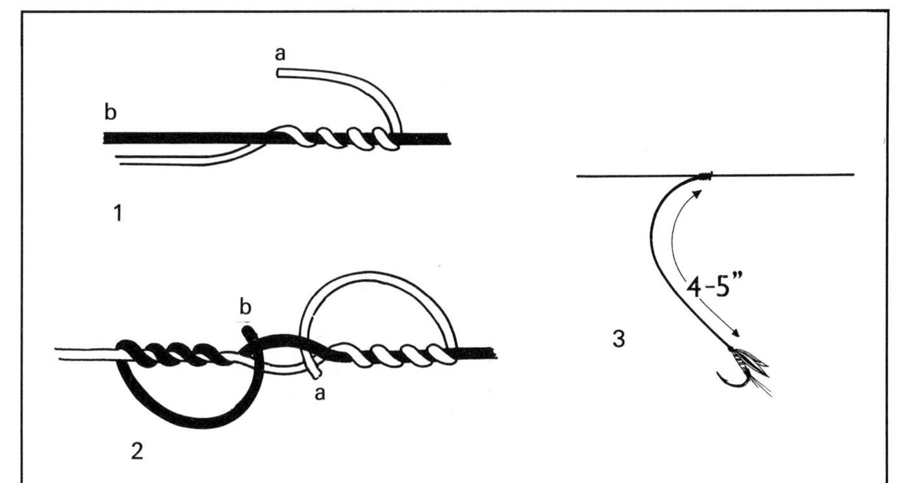

The Blood Knot for joining two lengths of nylon. *1.* The two ends are laid side by side, overlapping. End (a) is twisted four to six times round end (b). *2.* End (a) is now brought back and goes through the junction of the two lines. Line (b) is twisted round line (a) and is brought back in the same way but goes through the junction in the opposite direction to (a). The knot is then snugged down and pulled tight and the ends trimmed. *3.* To make a dropper, one end is left uncut for four to five inches

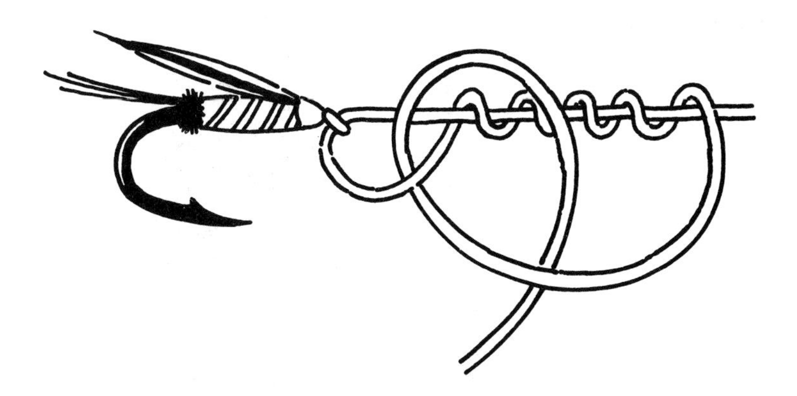

The Half Blood or Clinch Knot is useful for tying on a fly, the end tucked through one loop and then through the other gives a very strong grip

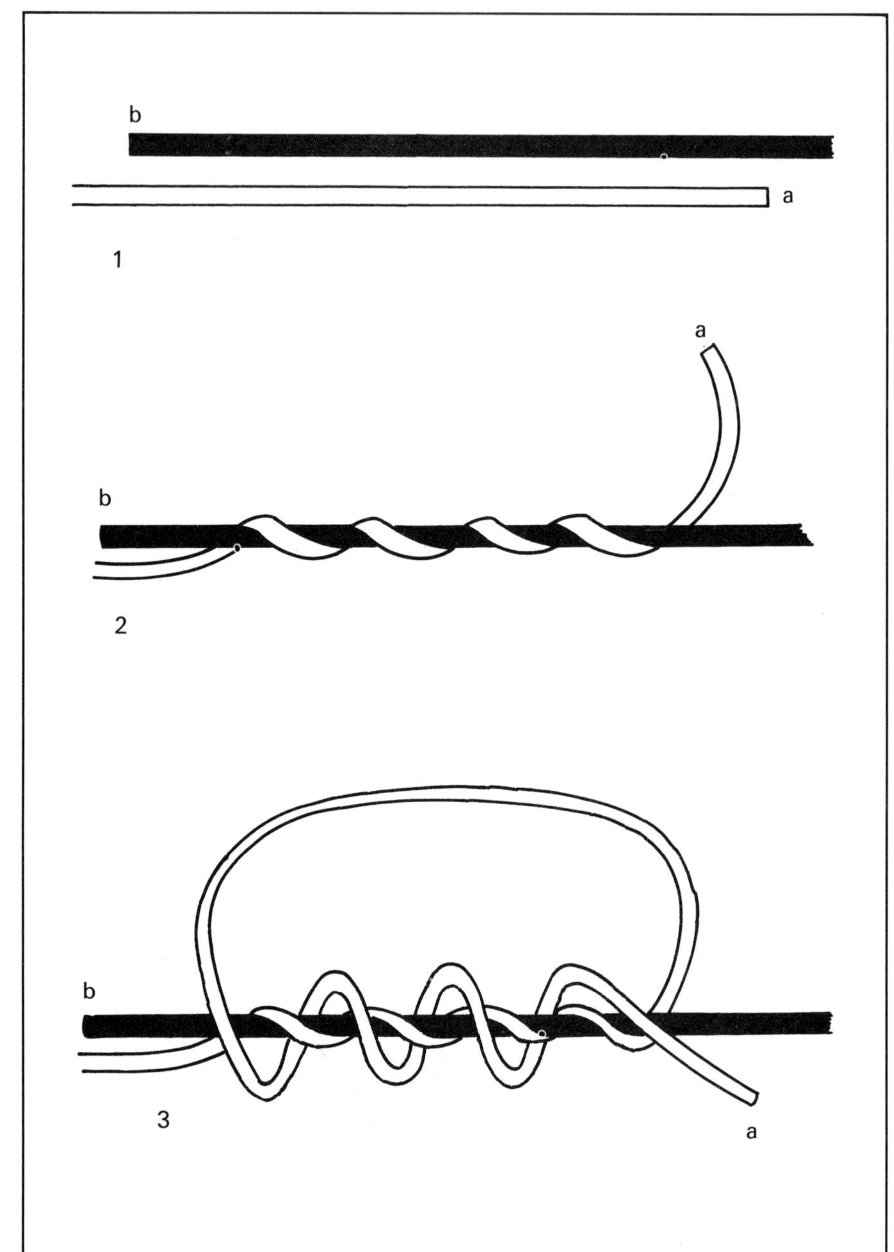

The Double Twist Knot is, on average, stronger than the Blood Knot, and was first known to Blagdon fishermen in the 1930s. In the 1970s a similar knot was known as the Grinner. *1.* The two lengths of nylon to be joined are laid side by side allowing for an overlap of about 8 inches each. *2.* The end (A) is wrapped round the length (B) four, five or six times, the more the stronger. *3.* The end (A) then comes back and twists over the first wrapping three, four or five times and the knot is snugged down. The same process is now carried out on end (B) and then the two knots are pulled tight and are jammed hard one against the other.

Make sure that knots are moistened a little in the mouth before they are tightened

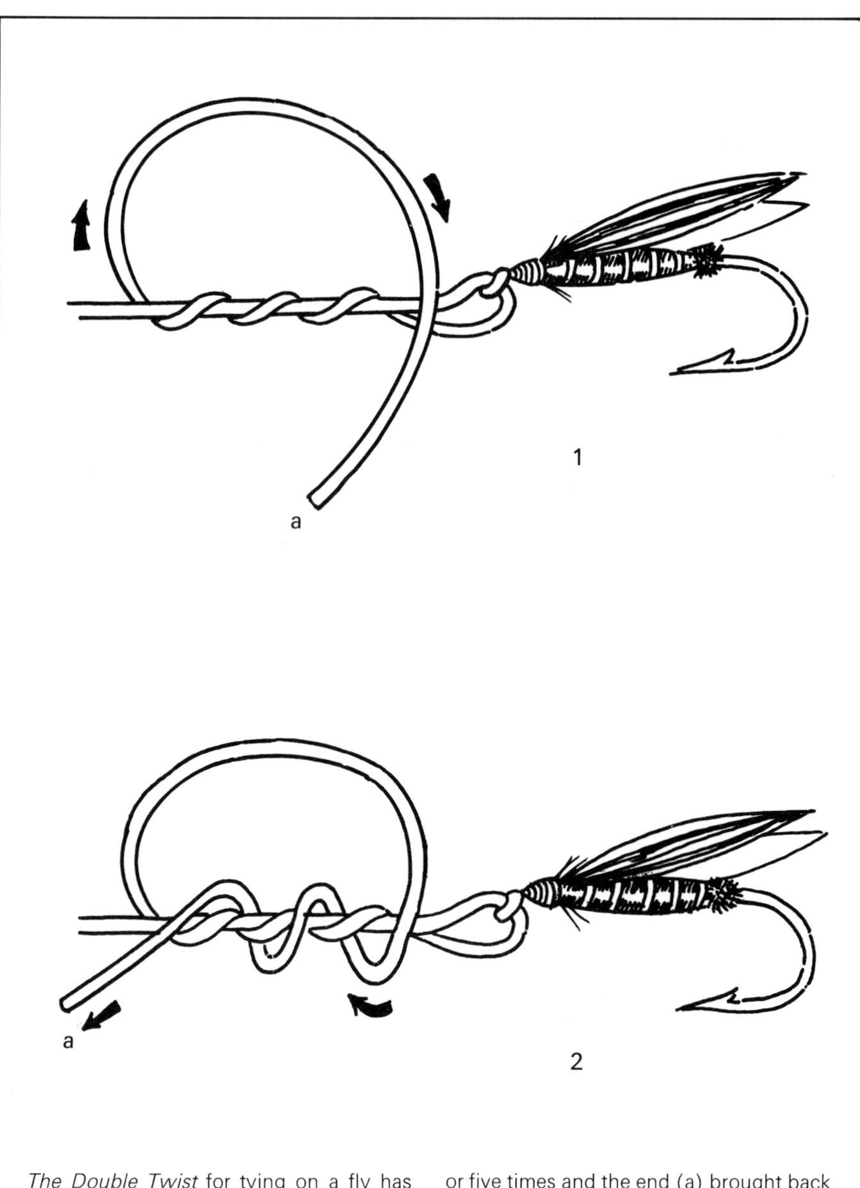

The Double Twist for tying on a fly has about the same test strength as the Half Blood but some fishermen find it slightly easier to tie. *1.* The twist is made three, four or five times and the end (a) brought back . . . *2.* and twisted inside the first loop, two, three or four times, snugged down, the knot moistened and pulled tight

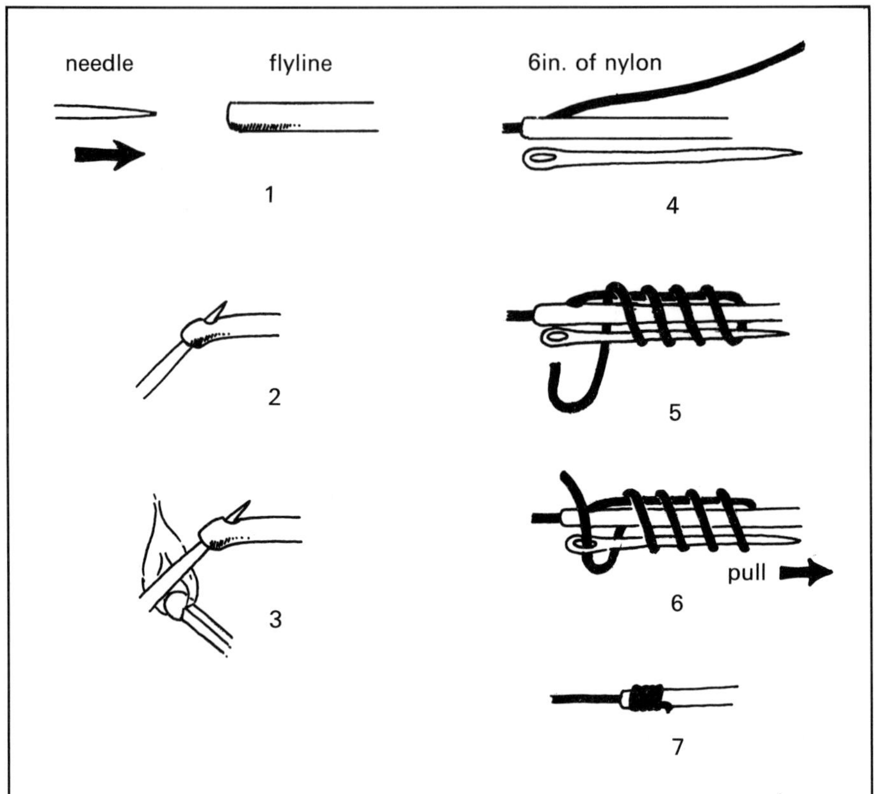

Needle Knot for Trout Fishing. 1. A fine needle is inserted into the middle of the end of the fly line. *2.* The needle point is brought out of the line at a place some four to six millimetres (about $\frac{3}{10}$in.) from the end. *3.* The needle is heated by a lighted match or gas lighter until the plastic of the line is slightly softened. The heat is then removed and the hole in the line made by the needle is allowed to set, a matter of about half a minute or so. The needle will then come away easily. *4.* The butt of the nylon leader is then inserted through the hole in the line and about six inches pulled through. *5.* The nylon is then wrapped round both the needle and the line about four or five times and then . . . *6.* . . . put through the eye of the needle which is then drawn through the loops in the direction of the arrow and . . . *7.* . . . the knot tightened, the end trimmed, and varnished

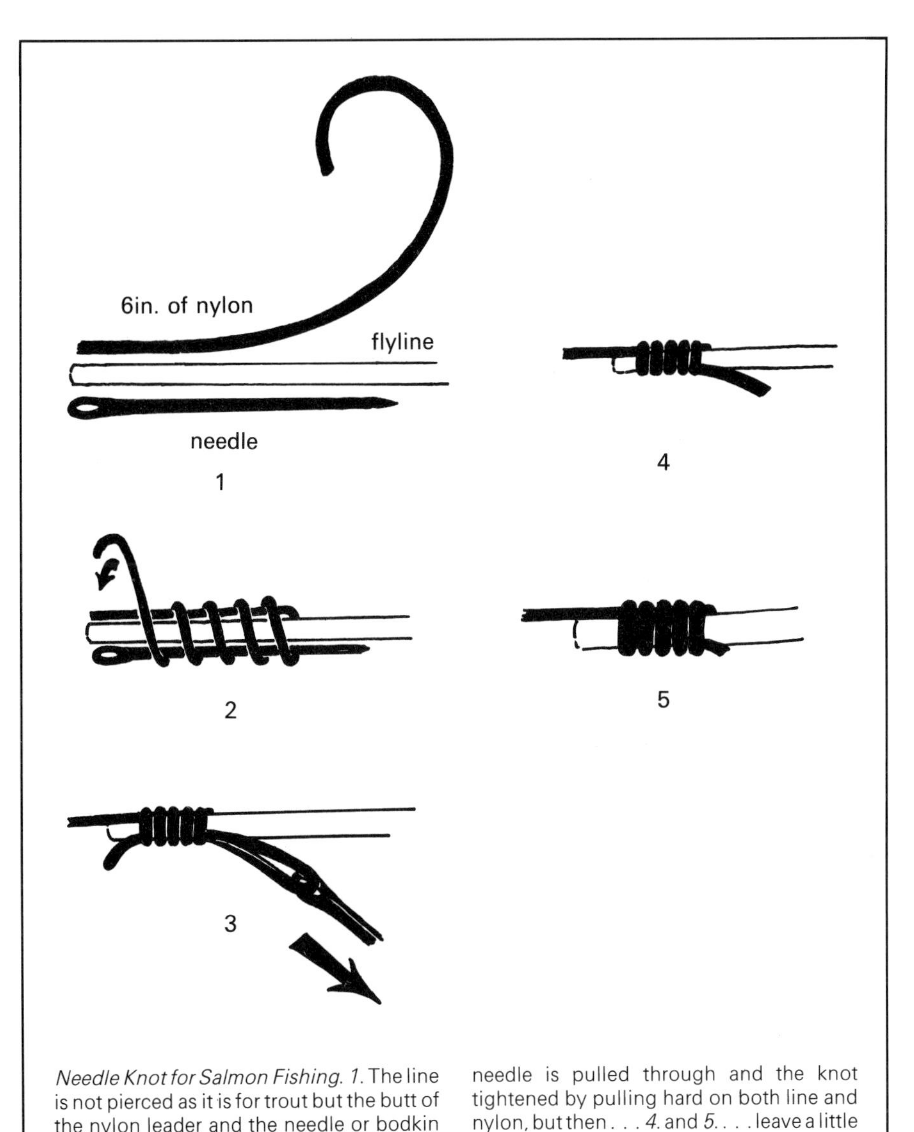

Needle Knot for Salmon Fishing. 1. The line is not pierced as it is for trout but the butt of the nylon leader and the needle or bodkin are simply laid alongside the end of the line. *2.* The nylon is brought back over both line and needle four, five or six times and the end of the nylon is then inserted through the needle eye, and then . . . *3.* . . . the needle is pulled through and the knot tightened by pulling hard on both line and nylon, but then . . . *4.* and *5.* . . . leave a little of both line and nylon projecting from the finished knot and give it two coats of varnish. This should be strong enough but some prefer to use a strong adhesive instead of varnish.

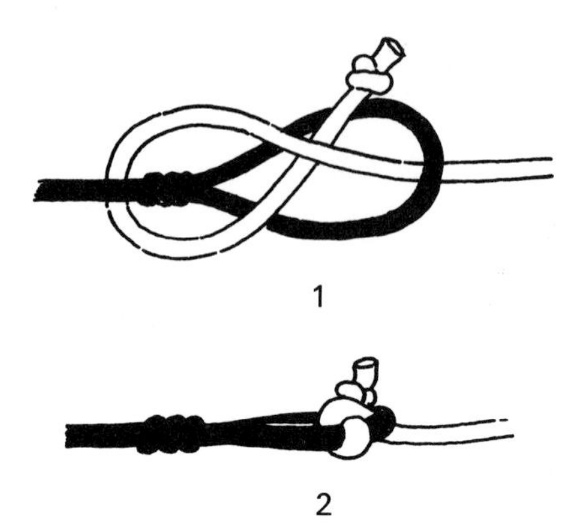

The Stopper Knot. Seamen call it a Sheet Bend. It is the simplest and easiest way of attaching a fly line to the loop in the butt of a leader. *1.* A simple granny knot is tied at the end of the line which makes a figure-of-eight knot in the nylon loop. *2.* The stopper knot in the line should be worked up close against the tightened figure-of-eight

The Figure-of-Eight Knot has several tyings, this is the one used by the casting champion, the late Eric Horsfall Turner, as described by F.W. Holiday. It needs practice

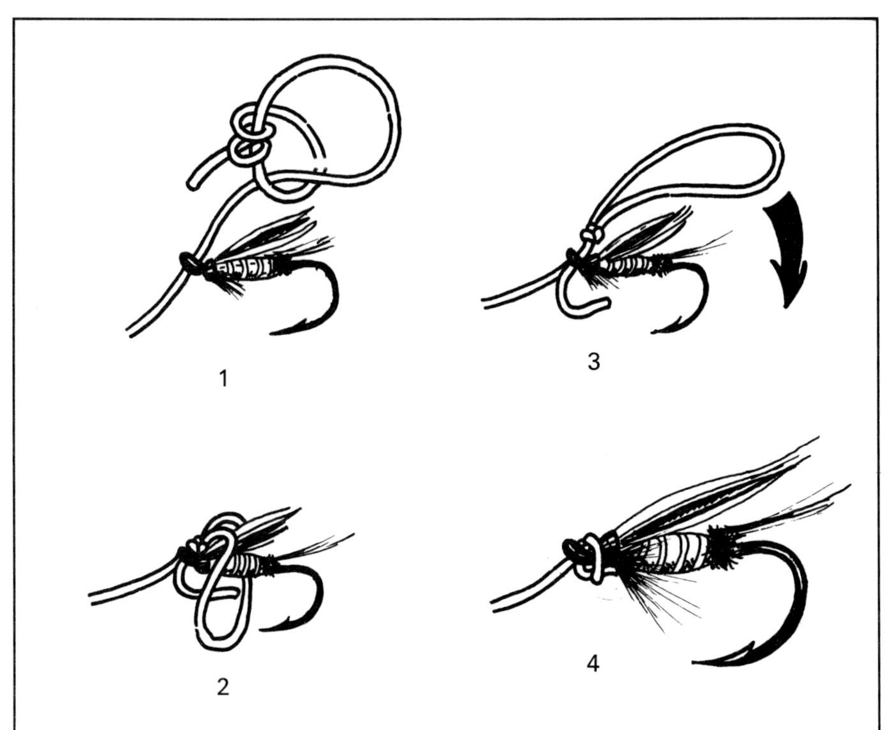

The Turle Knot invented by Major W.G. Turle of Newton Stacey (1840–1909) is useful for attaching the leader to the fly, especially the Tucked Turle for salmon flies. *1.* The fly is threaded on to the nylon, a loop is made and a double overhand knot tied as shown. *2.* The loop is now brought over the back of the fly and at the same time the stopper knot brought up against the eye of the hook. *3.* The loose end of the knot is now tucked under the body of the hook so that it is trapped there when . . . *4.* the loop is adjusted and pulled tight.

The Turle knot is very strong but has the disadvantage that the whipping on the eye of the hook can be damaged if the knot is pulled hard by a big fish

The Big Fish

Last September I put a fly over a quiet dimple under the far bank, and a great neb came up and absorbed it and turned down. When I tightened, after a delay caused more by shock than good timing, I felt momentarily that I had hooked a brick wall. Then there was a vast boil and an explosion and a huge trout leapt clear of the water, skeetered along on his shovel of a tail and came down fairly and squarely and conclusively on my 5X nylon.

He was a big fish. A very big fish, certainly over four pounds, and yet, as I watched the waves spreading where he indignantly shouldered his way upstream like an All-Black forward driving through a maul, I was not altogether sorry. A little sad at my own usual incompetence, perhaps, but this visitor from the Kennet, searching for spawning grounds, was right out of his league. He had nothing in common with my lively little trout. He made my river look like a ditch. I was glad to see the last of him.

Sour grapes, you may say, but I really do not think so. Had I lost as large a fish on the Kennet, I should have been more than sad. There such a fish would have fitted into the pattern. He would have been expected, and the angler would have been equipped to deal with him. Not that equipment is enough. The margin of human error is wide, and we are all potential bunglers with a fly rod in our hands.

Howard Marshall, *Reflections On A River*, Witherby, 1967

L

Lake Fishing The great expansion in the number of trout lake fisheries began shortly after the end of the Second World War. There were several reasons. Men returning from the war who were looking for fishing found that most of the best fly fishing on the chalk streams was virtually unobtainable. At the same time, in spite of the continuation of many restrictions, such as rationing, the country was becoming more prosperous and the population more mobile as the number of cars on the road increased by several hundred thousand a year. Many servicemen, used to an outdoor life, returning to factories, shops and offices in towns, sought hobbies that would take them into the country at weekends. They turned to golf, mountaineering, camping, hunting and to fishing. Some fishing clubs were almost swamped by applications for membership in the latter part of the 1940s.

It was at this time that Alex Behrendt opened his pioneer fishery at Two Lakes in Hampshire. His approach to the fishery, to the landscaping around the lakes, and the size and quality of the trout, set new standards which had not been reached before. His success was contagious. Many came to learn and to follow his example. New trout lakes, some excavated, some in flooded quarries, began to spring up not only in Hampshire in the chalk stream country but in many other places within reasonable distance of the big towns. The arrival of the motorways accelerated the process in which the reservoirs shared.

The attraction of the small trout fishery lies in its intimate nature, the narrow inlets and bays of a lake that is not much wider than a river, the water glimpsed through screens of flowering shrubs and evergreens, all carefully planted, all designed to give the impression that the angler is alone in the wild. The number of anglers who can fish on any one day is or should be limited, whether the waters are on a subscription or day ticket basis. Subscription waters have an advantage because the anglers who come on fixed days get to know each other and a club-like atmosphere develops. Day ticket waters can at times be crowded and occasionally the unwritten laws of lake fishing can be broken by those who are new to fly fishing habits.

As well as being a pleasant place to be, where one can have a picnic by the water's edge, the important factor in the success of a private fishery is the control which the fishery manager or proprietor can exercise over the rods and the quality of the fish that they can catch. On the best private lakes fish are stocked at between 140 to 160 to an acre, about twice the density of those stocked in the reservoirs. On a small lake, most of which can be reached from the bank, the lake fisherman has a considerable advantage. In addition, skilful fishery management techniques can provide strong and healthy fish, mostly rainbow, which average well over 2lb.

Lake Fishing: Payments and Rules On a subscription fishery, the fisherman will generally pay his subscription some time in the winter before the season opens. Where there is a waiting list of potential subscribers he will often pay at the end of one season for the next. This will give him the right to fish for a specific day or days each week during the season which will last, approximately, from March or April until September or October. The best trout fisheries have rules which are strictly enforced. The rods are generally warned about any breach of the rules to begin with but a serious offence – such as ground baiting or fly-maggot fishing on a fly only water – will be met with an instant ban from the fishery. Even if the offence happens during the first week of the season, the subscription will not be returned. Action of this kind, however, is exceptionally rare.

Behrendt's rules for a subscription fishery have been widely applied by many owners. The following are fairly standard:

1. Rents to be paid in the October previous to the fishing season. The payments of rent is considered to be an acknowledgment of the rules, and rent, once paid, is not returnable.
2. No water authority licence is necessary as the fishing is covered by a general licence
3. Fly fishing only is permitted. Only one fly must be attached to the cast. No hook to be longer than 2cm.
4. Rods are not entitled to more than one visit per week. A day or a part of a day is counted as one visit. Each rod is booked for one particular day of the week and any change must be by agreement with the owner
5. All rods and their guests or visitors are at the fishery entirely at their own risk
6. The management does not take responsibility for any disaster which may strike the fishery or the fish – flood, drought, disease, etc. – which may make fishing impossible
7. All fish caught must be recorded
8. Every trout caught must be killed, irrespective of size. The bag limit is two brace per rod per day. Only trout from a pound upward are counted. Trout under a pound can be kept without being entered in the log book or being counted as part of the bag, but rods are asked to try to avoid catching undersized fish. When the bag limit has been taken, fishing must stop
9. Permits are not transferable. Rod sharing is permitted but only one rod may be used at the time and only one rod's limit of fish may be killed by rod and guest together
10. Each rod may purchase four guest tickets per season, which entitle the guest to the same bag limit as the season rod. Rods are asked not to invite guests who are fishing novices and particularly not to bring children or dogs
11. The use of boats, wading, or standing in the water is not allowed
12. The use of transistor radios at the fishery is forbidden. Car radios may be used providing the broadcasts are not heard outside the car
13. Day tickets, or other short-term tickets, are not issued
14. Fishing is from 9 a.m. to one hour after sunset

Rule 3 means that the largest fly is probably an 8 or 9 longshank, mostly used for fishing damselfly nymphs. Rule 5 and rule 6 are fairly obvious and managements have insurance policies covering most if not all risks. Rule 8 is more interesting. According to many fishery managers trout which are caught and returned to the water may die, may suffer a setback to growth rate, or may become more difficult to catch. An experiment at Bayham Abbey Lake in Kent which allowed anglers to return unwanted fish was given up after two years for these reasons.

Apart from the published rules there is also an unwritten code of behaviour.

Fishermen must not leave litter, reserve places by the lake with staked landing nets or chairs, or start fishing too close to another rod.

The following are the rules on a fairly typical day-ticket water:

1. Fishing is permitted from 9 a.m. Earlier only by prior arrangement
2. Wading is prohibited – it is not necessary
3. Fishing with fly (including nymph) and feathered lures only is permitted
4. The limit to be taken by one rod in one day is four fish. Fish under 1lb do not count towards the limit. No fish caught will be returned to the water
   Fishery permits must be obtained from the headquarters before fishing commences, or names must be left at the office. These are issued on condition that a full and accurate return be made on the form provided. Please weigh in all fish at the headquarters before leaving the premises. Nil returns *are* required
5. The use of transistor radios and the exercising of dogs at the fishery is strictly prohibited
6. No responsibility will be taken by the management for the safety of any fisherman or their belongings whilst on the premises
7. Only one rod to be in use at any one time. This must be strictly observed. No fishing close to another Rod without prior consent
8. Stocking takes place on a weekly basis, depending on the number of fish caught

Rule 3 means that any fly can be used. There is in general no restriction on hook sizes on day-ticket water, otherwise the rules are along the same lines as a subscription fishery. In the case of clubs leasing a trout fishery the members themselves make or approve the rules at the annual general meeting.

Lake Fishing: Dry Fly Lake trout, because of their environment, the type of food, and in many cases the depth of water, will not rise as readily to the dry fly as river trout. Most of their food – a reasonable guess from stomach contents and it can only be a guess – is that some 80 per cent is taken from near or on the bottom or in weed beds. It will vary a good deal from time to time, according to the lake and the insect population, but only between 5 to 20 per cent at the most will be taken from near or on the surface. These figures are unreliable. They indicate trends.

There are times when trout will feed avidly on or just under the surface to a rise of plankton, chironomid, sedge, or the occasional pond or lake olive, but these are comparatively rare. When selective rises take place they generally do not last long but while they last a wet fly is less effective than the dry.

For several years William Nicholson fished only the dry fly at the Two Lakes fishery, casting to the rise, though the rise was not necessarily a take to a surface fly; but, for example, a bulge, taking the pupae under the surface. The rise merely indicated the presence of a trout. William Nicholson cast a dry fly into that area. He used small flies, about size 16, a fine leader point, about 3lb breaking strain, and a small flexible cane rod of about 7½ft. His flies varied but were mostly small olive duns. With this technique he took a number of fish up to 5lb, some more, and his catch during the season was only slightly below those of the best wet-fly fishermen.

On one evening during a hatch of chironomid, he fished a dark-coloured dry fly into the area of the rise, letting the fly stand stationary on the water. On the opposite bank another fisherman was fishing a dark-coloured midge pupa, casting out and then moving it slowly back. Nicholson took two fish on his stationary dry fly during the rise, the moving midge pupae patterns took none. This does not prove anything except that there are times when the dry fly can be effective.

Useful flies for the dry-fly fisherman are the Black Gnat, Greenwell, Blue Upright, a beetle fly such as Terry's Terror, and in August an Ant or a Daddy Longlegs.

The important thing for the fisherman is to keep close watch on the water and if he suspects that the dry fly will work then he should at once switch over: there is no need to put floatant on the leader or the leader tippet, only on the fly.

For boat fishing with a dry fly, dapping is much the more deadly method. A bank fisherman can sometimes take an unlikely fish by floating his fly, letting it drift with a cross wind, and keeping it company by following it along the lake. The lightest tackle is needed and in a float of that kind the leader will obviously have to lie on and not under the surface.

Lake Fishing: Stalking Fishermen with good eyesight have developed the technique of stalking lake trout and fishing for individual fish. Some remarkable results can be obtained. The first essential is the ability to look through the water, disregarding the surface, for which polarising glasses are needed, especially those with side-pieces that black out light. The fisherman will walk slowly round the lake, moving 'as slow as a heron', until he sees a sizeable fish. There are then two methods of presenting the fly.

The first method is that pursued by Barry Welham at the Two Lakes fishery in Hampshire, given in an interview published in later editions of T.C. Ivens's *Still Water Fly Fishing*. This is a summary:

> The cruise path of the fish is established. After the fish has passed, continuing on its way, a weighted nymph is cast just beyond the cruise path and allowed to settle. When the fish reappears – it may be many minutes – the nymph is brought up from the bottom by a slow retrieve so that nymph and fish coincide, or at least the nymph becomes visible to the fish which does not have far to move for a take.

The excitement and tension can be great. Some idea of this is given in Conrad Voss Bark's *Fishing for Lake Trout* (Witherby, 1972).

The other method was described in an article in *The Times* of 15 September, 1983, concerning the remarkable catches of large trout made by Bill Sibbons in Hampshire lakes. He gave a demonstration at Lapsley's fishery, near Fordingbridge, using a carbon fibre rod, a # 7 line tinged slightly green, and a long leader, between 10ft–15ft. The key to this method is the use of an exceptionally heavy fly, the Lead Midge:

> As soon as he sees a cruising fish he casts accurately and fast, dropping the lead midge a foot or so in front of the fish's nose. Although the fish is cruising he can cast to it twice or even three times, letting the midge sink, moving it back fast. The fish will look at it, sometimes turn away slowly as if indifferent, sometimes coming for a closer look, sometimes taking straight away. If there are too many refusals, the lead midge is changed for a leaded shrimp or a damsel fly nymph, in case these prove more attractive, but the first choice is the lead midge.

Lake Fishing: Wet Fly and Nymph The standard techniques of fishing wet fly and nymph are more or less the same as in reservoir fishing, with certain practical adjustments; for example, there is no need for deep wading or long casting; indeed long casting over small well-stocked waters is likely to reduce the chances of taking a fish rather than increasing them. Reservoir fishermen who come to lake fishing for the first time often find difficulty in adjusting to more delicate methods of presentation.

Most lake fishermen will, on average, cast no more than 15 yards, some much less, for the fish are inclined to feed in marginal weed beds which are full of insect life and have not been disturbed by wading. A leader of about 10ft on a floating double-taper line is generally used, depending on conditions. Surveys at two reservoirs and two private lakes show a preference for the floating line whenever possible but those who preferred this method admitted that there were times when the fish were lying deep when a sinking line was needed, even though some did not carry them.

In the early 1970s, David Jacques carried out a survey of the flies in use at Two Lakes. The two most popular were Iven's Green Nymph and the Peter Ross, followed closely by the Invicta and Dunkeld. The Iven's Green and Brown Nymph was, however, first choice every time it was mentioned. The sizes varied from 14s to 8s.

Most of the fishermen who replied to Jacques' questionnaire confessed they were puzzled by the apparent lack of uniformity in the trouts' responses to artificial flies. Whether the flies were of the traditional wet fly type or imitation bait patterns there seemed to be the same reaction; flies that were successful one year were failures the next. Various explanations included one that might account for it: the number of fish pricked and lost on the popular pattern one year would avoid it the next. Many, however, refused to believe such an explanation, pointing out that many new stock fish behaved in this way and that in any case a large over-wintering trout was unlikely to remember a pattern he had seen six months earlier.

The following is a fairly typical example of some of the replies to another questionnaire in the late 1970s:

I fished the whole day. I started with a new pattern of a crane fly, which was bad judgment as there were very few naturals on the water, though there had been. I then fished for an hour or so with a weighted pupa pattern, a good one I had fished many times before with success. I then put on an unweighted pattern and fished this with a greased leader, then an ungreased leader. I moved round the lake. I moved to another lake. I switched to a Killer Bug, followed by a small Butcher, and a Black and Peacock Spider. Nothing at all. I was bewildered. I didn't know what to do. This took me most of the day. Quite a few other rods were blank. One or two who were fishing on the bottom with a sinking line had one or two fish. I assumed that the fish were bottom feeding. I had a sinker but I didn't use it because I prefer a floater. At last, in desperation, for I needed just one fish which I'd promised to a friend, I took out my sea trout box and picked out a huge hairwing fly with mixed red, brown and orange hair, about two inches long, a great bushy thing on a low-water salmon hook, a number 4 or 6, casting this a long distance on a floating line and stripping it back fast just under the surface. On the second or third cast – bang! – a lovely two pounder. Don't ask me to explain. I can't. It was against the rules, so don't give my name.

To many, however, and to the man who wrote the above report, the unpredictability of fishing was one of its greatest charms.

> Too often we see a trout following our fly and then turning away at the last moment. On one such occasion . . . I twitched the fly sharply two or three times and was rewarded by the beautiful sight of the fish grabbing the fly as a cat would an escaping mouse. I have repeated this seemingly infallible manoeuvre many times since, always with one of two results: either the trout grabs the fly or it flees the scene in panic.

Lake fishermen have found that it is important to balance the size of fly and tippet to the kind of water that is fished. Although all rules about fly fishing are made uncertain by exceptions, the general belief is that the clearer the water the finer the nylon and the smaller the fly. Fishery managers will often advise the use of 7lb breaking strain nylon in lakes where 10lb fish are liable to be caught. Many of the most successful lake fishermen use nylon of 3lb breaking strain only, but, significantly, also use a flexible rod rather than a stiff one. Many believe also that large flies are less attractive than small when fished close to the surface but larger flies are more attractive when fished on sinking lines close to the bottom.

Summing up his survey, which was published in *Development of Modern Stillwater Fishing* (Black, 1974), Jacques concluded that success appeared to come from:

— persistence
— frequent changes of fly
— frequent changes of methods of presentation
— minimising the danger of frightening fish through casting over them

When fishing with a floating line and retrieving small wet flies or imitation bait patterns – Ivens' deceivers – there is always the problem of seeing the take. These flies are retrieved slowly. The end of the floating line registers the take, acting as a float does in coarse fishing; but not always.

Observations at a clear-water lake, at Nether Wallop Mill, in Hampshire, in the 1960s, showed that many trout would annexe an angler's nymph while cruising slowly and eject it at once without any take being visible on the line. The takes were gentle casual pick-ups which were almost immediately ejected. There was no violence, no chasing the fly, no savage takes.

From this it might well be concluded that there is a disadvantage in moving the fly too slowly, especially if the fly is a hard one – such as a pheasant tail nymph – but on the other hand it was clear from the observations that any fast moving small nymph did not evoke any reaction, presumably because it was not worth chasing.

The smash-takes experienced by many fishermen when using quite small flies may be because the trout is moving in the opposite direction to the retrieve, will feel the hook, and then accelerate. This can be so unexpected that a considerable sudden strain can be put on the tippet which results in a break. One way to try to avoid smash takes is in the method of the retrieve. The rod should be level with the water, pointing directly towards the fly, when the retrieve is started. The hand holding the line must hold it very gently. If the take is gentle the rod can be raised quickly and the fingers tightened on the line.

1. The oldest known fishery – the Hungerford town water, given to the Commoners of the town by John of Gaunt, Duke of Lancaster (1340-1399) as a reward for sheltering his army during the Wars of the Roses. This is the Wine Cellar Pool.

Source: *The Story of An Ancient Fishery* by E.L. Davis, published privately by the Hungerford Town and Manor Trustees, 1978. Photograph by Conrad Voss Bark.

2. 'The most crystalline stream you ever saw' – Charles Cotton's Dove at Dovedale just below the Beresford Dale water where he and Izaak Walton went fishing.

Source: *Charles Cotton and His River*, by Gerald Heywood, Sherrat and Hughes, Manchester, 1928. Photograph by Conrad Voss Bark.

3. Conversation piece at Blagdon — the Somerset reservoir which set the standard for all subsequent large-scale stillwater fishing. Photograph by Conrad Voss Bark.

4. The Test at Bossington – the fast stretch just below the Mill House at the end of the Houghton water where Halford and Marryat carried out their experiments which led to the adoption of dry-fly fishing.

Source: Halford's writings, and by courtesy of Mick Lunn of the Houghton Club. Photograph by Conrad Voss Bark.

5. Early morning on the Wilderness water of the Kennet where John Goddard set up his underwater cameras to take the pictures which were published in *The Trout* and *The Fly*. Photograph by John Goddard.

6. The Court Reach of the Wiltshire Avon where Frank Sawyer was water keeper and where the first pheasant tail and grey goose nymphs were fished. Photograph by Graham Swanson.

7. Plunket Greene's Bourne at Hurstbourne Priors at the place 'where the little iron blues came bobbing down under the trees below the Beehive Bridge'.

Source: *Where the Bright Waters Meet*. Photograph by Graham Swanson.

8. The favourite water of G.E.M. Skues – the Abbots Barton fishery of the Itchen, the Park Stream with Duck's Nest Spinney on the left of the picture, the site of the fishing hut, Piscatoribus Sacrum, just behind where the photographer was standing.

Source: *Itchen Memories* and the other works of G.E.M. Skues. Photograph by Graham Swanson.

Pale Watery Dun (m), *Baetis bioculatus*

Iron Blue Dun (f), *Baetis niger*

Blue Winged Olive (f), *Ephemerella ignita*

Hawthorn Fly, *Bibio marci*

Iron Blue Spinner, *Baetis pumilus*

Mayfly Dun (f), *Ephemera danica*

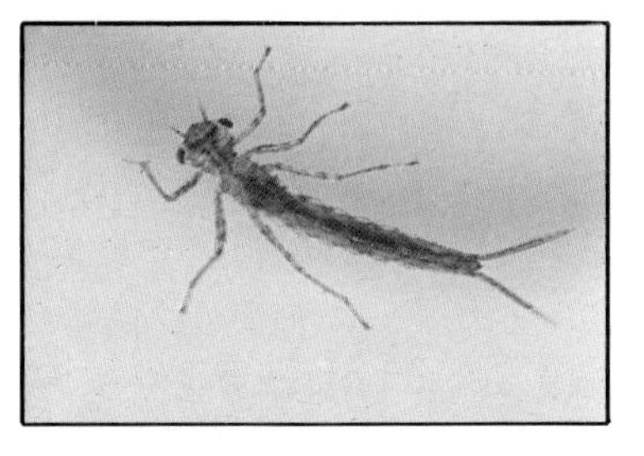

Damselfly Nymph, *Odonata*

Large Dark Olive Nymph, *Baetis Rhodani*

Blue Winged Olive (Sherry Spinner)

Black Gnat (m), *Bibio Johannis*

Cinnamon Sedge, *Limnephilus lunatus*

Grannom, *Brachycentrus subnubilus*

9. In the late 1960s came the breakthrough in underwater macrophotography pioneered by a great practical angler, John Goddard, which gave for the first time the classification and pictures of living insects of rivers and stillwaters together with their matching artificials.

The photographs and descriptions of the insects are from the original illustrations in *Trout Fly Recognition* (1966) and *Trout Flies of Stillwater* (1969) by courtesy of John Goddard.

10. Early artificials. Photographs by Dermot Wilson.

(a) Some of the earliest flies known to have survived – Yorkshire wet flies tied to gut taken from a fly wallet dating back to 1840. From The Flyfishers' Club collection.

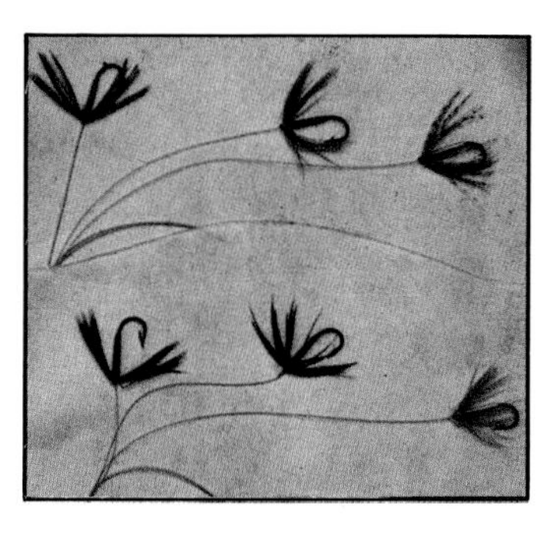

(b) Scottish Border spider patterns in a wallet in the 1905 edition of W.C. Stewart's *The Practical Angler.* They are (clockwise) grouse, dotterel, partridge, starling, black and red spiders. From The Flyfishers' Club collection.

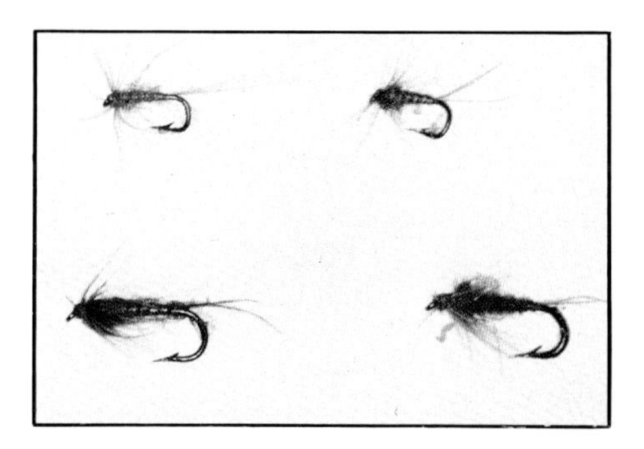

(c) Nymphs tied by G.E.M. Skues on 15 and 18 hooks, date unknown, probably early twentieth century. From The Flyfishers' Club collection.

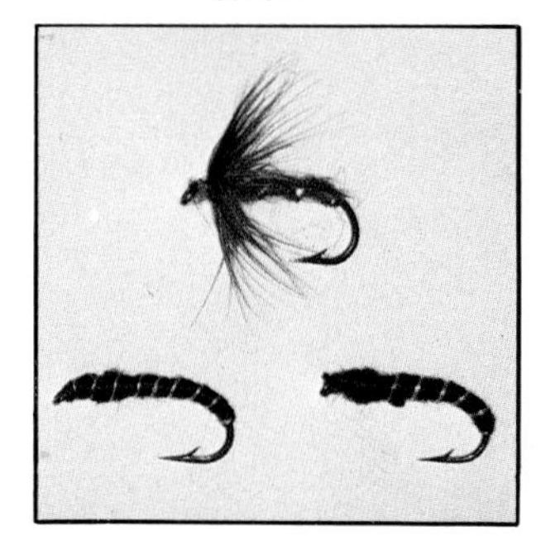

(d) The originals of the Grenadier and (*below*) Blagdon Buzzers, designed and tied by Dr Bell of Blagdon in the 1920s or 1930s. From The Flyfishers' Club collection.

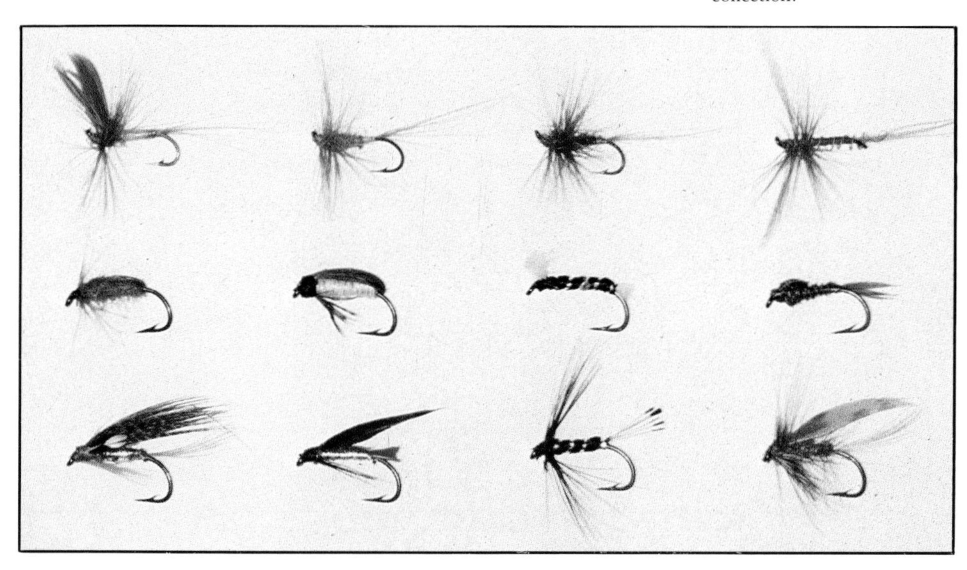

11. Modern trout flies for rivers and lakes – 12 popular patterns from the Farlow list. Photograph by Dermot Wilson.

Blue-Winged Olive	Tup's Indispensible	Blue Upright	Lunn's Particular
Amber Nymph	Corixa	Blagdon Buzzer	Pheasant Tail Nymph
Dunkeld	Butcher	Black Pennell	Invicta

12. Reservoir and sea trout lures. Photographs by Dermot Wilson.

(a) The White Marabou Lure, four to five inches long for deep water fishing on reservoirs dwarfs a Whisky Fly and an Ace of Spades which are fished closer to the surface.

(b) Double-hook Demons and Terrors for Sea Trout fishing – a Dr Evelyn Lure of the 1950s above Hugh Falkus's Sunk Lure.

(c) Wooden lures for surface fishing – an American Popper Bug for stripping in on reservoirs (*above*) and a deadly-looking Wake Lure designed by Hugh Falkus for sea trout.

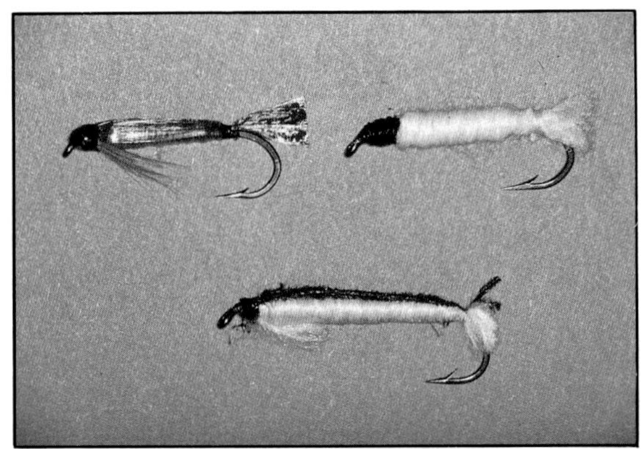

(d) Minnow flies for stillwater trout. Richard Walker's Polystickle (*top left*) next to a Baby Doll and (*below*) a Minnow Fly from Blagdon in the 1930s.

13. Salmon flies: A complete contrast – the highly decorative Popham, tied to gut, dating from about 1870, and a brilliant imitation bait lure, Peter Deane's Black-Eyed Prawn.

If it is a violent take and the line speeds away it is allowed to do so before strain is put on by raising the rod slowly and tightening pressure on the line with the fingers, again slowly. It sounds complex. With practice, it becomes instinctive.

Lake Fishing: Fanning the Casts Surveys have shown that one of the causes of failure in lake fishing is the disturbance caused by casting, especially frequent casting and long-distance casting towards the middle, sometimes well beyond the middle, of the lake. Even a # 3 line makes a crack and a shadow on the surface of calm water and most lake fishermen use # 5 or 6.

One well-known fishing writer who came to fish a small private lake in Hampshire began to cast long distances. He was using a shooting head and his casting was very pleasant to watch but no fish took. However, he soon realised what was happening and began to use a different technique, fishing close in, using a much longer leader, and was successful. Fishing close in means fanning the casts. Whether a fisherman likes mobile fishing, moving slowly along the bank, or whether he prefers to settle in one spot for a while, sometimes indeed settling down on a camp stool or chair, the technique of fanning the casts is the same.

The first cast will be made with a very short line along the bank, either to the left or the right, dropping the fly a yard or so out from the bank not more than a few yards away from the fisherman who, of course, should be taking cover behind screens of foliage or rushes and wearing clothes which blend with his surroundings. Having put the fly to the left he will try the right, and then, still using the short line, will fan the casts out in front of him. After he has covered the water close in he will lengthen line and repeat the process. When using a small fly, imitative or traditional, he will let the fly sink before beginning to retrieve.

The value of allowing the fly to sink is twofold. Many takes come to a sinking fly without being retrieved. The disturbance caused by line crack and shadow may well have scared one fish which has been cast over but other fish may well be cruising into the area which have not observed the disturbance. This method is summed up in the old saying: let the fish have a good look at the fly first.

There is a certain amount of controversy here. Most flies, unless they are very heavily hackled, will sink slowly. Should they be weighted? Some say yes and some no. It will depend to a great extent on the depth of the water the type of fly and one's own personal preference.

Lake Fishing: Sinking Lines A large proportion of lake fishermen (about a third, according to one survey) carry a sinking line; but most of those who do so are inclined to use a floating line first and only put on a sinker if conditions are very dour, the water cold, and few fish to be seen near the surface. Observations at several small lakes suggest that at any one time about six or seven fishermen out of ten will be using a floating line, perhaps one or two with a sink tip, which is a natural compromise between the two methods. The reasons given for using a floater are:

— it's more fun
— I like to see the take
— it is a much more certain way of hooking a fish
— if you use a sinker the fish pretty well have to hook themselves and when you fish a fly you want to see what's going on.

With a sinking line one does have a chance of reaching fish that are feeding deep, which frequently happens, and it is noticeable that these are often big two-winter trout rather than stock fish. This has been noticeable in reservoir fishing where sinking lines are used much more frequently than floaters.

The problem of hooking weed can be irritating, especially if there are many snags about. To avoid snagging, many fishermen use flies that are weighted to fish with the hook point uppermost (keel flies) or else flies that fish the usual way up which have a bristle tied at the head that projects downwards and over the point of the hook, thus lifting the hook over a snag when it comes to it. A third way, of course, is to use a naturally buoyant fly with cork or deer hair in the dressing. If the line is being retrieved along the bottom a buoyant fly may well be above the obstructions, or that at least is the theory.

The general tendency in fishing deep on lakes is to use larger and more visible flies. For example, a white lure, or a Coachman, which has white wings, will frequently be more successful than a small dark nymph, and many fly dressers who fish a deep nymph will put a small white tag somewhere on the body to make it more visible.

Lake Fishing: The Late Hatch Most lakes do not open for fishing until well after breakfast but the evening is another matter. Quite a few stay open until dusk, often an hour after sunset, and an evening rise frequently produces fish in the last hour or so for anglers who have been fishless all day.

It is always dangerous to generalise but with that proviso in mind one can say that there are two kinds of evening rises and therefore two ways of fishing them. The first is a hatch of small black flies, chironomids (midge) or of small white flies (caenis). The flies, as a rule, can be seen and identified, but the problem in fishing either a surface or sub-surface pattern is simply a numerical one. There are times when caenis and chironomids will be hatching in countless numbers and the trout will be cruising along souping them up in almost hundreds at a time. What chance has one artificial in these conditions? It is often very frustrating. If one tires of fishing the imitative patterns, either the pupa or the hatched fly, the alternative is to strip a large lure through the area of the hatch in the hope that some trout or other will lose its temper with the intruder and try to do away with it. This is more exciting for the fisherman than casting out a tiny pupa and waiting in the growing darkness for something to happen. On the other hand . . .

The second type of rise is to a hatch of sedge. This produces some very exciting fishing indeed. Many sedges scuttle over the surface of the water after hatching to gain speed for the take-off. During a sedge rise, one should use fairly strong nylon and a large palmer fly, treated with floatant, cast out and retrieved at a good speed over the surface of the water, thus creating a wake and drawing attention to itself. The takes are savage and violent and one needs to point the rod at the fly before lifting into the smash.

Lambourn The River Lambourn is a chalk stream that rises on the Berkshire Downs and flows into the Kennet near Newbury. It can sometimes be glimpsed by passengers in cars riding the M4 motorway, which crosses the river just above the water fished by Howard Marshall, commemorated in his *Reflections of a River*, published by Witherby in 1967:

Always I shall come back to the little River Lambourn. The fact that I am fortunate enough to live on its banks is beside the point. If I lived a hundred miles away I should still return to this limpid stream and its golden trout.

Most of the Lambourn is now private fishing. Howard Marshall's water at Easton has been taken over by a syndicate. Apart from industrious local enquiries, it is doubtful whether there is now any way of fishing the Lambourn for someone who does not own a stretch. This is a pity. It is one of the most charming little rivers in Southern England.

Lane, Joscelyn Published in 1954 by Seeley Service, Colonel Lane's book *Lake and Loch Fishing* set high standards in the study of the development of stillwater fishing techniques. He was among the first to produce good fly dressings of lake olive nymphs, damselfly nymphs, shrimps, water boatmen and stickleback lures. His trimmed hackle sedges preceded those of Richard Walker and other fly dressers. A thoughtful and useful book.

Lapsley, Peter A former army officer, for some time owner of what is now Rockbourne fishery, near Fordingbridge, and author of several useful books on lake fishing. His best book, *Trout From Stillwaters* (Benn, 1981) with a foreword by Richard Walker, gave a detailed and comprehensive picture of every kind of stillwater fishing, on lochs, lakes and reservoirs, bank fishing and boat fishing:

As an advocate of flexibility I have sought to consider all aspects of fly fishing for stillwater trout, from the fish themselves, their environments and food, to the various forms of tackle, techniques and tactics used in their capture.

His choice of flies is also given in *The Bankside Book of Stillwater Trout Flies*, published by Benn in 1976, with a new and enlarged edition in 1981.

Last Hope A fly designed by John Goddard to suggest a pale watery but it is also useful in a caenis hatch and when trout are smutting:

Body: natural stone or buff colour condor herl but in the absence of condor a light-coloured or off white silk or wool might do
Whisks: four to six fibres of honey dun cock
Hackle: very short cream cock
Tying silk: pale yellow
Hook: 18–20

Lawrie, W.H. A great authority on the history of anglers' flies, Lawrie's *A Reference Book of English Trout Flies* (Pelham Books, 1967) is the standard work, giving dressings of some 700 flies from the 15th century onwards, created by more than 70 anglers and fly dressers from the author of the *Treatyse* to those of our own time. An earlier work, *Scottish Trout Flies*, is also invaluable for reference purposes. Lawrie's *Border River Angling* (Oliver and Boyd, 1939) is a useful book dealing with classic wet fly methods.

Lee, Art An American fisherman whose book, *Fishing Dry Flies For Trout on Rivers and Streams* (Atheneum Publishers, New York) has had some influence in Britain. He concentrates on presentation of the fly rather than precise imitation of the natural insect, and as a result of his experience recommends fishing the dry fly across or slightly downstream rather than in the traditional upstream fashion. His book was published in 1983 after some 30 years experience of fishing the Catskill rivers and other American streams as well as the River Test in Hampshire.

Lewis, Isle of The wild country of this Hebridean island provides some excellent salmon fishing on the Fhorsa river on the Uig Lodge estate. Renton Finlayson of Bonar Bridge, Sutherland, has letting. There is good sea trout fishing also in the sea pools.

Little Red Sedge A pattern of a sedge fly made popular by G.E.M. Skues which can be fished whenever sedges are hatching.

Body: dark hares' ear
Body hackle: red cock tied in at the shoulder and taken down sparsely to the bend
Rib: fine gold wire binding down the body hackle
Wing: rolled landrail or substitute landrail tied sloping well back and close to the body
Front hackle: red cock tied in front of the wing
Hook: the usual size is 14, but it should be larger when the sedges are about

Lines The first fly lines were made of horsehair, then mixtures of silk and horsehair, and in about the 1860s of dressed silk, a dressing made by various mixes of oils and varnish. By the 1960s came plastic lines covering a synthetic core. The advantage of plastic is that the lines can be made of different densities with a specific gravity lighter or heavier than water; and unlike silk a plastic line does not need to be dried out after use.

The line weight, in grains, of the first 30ft of line, (the working weight of the line excluding the tapered point) is now marked on all line cartons, under scales agreed by the Fishing Tackle Manufacturers Association (FTMA) in Britain, and by the American Fishing Tackle Manufacturers Association (AFTMA). The appropriate line weights are also marked on fly fishing rods so that the line weight can be matched, in most cases correctly, to the casting capacity of the rod. With the advent of carbon fibre/graphite rods in the 1970s some manufacturers marked their rods with inappropriately wide ranges of casting weights. This has now largely been corrected.

Line marking codes range from one to eleven. There are allowable weight tolerances of something like 10 to 20 grains. Under the code, a # 4 line would weigh about 120 grains; a # 5, 140; # 6, 160; and so on.

Marking codes also indicate the type of line: L, level; ST, single taper; WF, weight-forward taper, DT, double taper; F, floating line; S, sinking line; FS,

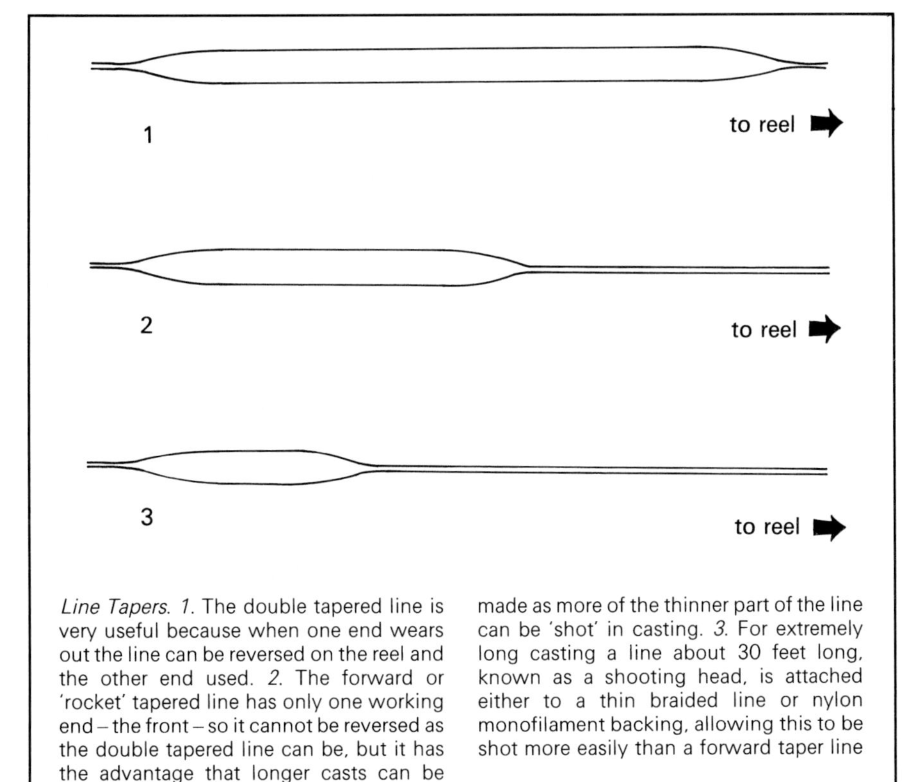

Line Tapers. 1. The double tapered line is very useful because when one end wears out the line can be reversed on the reel and the other end used. *2.* The forward or 'rocket' tapered line has only one working end – the front – so it cannot be reversed as the double tapered line can be, but it has the advantage that longer casts can be made as more of the thinner part of the line can be 'shot' in casting. *3.* For extremely long casting a line about 30 feet long, known as a shooting head, is attached either to a thin braided line or nylon monofilament backing, allowing this to be shot more easily than a forward taper line

sink tip line; I, intermediate. Under the codes, a line marked DT6F is a double taper floating line for a six-weight rod; a WF6S a weight forward sinking line for a six-weight rod; and so on.

Line Care Scum, grease, algae and microscopic particles of grit are picked up by lines and can damage the line surface. In the case of floating lines this will increase their weight to the point where they will begin to sink. The use of a cleaning pad, generally supplied with the line by the best manufacturers, is recommended from time to time.

Plastic lines can also be damaged by various chemicals, oil, petrol, detergents, insect repellants, and certain kinds of line floatants. They can also be damaged by excessive heat, such as leaving the line in the back window of a car in direct sunlight for many hours. Worn rod rings can slice a line to pieces in no time at all. Bad casting, treading on the line with nailed boots, and pulling it violently from branches and brambles, are the most common form of damage.

Some fishermen with experience of the old silk lines affirm that, if properly treated, a silk line would last three times longer than a plastic line but admit, sometimes reluctantly, that a plastic line is less trouble to use.

Line Colour *The Angling Times* columnist, Richard Walker, campaigned during the 1970s for the use of dark-coloured fly lines, suggesting that white lines created too much flash and frightened the fish. Theodore Gordon in America said much the same thing 60 years before. He much preferred a black line.

In *The Trout and the Fly*, by Brian Clarke and John Goddard (Benn, 1980) underwater photography was brought in aid:

The white flyline, though it causes a degree of flash in the air, is most of the time less visible to the trout. But it falls like a flash of white lightning across all the water surrounding the trout . . . across the mirror . . .

And Clarke and Goddard came to this conclusion:

There can be little doubt . . . that white or light-coloured fly lines should not be used when trout are close to the surface.

Critics have pointed to certain apparent discrepancies. How often does a fly line fall across a trout's window? If the line is '*most* of the time less visible to the trout' might this not compensate for the times when it is not?

The case for white lines was put in a letter on the subject from Rod Towsley of Scientific Anglers, the big American line manufacturers in Michigan:

About two years ago (1963) our Michigan outdoors television show anchored a skin-diver type photographer at the bottom of the Manistee river. This gentleman took pictures of various-colored lines floating over him on the surface, and there was no question: all the light colours presented a much less distinct image and the ivory was almost invisible. I'm uncertain whether the fish's eye would get the same effect, but there you have it. One last factor: how often does the line itself pass over the fish?

So far as is known, no other evidence is available. By the 1980s various new colours were in use, including bright red and yellow lines and brown lines with brightly coloured tips.

Lunn Three generations of the Lunn family have been river keepers on the Houghton Club water of the Test at Stockbridge. The first, W.J. Lunn, began work at Houghton in 1887 at the age of 20 and retired 55 years later in 1932. Even at an early age he was a fine practical naturalist and Halford and Marryat and others frequently consulted him and took his advice. He was a splendid fly designer and tyer, had an almost unrivalled knowledge of the ecology of rivers, and so many fishermen relied on his judgements that it was not surprising that J. Waller Hills wrote about him and his life and times in *River Keeper*, first published in 1934.

Alfred Lunn, his son, took over from him in 1932, when W.J. Lunn retired and was responsible for the layout of the hatchery and the stews at Stockbridge. One of Alfred Lunn's many achievements was the substitution of borehole water for stream water in the rearing of fry, which increased the survival rate from 50 to 80 per cent.

When Alfred's son, Mick Lunn, took over in 1963, he had already absorbed an enormous amount of river lore as part of his family background but was never content to rest on tradition. He made considerable advances in modern

Mick Lunn

methods of fish farming, studying the use of chemicals and the improvement of fish diet.

Lunn's Particular One of the famous flies designed by W. J. Lunn, tied first in 1917 as a suggestion of an olive spinner. It gained the title *particular* because it was said to have the quality of attracting shy feeders when the trout were being particular about their choice of fly.

Body: undyed hackle stalk from a Rhode Island red cock
Hackle: medium Rhode Island cock
Whisks: four fibres from the same bird, rather long
Wings: two medium blue hackle points tied on flat and at right angles to the body – the spent position
Tying silk: dark red
Hook: 14

Many fly dressers like to clip a V in the hackle underneath so that the fly floats in the surface film. Some fishermen like to fish a Particular upstream wet, on the assumption that trout prefer drowned flies.

Lunn's Spent Gnat *See* Mayfly.

Loch Hope A Sutherland loch some eight miles long, not too wide and with good shallows. A quick run into the sea brings in fresh and vigorous sea trout of six and seven pounds or more which take out line like a torpedo. Dapping on the drift is the main method, using a black parachute fly or palmer, though preferably the local fly, a Willie Ross. The Altnaharra Hotel has good beats on Hope for visitors and also on Loch Naver, which from time to time will produce heavy salmon of 20–30lb. Dappers must be careful to have a reasonable breaking strain of nylon.

Ghillies and boats are provided by the hotel and beats are fished in rotation, with occasional outings for salmon on the Mudale and Mallart, productive tributaries of the River Naver.

Loch Lomond A great loch for pleasure boating as well as fishing, Lomond has plenty of room, for it is the largest freshwater loch in Scotland, 24 miles long and several miles wide. Salmon are taken in many areas but the most popular place is the south shore between Balloch and Balmaha. It is spinning early in the season but fly only on the Endrick Bank from May. Boats and permits can be obtained at Balmaha, Balloch and Luss and hotels along the lochside can also make arrangements for the fishing. The loch is so big and the lies so widespread that a local boatman is essential if one is to feel confident of covering fish. There is good sea trout and brown trout fly fishing on the drift with a team of two or three flies on the cast, and when the water is clear, which it generally is, quite small flies will bring up the fish. Because there are big fish around it is advisable to have a flexible rod and not fish too fine.

Loch Maree A deep loch in Ross and Cromarty which lays claim to being 'the fairest in Scotland' and which certainly produces some record sea trout. Geoffrey Snutch gives this description:

The loch is in a magnificent setting in Wester Ross, bounded on the inaccessible northerly shore by wooded slopes tumbling sheer from the bare faces of Slioch mountain, where circling eagles are sometimes seen. The road follows the southerly shore through unspoilt woods and rocky moorland. About eleven and a half miles long and two miles wide at its broadest point, Maree is studded with wooded islands which add much to its beauty and also its fishing potential.

The fishing is for sea trout and salmon, which ascend the short and often productive outfall river Ewe from Loch Ewe and the sea, at the northwesterly end, on their passage to the feeder streams around Kinlochewe at the head of the loch. Salmon fishing is by trolling during June. Conventional trolling gear and methods are used and can be productive, although salmon are taken also on the dapped dry fly through July to September which constitutes the method and season for sea trout fishing.

The major part of the fishing is controlled and organised from the Loch Maree Hotel, situated half way along the southern shore. Ten outboard motor boats and their attendant ghillies are employed to take the angler to dap the sea trout drifts around the ten hotel beats, bearing names such as Coree, Grudie and Fool's Rock. Ash Island is reckoned the best and to produce the biggest trout. An example is the cast of a 22½lb sea trout in the lounge of the hotel, which may be a record. The trout can be large, but average 2lb. In the rotation, the far beats are not popular because of the boating time needed to reach them and return, but one far beat enjoyed a brief popularity due to several appearances of a naked female bather. She was called 'the Naiad', but apparently was far from Greek in other respects to the lucky observers.

The fishing at the head of the loch is by boat from Kinlochewe, and ghillies are not normally provided, which some anglers may prefer.

Lochy and the Western Highlands A vast area with dozens of salmon and sea trout rivers and lochs, and some of the sea trout lochs like Eilt, Shiel and

Morar, are among the most productive in Scotland. The mountains – here is Ben Nevis, 4,408ft (1,344m), the highest in Britain – are most spectacular with fairly short fast flowing rivers, rocky gorges, some fed by freshwater lochs, and some of the sea lochs into which they run are so steep-sided they give the impression of Norwegian fjords. A good centre is Fort William with the tackle shop there being able to make a number of reservations for rods. A good stretch of the Lochy is available but is soon booked up. The Spean Bridge Hotel has water on the Spean, the main tributary of the Lochy. For Eilt and Morar the centre is the Loch Morar Hotel. It is worth remembering when considering the fishing that practically all these West Highland rivers depend very much on water levels.

London Reservoirs There is some good stillwater fishing in the London area, not to be despised at all, in spite of the built-up areas all around. The Barn Elms reservoir near Hammersmith Bridge has good fly fishing on day tickets which can be purchased at the reservoir, and so has Walthamstow. Further out towards the country is Kempton Park, near the racecourse, which also provides day ticket fishing. Most of the other London reservoirs are let to clubs.

Lune The River Lune rises on Ravenstonedale in Cumbria where it is a wild and open moorland stream. Well past Sedbergh it turns down into the valleys and broadens out, flowing through farmland, joined by small streams, on past Kirkby Lonsdale and Hornby, glimpsed briefly by motorists on the M6 motorway as it goes into the estuary at Lancaster.

The Lune is a wonderful mixed fishery. Oliver Kite had a splendid few days there with Reg Righyni and Arthur Oglesby (*A Fisherman's Diary*, André Deutsch, 1969) during which he caught one roach, nine brown trout to 2lb 6 oz, eight sea trout, including three three-pounders, and two salmon together weighing 20lb. He caught his two best sea trout – in Lancashire they are called morts – in blazing sunshine in mid-afternoon, taken on a small and sparsely dressed nymph. The country is lovely and open with a variety of secluded valleys and the up-stream wet fly fishing for trout in the classic style is among the best in the North Country. In recent years, from the late 1970s, the salmon runs have declined as they have in so many other rivers.

Visitors are well catered for on the Lune and tackle shops at Lancaster, Halton and Sedbergh are useful centres for permits. Many hotels in the upper reaches in Cumbria and Yorkshire can arrange fishing for guests, including the Royal at Kirkby Lonsdale, the Barbon Inn at Barbon, The Bull at Sedbergh, among others.

Lures Lure fishing was probably carried out by the ancient Egyptians and the Chinese several thousand years ago. Jacques records that Homer wrote of fishing rods, hooks and casting in the twelfth century B.C. The Greeks used what they called a plume, rather similar to the feathers that the Cornish use for mackerel.

The Romans also fished plumes and it is not unlikely that they brought the habit over to this country during the colonisation of Britain. Fishing for salmon with a 'dubbe' is mentioned in the *Treatyse of Fysshynge* in 1496 though what a dubbe on a hook looked like is uncertain. A hundred years later several writers were describing flies for salmon which had several 'wings'.

The plumes, dubbes and wings give a tantalising glimpse of feathered lures that were dressed according to an oral tradition that was passed down from one fishing family to another, changing little over many centuries.

The modern lure has developed from the artistic creations of early Victorian fly dressers, leading up to Kelson, but definition is difficult. Salmon and sea trout flies are visibly lures though it may be that at least some patterns might give the impression of small fish. In reservoir fly fishing many large double and treble-hook lures are specially designed as a result of American influence – for example, the popper bug and the lead-headed jig, known here as a Nobbler. The more one tries to define a lure the less likely we are to succeed except in the broadest terms – that it is almost any creation of fur and feathers that is not a copy of an insect.

An interesting comment on reservoir lures was given by Richard Walker in an article in *Trout and Salmon*, republished in *Dick Walker's Trout Fishing* (David and Charles, 1982):

> There is a great deal of debate about the ethics of lure fishing. I should be sorry to see any restriction placed on it in large water-supply reservoirs and other sheets of water of comparable size, where there is no evidence that its use leads to too high a catch rate. When trout are eating fry, or when they are obviously not eating insects, the use of an appropriate lure may catch a fish or two and save an angler, who may have travelled a long way, from a blank day. In these conditions, using a lure is perfectly reasonable.
>
> I am, however, sorry for the anglers who have no ideas beyond casting out a lure as far as possible and stripping it in as fast as they can, regardless of what the trout are doing. They don't know how much pleasure they are missing. That they often catch a lot of fish is undeniable, but they never learn what fly fishing is really about.

Sources: Bob Church, *Reservoir Trout Fishing* (2nd edn., Black, 1983); *Stillwater Flies: How and When to Fish Them* (ed. Goddard, Benn, 1982); and David Jacques, *The Development of Modern Stillwater Fishing* (Black, 1974).

Lyd A small tributary of the Tamar, rising on Dartmoor, creating picturesque falls in the National Trust area of Lydford Gorge, then passing in a sequence of pools and stickles through farming valleys to join the Tamar south of Lifton. Though small, the Lyd has an excellent run of sea trout from late June, early July, and a small run of salmon. The Arundell Arms at Lifton has several miles of fishing for hotel guests.

Lyn A small Exmoor stream in *Lorna Doone* country. Fishermen should avoid the tourist area of Watersmeet. There is good fly fishing for small trout around Rockford, where permits may be had, and then two little rivers, East and West Lyn, join up and speed down a steep wooded and rocky gorge to the sea at Lynmouth. Salmon do run up the Lyn, the South West Water Authority issue permits, but it is mostly local inhabitants who know when best to fish.

Extase

The appeal of a sport – being simply an appeal to age-old inherited instincts – is never experienced in its full perfection unless there is involved some call upon the craft of the wilderness, that faculty of appreciating the ways of bird and beast, and fish and insect, the acquirement of which was, through countless centuries, the one great primary interest of primitive man.

J.W. Dunne, *Sunshine and the Dry Fly*, A and C Black, 1924, 2nd Edn. 1950

For the reluctant town dweller (of the early 19th century) fishing represented an escape from the dull world of reality. It was not long before this new feeling crept consciously or unconsciously into our angling books. The works of Viscount Grey of Fallodon, H.T. Sheringham, William Caine and others owe their abiding charm to the joyous sense of escape that runs through them. Escape is a poor word with something of the Freudian jargon clinging to it; the Greeks had a nobler name for it, and called it ectasy; a standing aside, a withdrawal from the common world.

H.B. McCaskie,' *The Guileless Trout*, Cresset Press, 1950

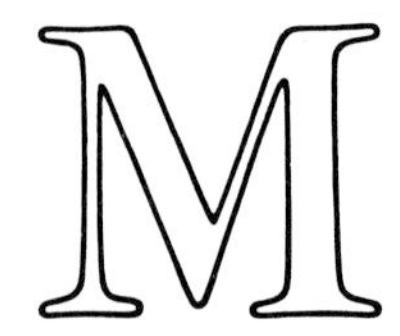

McCaskie McCaskie's Green Cat Fly, mentioned by G.E.M. Skues (*see* Courtney Williams) was designed by Dr Norman McCaskie, author of *Fishing – My Life's Hobby* (1950) which contains an 11-page introduction by Skues. McCaskie's Corner on the Abbots Barton water, named after him, was taken over for Winchester town development in the 1970s and is now (1986) closed to fishermen. Dr Norman McCaskie's brother, Dr H.B. McCaskie, also a fisherman, was the author of *The Guileless Trout*, also published in 1950. **Source:** Jocelyn Godley, and others.

McLaren, Charles Author of *Fishing for Salmon* (John Donald, Edinburgh, 1977) and of other books on fishing, Charles McLaren is a great exponent of long casting and the use of fine tackle to take shy fish in clear water. He won a number of English and Scottish fly casting championships and in the 1970s opened his own fly fishing school at Altnaharra, Sutherland.

Mallard and Claret A wet fly for trout in use almost everywhere, abroad as well as at home, mostly for lake fishing, for fishing the drift, and for sea trout:

Body: claret-coloured seals' fur or wool, ribbed with fine gold wire or gold tinsel in the larger sizes, sometimes with a small gold tag
Tail: golden pheasant tippet
Wings: two strips of dark bronze mallard
Hackle: red cock
Hook: 14 for lake trout, up to 8 or 6 for sea trout

March Brown (*Rhithrogena haarupi*) A pleasant-looking ephemerid fly, about the size of the Large Dark Olive, with noticeable speckled wings. Localised distribution: Wales, Devon, Yorkshire and parts of Scotland. Fished dry on rivers like the Usk, a good artificial can be deadly. Jean Williams, of Sweet's Fishing Tackle, Usk, Gwent, changes the body colours of her dry March Brown because of the way the natural fly varies in colour:

Body: hare's ear, or red or yellow or green wool
Rib: fine oval gold tinsel
Tail: four or five reddish fibres from a cock pheasant's tail
Hackle: one brown partridge hackle in front of two medium red cock hackles, the partridge, which gives the speckled look being slightly longer than the red cock
Hook: 12 or 10

Jean Williams also has an interesting pattern of the nymph of the March Brown, imitating the male:

Body: weighted with fine lead wire
Tail: short cock pheasant tail fibres
Body: first half, the abdomen – cock pheasant tail fibres; second half, thorax – hare's ear and red wool fibres mixed together
Casing: fibre strips over the top of the thorax taken from the very darkest cock pheasant tail fibres
Hackle: grouse
Hook: 12

The female March Brown nymph is similar but the red wool is absent from the thorax, which is plain hare's ear, and the tail fibres and throat hackle are not pheasant but partridge.

The wet fly March Brown is similar to the dry but with less hackle and the addition of strips of feather taken from the tail of the hen pheasant, sloping backwards, with a brick-red wool body.

The Silver March Brown is the same as the standard wet fly but with a body of bright silver tinsel, sometimes ribbed fine silver wire.

Marryat, George Selwyn Once described as 'the finest fly fisherman in England', G.S. Marryat was the son of an army officer, went to school at Winchester, served as a Guard's officer in India and Australia, and retired from the army in 1870 when he was only 30 years old. Most of his time for the next 26 years was devoted to fishing. He was involved with H.S. Hall in improvements to the eyed hook which had been introduced in an early form some 40 years before. Marryat met Halford by chance – a meeting described by Donald Overfield in *Famous Flies and Their Originators* (Black, 1972) – which began their partnership. Marryat, to begin with, knew far more than Halford about the dressing of floating flies. Halford certainly thought that the result of their researches should be published under their names. For some reason, Marryat refused. It is possible that this might have been because of Halford's rigid insistence on the use of the dry fly at all times. Marryat, so far as we know, did not share this view. A box of Marryat's flies in the Flyfishers' Club museum in London contains many wet fly patterns.

Marryat died in 1896 and is buried near Izaak Walton in Winchester Cathedral.

Marshall, Howard (1900–1973) Howard Marshall's only book on fishing, *Reflections on a River* (Witherby, 1967) was widely admired for delicate and perceptive essays that took their inspiration from the River Lambourn. He was interested in fishing all his life and was the co-founder, with Bernard Venables, of the *Trout and Salmon Magazine*. In his last years Marshall lived at Easton Lodge, Easton, near Newbury, close to the Lambourn, whose charms he shared lavishly with his friends. His favourite flies were the Greenwell, the Gold-Ribbed Hare's Ear, the Blue Upright, and the Little Red Sedge.

Marshall became famous for his radio commentaries for the BBC on great national and sporting occasions. He was educated at Haileybury and Oriel College, Oxford, became a sports writer for *The Daily Telegraph*, and joined the BBC in 1927. One of his many famous commentaries was on the Coronation of King George VI in 1937. He was Director of War Reporting for the BBC from 1940 to 1945, died in 1973, and is buried in Welford churchyard, not far from the Lambourn.

Martin, The Rev. James A great advocate of dry-fly fishing, James Martin was the author of *The Angler's Guide*, published in 1854, which among other things gave this advice:

> Never throw your fly on the water in a wet state, for if you do it will sink the moment it gets there, which is not well. To prevent this, whisk it once or twice through the air before you let it fall on the water . . . so that it shall appear in its descent exactly like a real fly.

Howard Marshall

Mayfly In America all ephemerid flies are called mayflies, in Britain only three – the most important being the big mayfly, *Ephemera danica*. The two others are the less frequently seen, *E. vulgata* and *E. lineata*. The hatches vary from year to year and place to place. The chalk streams are liable to have very profuse hatches during the last week in May and the first week in June and in certain years there are very heavy hatches indeed: in some places where a road is near a river passing cars have their windscreens spattered with insects to such extent they have to stop and wipe them off.

The mayfly occurs in other districts apart from the chalk streams – in the West Country, Wales, in parts of northern England and Scotland but the hatches are generally sparse, nothing like the abundance of fly in the Hampshire–Wiltshire area.

The comon name for the mayfly dun is the Green Drake and for the spinner the Spent Gnat.

In recent years the most popular flies to suggest the Green Drake are Peter Deane's Shadow Mayfly and Lee Wulff's Grey Wulff. The Wulff pattern is most likely taken by the trout as an emerger. There is no such doubt about the Peter Deane Shadow Mayfly which floats very high on the water. This is Deane's Shadow Mayfly dressing:

Body: none
Body hackle: palmered grizzle cock, long, from eye to bend
Whisks: none
Wings: two red cock hackles, points clipped square, standing up well from the body, tied in about half way between the centre of the hook and the eye
Hook: 10, longshank

At times a badger or grizzle hackle can be used for the wings but the original is red game cock, the hackle points curving inwards towards each other. Peter Deane writes:

I was taught to tie the Shadow Mayfly by post by J. Arthur Palethorpe of Hungerford Priory in 1950. Believe me it was the only fly tying lesson I ever had and I trust the last as he was an extremely hard taskmaster. In the hand it looks nothing like a real mayfly and it took me some 16 years after I first tied it before I had sufficient confidence to use it myself, and what a surprise when I did so! It is most effective and creates an illusion or impression of a fly, possibly because it casts the right kind of shadow.

There are many other patterns of mayflies. This is the French Partridge, a traditional pattern:

Body: cream-coloured floss silk or raffia, ribbed black or claret tying silk
Whisks: red cock
Hackles: two – the inner hackle being red cock, four or five turns, in order to give the fly support on the water, and in front a couple of turns of the soft feather from the back of a French Partridge.
Hook: 12 or 10 longshank

Among other dressings are Horace Brown's Fore and Aft fly, and Skue's Straddlebug:

Body: raffia
Whisks: brown mallard
Ribbing: fine gold wire
Hackle: ginger cock palmered from the eye of the hook to the bend, held down by the gold wire
Wings: none
Hook: longshank 12 or 10

The emerger pattern, the Grey Wulff, suggests the nymph in the act of ecdysis:

Body: blue-grey seal's fur
Tail: fibres from a grey-brown bucktail with white points
Wings: fibres from a bucktail with white points, divided, fairly short, pointing upwards and forwards
Hackle: dark blue-dun cock
Hook: longshank 10 or 11

The overall impression is of a grey fairly colourless pattern, only the white points noticeable. For both dun and spinner combined, depending on the set of the wings, the best and easiest tying is still Lunn's Shaving Brush:

Body: thin white wool ribbed with black or brown tying silk, the closest turns at the head
Whisks: two or three fibres of teal, grizzle or pheasant tail according to taste
Wings: grey hackle points tied forward and divided for the spinner, and for the dun grey hackle and black mixed thickly to give a nice bushy appearance
Hook: 12 or 10 longshank

Veniard's dressing of the Spent Gnat is also good:

Body: White floss silk or dun-coloured raffia
Tail: three cock pheasant tail fibres
Hackle: badger cock
Wings: dark blue dun hackle points, tied spent
Hook: 12 or 10 longshank

And at times one can hardly do better for a Spent Gnat than John Goddard's:

Body: natural raffia
Tail: three fibres from a cock pheasant's tail
Rib: fine oval silver

Wings: a very stiff black or dark blue cock hackle wound in the usual way, the hackle then split into two equal halves and tied spent
Hook: 12 or 10 longshank of fine wire

Mayfly Nymph There are various opinions about the use of a nymph during the mayfly season. On many chalk streams nymph fishing is not allowed, or allowed only after the mayfly season is over. Skues has an account in *Nymph Fishing for Chalk Stream Trout* (A and C Black, 1939) which is not altogether encouraging. He thought trout seemed to snatch at the mayfly nymph as if afraid of it, and did not take it calmly as they did the nymphs of the smaller ephemerids. However, he did record the case of an angler on the Kennet who had caught far more than any others in his party on a mayfly nymph, but Skues was careful to say he did not know how the nymph was fished.

An outspoken rejection of fishing a mayfly nymph during a hatch is in Oliver Kite's *Nymph Fishing in Practice* (Herbert Jenkins, 1963):

If I can't catch them with [a dry Mayfly] I give them best although I know there are days when trout taking the natural Mayfly can be damnably difficult. The point is they do take it, and for me, personally, deceiving them is part of the challenge. In such circumstances it would be spiritual prostitution for me to put on a nymph on a No 5 hook [Redditch scale 10] and use this to butcher trout with. For that is what using a large Mayfly nymph amounts to, in my opinion.

Midge (*Chironomidae*) A large family of mostly non-biting midges or gnats. There are some 400 types, all belonging to the order of two-winged flies (*Diptera*). On stillwaters, midge are a major trout food and on rivers are of growing importance. The midge larvae, known as bloodworms, because of their colour, live on or near the bottom, and are sometimes copied by a thin thread of red wool or red rubber on a hook, fished deep. The more usual method is to fish the pupae. These rise to the surface with a wriggling motion and then hang in the surface film before ecdysis. The winged midge can sometimes be seen in a swarm of flies, generally of a dark colour, rising and falling in their mating dance by the edge of stillwaters. The larger ones can sometimes be identified on sight by the slight hooked shape of the body.

Midge were frequently taken by using spider patterns prior to the 1920s. The first artificial that was specifically tied to imitate a midge, so far as we know, came from Blagdon in the 1920s, or earlier, possibly tied by Willie Cox, a scenic artist at the Bristol Theatre Royal. The best known, however, which was tied a few years later, was Dr Bell's Blagdon Buzzer:

Body: black wool, thickening towards the thorax and head
Ribbing: thin silver tinsel
Head hackle: a small fluff of white wool on top of the hook
Hook: 12 or 14

In *Lake Flies and Their Imitation* (Herbert Jenkins, 1960) C.F. Walker emphasised the great importance of midge pupae patterns and used gut or nylon for the abdomen and ostrich, condor or peacock herl for the thorax. In *Fly Fishing Tactics on Stillwater* (Frederick Muller, 1966) Geoffrey Bucknall introduced the Footballer:

Body: alternate turns of black and white horsehair carried round the bend
Thorax: mole's fur
Head: peacock herl
Hook: 14–16

One of the most elaborate of all midge dressings is John Goddard's:

Body: according to the colour of the midge being imitated, black, brown, red or green maribou silk, ribbed silver lurex, then covered with PVC
Tag: white hen hackle fibres projecting about one-eighth of an inch, tied in well round the bend of the hook
Thorax: green peacock or buff condor herl
Head filaments: loop or bunch of white hen hackle fibres tied through the thorax to face upwards and forwards over the eye of the hook
Hook sizes: 16, 14, 12

An interesting variation was Frank Sawyer's Bow Tie Buzzer which had detached head filaments. For river fishing, most anglers use a small Black Gnat or flies such as Kees Ketting's Duck Fly or the Blae and Black.

A new development of the midge pattern for lake fishing came in the late 1970s. Steve Hare of the Hucklebrook Trout Lake, near Fordingbridge, designed a midge pattern made almost entirely of lead wire. It was at first used to reach deep-lying river trout in fast water but its advantage for lake fishing were soon realised. This was the original Steve Hare dressing:

Body: turns of lead wire
Hackle: a fluff of white deer hair at the head

Based on this, Bill Sibbons, a portrait painter with a studio near Fordingbridge, who had experience of fishing Two Lakes, Damerham and Rockbourne, developed this:

Abdomen: lead wire over a base of brown tying silk, the lead turns slightly apart to give the impression of the ringed body of the natural
Thorax: mole fur
Head: a small fluff of white deerhair, or similar
Hook: 14–10

A variation of this, giving a brighter appearance, was to use copper wire for the abdomen.

Midland Flyfishers Formed in 1931 with Courtney Williams as chairman. Owns salmon fishing on the Welsh Dee and has trout fishing on Shropshire brooks. Neville Chamberlain was president, 1934–1940, and, among others, Lord Cobham, 1964–1977.

Mill Brook A tiny chalk stream rising at Blewbury in Wiltshire and flowing into the Thames at Wallingford. David Barr writes:

The Mill Brook is believed to be the stream in Kenneth Grahame's *The Wind in the Willows*. For many years a good head of trout lived amicably with shoals of roach. A trout of 5lb 2oz was once caught on a sunken Dunkeld at East Hagbourne. Sadly, Mill Brook has become a winterbourne, drying up in times of drought. There are those who believe that this could be linked to the atomic activities at nearby Harwell.

Missionary Ancestor and inspiration of many a reservoir lure, the Missionary dates back at least 50 years if not more and is believed to have been first tied by

Captain J. J. Dunn for the Blagdon sticklebackers. Later, the pattern emigrated to New Zealand and after being ignored in its home country for a while became popular among Midland reservoir fly fishers.

Body: white wool
Tail: white cock
Wings: a few fibres of dark turkey tail with side strips of dark teal, extending well beyond the bend of the hook
Beard hackle: white cock
Hook: originally 8 or 10 standard size but now longshank is more usual

Mottram, Dr. J.C. An experimental fly designer of the late Halford period, Mottram broke away completely from conventional styles and pioneered the arts of creating illusions and suggestions: silhouette flies, and flies without bodies. Indeed, to a large extent, some of the exploratory work in his book anticipates findings of fly designers fifty years later. His Alevin Fly is no longer in use but the principles on which it was based were far in advance of his time:

Head: eyes made from black beads, one on either side of the hook
Body: strands of peacock herl with a topping of golden pheasant crest

His midge pupae had cork bodies to allow them to float just below the surface. He created new designs for many wet flies including a bare-hook reed smut:

> Of this nature are the new wet flies; their use entails a new kind of fishing, an art the practise of which requires much skill and wherein rules are logical, a science based on true observation rather than myth.

There are traces of two other great fly dressing innovators in that passage, Dunne and Deane, and indeed Mottram would have had a great affinity with both. Mottram was also tying nymph patterns more or less at the same time as Skues. His most remarkable designs, however, were of dry flies. Because the dry fly was seen from below, colour was not all that important:

> It may be said that objects almost without exception are recognised by their shape . . . so it follows that the dry fly dresser must pay more attention to the insect's silhouette, its outline against the sky.

Among his dressings were a Buoyant Olive Dun, a Transparent Jenny Spinner and a Silhouette Olive Dun. This is his dressing of the Jenny Spinner:

Tail: three long white cock hackle barbs (fibres)
Abdomen: a few turns of red-brown floss silk near the bend of the hook by the tails and the rest of the hook as far as the thorax left uncovered, which suggests the transparency of the body
Thorax: red-brown floss silk
Wings: a white cock hackle wound around the hook behind the eye four or five times; then the underpart of the hackle is cut, leaving the sides and top projecting, thus the fly will lie flat on the water and be kept afloat in the most natural manner; no floating hackle is used

Mottram was so unusual that many fishermen of his time – though not Skues – treated him with indifference or contempt, for this was in the middle of the Halford era when any flies as strange as Mottram's would be regarded as the work of a crank and without any value at all; it was not of much help either that Mottram's book in which he explained his theories came out at a time during the First World War when there was not only a paper shortage but a concentration of attention on other things. (The book, *Fly Fishing: Some New Arts and Mysteries*, was published by *The Field*, undated, but believed to be in 1915 or 1916.)

Muddler Minnow At least one and possibly several fly patterns that have become popular on Midland reservoirs in recent years have been designed by American fly dressers. Not all have been given the credit. This one was. The Muddler was introduced from America in 1967 by Tom Saville from a design by an American fisherman and instructor, Don Gapen of Minnesota. The Muddler, buoyant because of its deerhair body, was an immediate success as a reservoir lure, as an imitation of a small bullhead or minnow, and as a surface lure for sea trout fishing

Body: flat gold tinsel
Tail: turkey or hen pheasant fibres, well bunched
Head: deer hair spun round the hook and clipped to form an oval or round shape, some of the fibres lying backwards along the hook and mingling with the wings
Wings: bunched or rolled turkey or hen pheasant fibres, projecting from immediately behind the head
Hook: longshank 10–6

Munro Killer A salmon fly, originally marketed in the 1970s by Munro of Aberlour for the Spey, now popular on many rivers. It has affinities with the Stoats Tail and the Torridge Special. The Munro dressing:

Body: black wool or floss
Ribbing: two turns of round gold tinsel at the tail and three or four turns up the body
Whisks: none
Underwing: a few fibres of squirrel tail, the tips dyed yellow, not projecting much beyond the bend of the hook
Overwing: a few sparse fibres of black bear or black squirrel, long, almost twice the length of the body
Beard hackle: whisps of bright blue and hot orange feather fibres, not mingled, tied on either side of the hook
Hook: generally small doubles, 6, 8, 10 and 12

The success of the Munro is sometimes attributed to the presence of its long wings and touches of colour which are said to give it the appearance of an elver or small fish in the water. This could be so, but then quite a few flies, if sparsely dressed, can give that impression. It is probably more likely to be the sparse dressing.

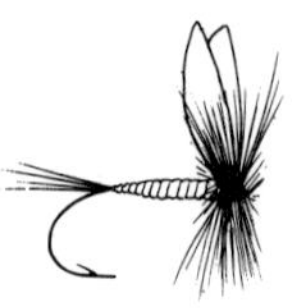

Cads and Poachers

When I was a small boy on the banks of the Usk fifty years ago, it was considered unsporting to fish for salmon (much less trout and sea trout) with a spinner whenever and wherever fish could be expected to be caught with a fly. As for using a natural bait like a prawn or a worm – well, only 'cads' and poachers admitted to any knowledge of such low and unsporting means of catching salmon when they refused an innocent fly.

L.R.N. Gray, *Torridge Fishery*, Nicholas Kaye, 1957

A dead fish remains a dead fish however it is killed. To suppose there is more merit in killing it on an unadorned fly rather than on a fly with a maggot attached is as ridiculous as supposing that, simply because a fly rod is involved, the use of fly maggot is any more creditable than the use of a worm or a dock grub, or a shrimp or a sand-eel, or any other legitimate lure fished with a fixed-spool reel.

Hugh Falkus, *Sea Trout Fishing*, 2nd edn., Witherby, 1975

Fishing with Mills bombs is prohibited. By Order.

Notice on the Bund Lake, Ypres Salient, 1917

Nadder A delightfully clear river rising on the borders of chalk stream country near Shaftesbury with good stocks of trout and grayling as well as coarse fish. Below Wilton it joins the Wylye and enters the Avon at Salisbury. The Tisbury, Burford, Teffont and Salisbury fishing clubs have good stretches for fly fishing. There is, on the whole, a sparse hatch of mayfly, but there are many midge, black gnat and sedge and, occasionally, profuse hatches of olives. The Nadder trout are known to be reasonably accommodating in their choice of artificial, a number of large trout are taken each year, and a five-pounder taken on a Wee McGregor near Compton Chamberlayne in 1983 by John Barclay of Sussex is a splendid example of what this small clear stream can produce.

National Anglers' Council The council represents the whole of the sport of angling and was established in 1966 to form a link between the sport and the Government and the Sports Council. Its main objects are to co-ordinate the views of angling in the promotion and development of the sport, and to co-ordinate grant aid applications. The Prince of Wales is patron. The council's executive director, P.H. Tombleson, summarises its work and history:

The Council has directly affiliated national bodies in membership, clubs, associations and individuals. The four national angling bodies – the National Federation of Anglers (coarse fishermen), the National Federation of Sea Anglers and the Salmon and Trout Association are foundation members, the fourth founder member is the Fishmongers' Company, one of the great twelve City of London livery companies.

The council is headed by an executive committee consisting of representatives of the major national angling bodies, the fishing tackle trade and non-affiliated anglers. This policy-making committee meets four times a year with sub-committees for detailed work. The council is funded partly by Sports Council grant and angling subscriptions. In turn it advises Sports Council on capital grant for the sport. By 1984 angling had received more than one million pounds in all types of grant aid. The N.A.C. also handles grant applications by member bodies which may be involved in national and international competitive events.

The main work of the council revolves around legislation which it watches closely, the Parliamentary angling lobby, protection of the sport from pressures from outside and direct negotiation with the many official and non-official bodies whose activities might affect angling.

It is closely involved in advising anglers how to meet anti-angling problems as well as developing a national angling coaching scheme with a proficiency awards scheme and advising on developments for disabled anglers. It runs the British Record (rod-caught) Fish Committee and the Sea Angling Liaison Committee of Great Britain and Ireland.

Ness A great area of the Highlands is drained by the River Ness and its feeder streams and lochs – Ness and Oich, Moriston and Garry. The town water at Inverness has permits for visitors from the local angling club. Further up river the Dochfour Estate lets rods on the Ness and, on the Moriston, the Glenmoriston Estate. Rods on the Oich may be obtained from the fishing tackle shop at Fort Augustus. The Garry is largely private.

There is good trout fishing but the salmon vary considerably according to the height of the water. In the lochs, especially Loch Ness, mostly fished trolling from boats, local knowledge is essential.

Netboy, Anthony The standard textbook on the salmon, covering the North Atlantic seaboard on both sides, and containing invaluable information, is Netboy's *The Atlantic Salmon: A Vanishing Species*, published by Faber and Faber in 1968.

Nith A Border river, though a long one, the Nith rises near Dalmellington in Strathclyde, flows through New Cumnock, past Sanquhar and Thornhill to Dumfries and the Solway Firth. At most of these towns fishing can be had for association water through local hotels. The Drumlanrig Estate at Thornhill leases beats. The Nith has a good run of salmon towards the autumn, with sea trout in summer, and so does its tributary, the Cairn. The river is on the whole slow running but with occasional fast spates.

Nymph Fishing

A very exacting form of fly fishing, infinitely more exacting than the dry fly. (Oliver Kite, *Nymph Fishing in Practice*, Herbert Jenkins, 1963)

Nymph fishing has various meanings. On reservoirs the term is widely used to describe fishing an artificial representation of a variety of underwater creatures, larvae, pupae and shrimp. On rivers it is generally limited to the nymphs of the olives and iron blues in hook sizes no larger than # 14.

Nymph fishing on rivers was pioneered by G.E.M. Skues towards the end of the nineteenth century on the Abbots Barton water of the Itchen just above Winchester. Skues was a dry fly fisherman to begin with, a disciple of Halford. One day, however, he was fishing a dry fly to a trout which refused it several times. The fly was a poor floater and on the last cast it sank. The trout immediately took.

This experience led Skues to experiment with fishing the upstream wet fly and in due course to tie patterns of the nymphs which he found in the trouts' stomachs. All his nymphs were unweighted and were now what we might call emerger patterns which are generally fished in, or close to, the surface of the streams. Most of them were on size 15 or 16 hooks, very delicately and sparsely tied. Some of the originals are in the Flyfishers' Club Museum in London.

Skues came into conflict with Halford and the dry fly purists and this continued for most of his life. One day, Skues's friend, Sir Grimwood Mears, showed him some new patterns of nymphs tied by a water keeper on the upper Avon, Frank Sawyer. These were the size and shape of the Skues's nymphs but tied very simply with the reddish fibres from a cock pheasant tail twisted around fine copper wire.

These, as distinct from the inert emergers of Skues, were swimming nymphs, intended to be fished deep when the nymphs were active. Sawyer's patterns dispensed with the hackles that Skues's used to suggest the nymph's legs because when nymphs swim their legs are almost invisible, being held close to the body.

Skues was impressed, urged that Sawyer should be encouraged, and helped in the preparation of Sawyer's first book.

A new stage was now being reached in the development of the nymph. Skues, with his unweighted emerger patterns, had always insisted that nymph fishing was not to be considered as a separate form of fishing but one that was ancilliary to the dry fly. Whether this was to placate the purists is difficult to say. But with the arrival of the weighted nymph this could no longer be sustained. It was obvious that fishing a nymph pattern several feet below the surface of the water was very different to the dry fly.

In the atmosphere of the 1920s and 30s, the idea of a weighted fly seemed to many to be a contradiction in terms. No 'fly' could be 'weighted'. Sawyer found the same opposition that Skues found when he introduced his emergers. In some cases it was even more bitter and contemptuous, for Sawyer was a water keeper and did not have the skill to argue with his critics in the way that Skues could. In time Sawyer came to ignore remarks about fishing bits of metal and hardened himself to the bans on his weighted nymphs on many of the chalk streams. It was some consolation that Sawyer ultimately had the satisfaction of knowing that his pheasant tail had a world-wide reputation and was being sold and used in more than 60 countries.

Fishing the nymph was popularised by Major Oliver Kite in the 1950s and 60s. He describes it in his book, *Nymph Fishing in Practice* (Herbert Jenkins, 1963):

> When things were quiet when I was fishing at Choulston one day in the 1957 season he [Frank Sawyer] suggested to me that I might do better if I went higher up and tried my hand with a nymph. I had nymphs, shop nymphs, which I did not consider worth using. He gave me a couple of his small pheasant tail nymphs and I went off to see what I could do.
>
> Above Choulston is the famous Court Reach at Netheravon, just at the back of the cottage where I now live. There, below Haxton Bridge, I found a good trout swinging to and fro in a streamy current where it emerged from between two clumps of starwort. This trout refused various dry flies. I put on one of the nymphs I had been given, casting it accurately a few feet ahead of the trout. As it passed the fish's head without being taken I raised the tip of my rod to withdraw it. As I did so, I saw the trout turn, so I stayed my hand momentarily, then, as the trout turned back, I struck. And that was how I caught my first trout on the artificial nymph. That was also the inspiration of my nymph fishing technique.

The method of activating the nymph as it passes or comes near to the fish Kite called 'the induced take.'

> The nymph must be pitched sufficiently far upstream, according to the strength of the current, to enable it to sink to the fish's level by the time it reaches a point immediately upstream of it. Movement is imparted with the rod at this point and if the timing is correct both trout and grayling take the activated nymph almost involuntarily . . .

The technique, which Sawyer also used, depends not only on the timing but on acute underwater vision and is, therefore, by no means an easy method of fishing. Kite was not alone in thinking it was more difficult than fishing the dry fly. Ordinary dry fly tackle is used, with a 9ft–10ft leader. The point of the leader (the tippet) is left ungreased, and the butt and centre section of the leader are greased. These float on the water surface while the nymph and the ungreased tippet sink to the correct depth. It is a nice matter of judgment how long the tippet should be and how far upstream it must be cast to travel over the trout's nose. Those fishermen who cannot see their nymph underwater – and there are many – have to guess when the nymph is in position for an induced take. Both Sawyer and Kite could see the white line of the fish's mouth as it opened to take the nymph, or they would see the fish turn aside to take it. If the light is bad, or the fisherman's eyesight poor, then the middle section of the nylon above the sunk tippet is watched. If this checks or dips down 'through a hole in the water', as Kite put it, the strike must be instantaneous, otherwise the nymph will have been rejected.

Nymph fishing in practice, as outlined by Kite and Sawyer, has its own unwritten rules:

No artificial pattern larger than 15 or 14 is to be fished.
No nymphs of the big mayfly (*E. danica*) are to be used.
When the mayfly is hatching, the dry fly is obligatory.
The nymph must be cast upstream, or up and across, to trout in position feeding or likely to feed on the natural nymph.
The trout must be located and fished for. Fishing the water is forbidden.

See also entries under the Piscatorial Society, and Reservoir Fishing. **Sources:** the works of Skues, Kite, and Sawyer – an invaluable reference book – *G.E.M. Skues: The Way of a Man With a Trout*, Donald Overfield, Benn, 1977.

Nymph Patterns Modern unweighted emerger patterns which follow the Skues' principles are numerous, but the Hare's Ear nymph or the Gold Ribbed Hare's Ear are among the better known:

Abdomen: hare or rabbit fur ribbed with fine gold wire
Whisks: none, or a few short dun hackle fibres
Thorax: a slightly thicker dubbing of the hare or rabbit fur
Hackle: one turn, two at the most, of a short dun hackle
Hook: 14–16

For the nymphs of the pale watery Sawyer's Grey Goose tied unweighted is as good as any, otherwise:

Abdomen: pale grey fur or heron herl ribbed with yellow silk
Whisks: a few fibres of grey feather, very short
Thorax: a thicker dubbing of the grey fur or heron herl
Hackle: one turn, two at the most, of pale grey or pale grey-blue feather
Hook: 15 or 16

The Iron Blue is not unlike a hackled Dark Watchet:

Abdomen: mole's fur thinly dubbed on crimson tying silk
Whisks: very short dark-blue cock
Thorax: a thicker dubbing of mole's fur
Hackle: black or dark blue cock, one or two turns
Hook: 15 or 16

Nymph Patterns: Sawyer

Pheasant Tail:
Wire body: cover the hook evenly from head to bend with fine red-coloured copper wire, then build up a wire thorax, returning the wire to the hook bend
Body covering: using the wire as you would tying silk, tie in four red-coloured fibres at the bend, the fibres projecting no more than one-eighth of an inch beyond the bend. These represent the tails of the nymph. Spin the fibres round the wire and cover the body to the eye of the hook with the mixed fibres and wire. At the hook eye separate the fibres and wire. Place the wire behind the thorax. Bend the fibres back from the hook eye over the thorax and trap them behind with the wire
Trim off by a half hitch on the wire, or alternatively four turns, break off the wire, and varnish. Alternatively return the wire and fibres from behind the thorax to the eye of the hook and trim off by the eye

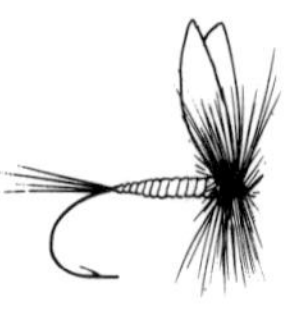

Ancestors

The taking of a salmon, when all the conditions were against it, and my weapon was a trout rod, looked so like a real achievement that for twenty-four hours I felt no need to justify my life. It was, I suppose, an atavistic sentiment, the lively ghost of some long-buried ancestral satisfaction. Before the Norsemen came to Orkney it was Pictish land; and my pleasure was so deep that its origin, I dare say, lay in the heart of a Pict who had gone fishing.

Erik Linklater, *A Year of Space*, reprinted in John Moore's anthology, *Best Fishing Stories*, Faber and Faber, 1965

There is romance in the Shetland lochs – and great history. One day I fished in the loch of Girlsta – the Geirhildavatan of the Norsemen – where Geirhilda, the daughter of Flokki, was drowned. Flokki was the discoverer of Iceland. And the loch has not changed by so much as one rock since his day. I fished Clousta Loch in a bronze sunset – with the heather in full bloom. It was a little too bright for fish – the air was too clear – but all around me on those rocky hills, waving against the blue sky, the purple heather seemed to be floating in a powdery mist of gold specks. For two years I fished the Shetlands.

Negley Farson, *Going Fishing*, the Clive Holloway Edn., 1981

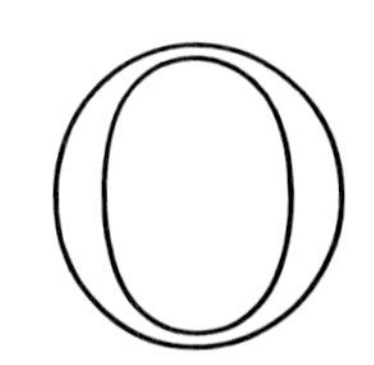

Ogden, James An inventive fly dresser of the mid-1800s who had a fishing tackle business at 28 Winchcombe Street, Cheltenham, and is best known for the design of that invaluable fly, the Invicta. He also claimed to have tied the first dry flies. The problem about that is best summarised by Donald Overfield in *Famous Flies and Their Originators* (Black, 1972):

That Ogden was the first to describe the dressing of the true dry fly there can be little doubt. He tells us in his book *Ogden On Fly Dressing* that he caused to be published in 1879 that . . . "I am confident that I am the originator of Floating Flies, having introduced them 40 years ago." This would pre-date Pulman by a matter of two years. A contender for the tying of the first dry fly is David Foster, the celebrated Derbyshire angler associated with the well-known firm of Fosters of Ashbourne. It is not inconceivable that Ogden and Foster were known to each other on the Derbyshire streams and during their meetings may well have discussed the mechanics of tying the floater, though this can be but pure conjecture. If Ogden was accurate in dating the introduction of his dry fly, then it seems he was ahead of Foster, for in the bicentenary booklet issued by the firm of Fosters in 1963, the winged dry fly as tied by Foster is listed as 1854. At a time so far removed from the actual period it is difficult to come to any definite conclusion.

Olive Dun A name given to several fly patterns designed to suggest most of the common olives of the Beätis species. The duns of these are also represented by a number of other patterns, including the Blue Dun, Greenwell, Olive Quill, Olive Upright, Blue Upright and Kite's Imperial. The pattern most likely to be an Olive Dun – and there are several – must have dark green about it somewhere:

Body: medium olive-coloured fur
Hackle: dyed olive-green cock
Whisks: three fairly long fibres of the same colour
Wings: starling primary
Hook: 14–16

Olive Quill The same dressing as the Olive Dun but with a stripped peacock quill body, dyed olive green. The Olive Quill is often used as a hackled pattern, without the starling wings.

Olive Upright The same as the Olive Quill but a West Country pattern. The stripped peacock quill body is dyed a yellowish apple green and it seems to be always used as a hackle pattern.

Orange Quill The dressing of the Orange Quill favoured by Skues when blue-winged olives were hatching is:

Body: pale condor quill, stripped so as to show no dark edge, dyed hot orange
Whisks and hackle: bright red cock
Wings: pale starling, rather full, as the natural insect has wings longer than the ordinary olive duns
Tying silk: hot orange
Hook: 13 or 14

Both J.W. Dunne and David Jacques were doubtful about the Orange Quill representing the sub-imago of the blue-winged olive, both of them thought it was more likely to suggest the imago, the sherry spinner. Photographs in the Goddard-Clark book (*The Trout and the Fly*, Benn, 1980) confirm their opinion.

Otter The River Otter rises in Somerset on the slopes of the Blackdown Hills, flows through Honiton and Ottery St Mary and into the sea by Budleigh Salterton. It is a small limestone stream, like its sister the Culm, and has a good head of wild brown trout and in places is now stocked with rainbows, all large fish, for the river is fertile and has a good hatch of fly.

Even when it gets to Honiton the Otter is quite small, only a few feet across, so that it has to be fished with care: a small rod, the lightest of lines, a fine tippet, and dry flies up to 18s or even 20s. The best patterns include the Pheasant Tail, Blue Upright, Beacon Beige for the duns, a Lunn's Particular or Sherry Spinner for the evening, and a very small Black Gnat, a Sedge, and a Terry's Terror in reserve. Fishing is mostly upstream, wet fly or dry. Several hotels have water, the best known being the Deer Park Hotel at Honiton. (See *West Country Fly Fishing*, edited by Anne Voss Bark, Batsford, 1983.)

Seaside visitors to Budleigh Salterton should enquire at fishing tackle shops for permits for sea trout fishing in and above the estuary.

Ouse (Sussex) A long tidal stretch of the River Ouse up to and above Lewes has a good run of sea trout in mid-summer but above is mostly coarse fishing. Tackle shops at Lewes, Cuckfield and Newhaven are helpful about sea trout permits.

Oykel A first-rate salmon river in the Kyle of Sutherland, not a large one, but prolific, sometimes even in low-water conditions. The river is in a low strath with birch woods and deer and a fishing hotel with good beats – the Oykel Bridge Hotel – just by the river. For spring fishing the Collie Dog and Garry Dog on aluminium tube flies are popular, the tubes giving way in summer to doubles and singles, Hairy Mary, Shrimp and Stoat's Tail, in sizes 6 and 8. Benmore and Assynt Estates have water and enquiries can be made through Renton Finlayson, estate agents, at Bonar Bridge.

Rivers

Fishing makes rivers my corrective lens; I see differently. Not only does the bird taking the mayfly signify a hatch, not only does the flash of colour at the break of the riffle signify a fish feeding, but my powers uncoil inside me and I must determine which insect is hatching and what feeding pattern the trout has established. Then I must properly equip myself and properly approach the fish and properly present my imitation. I am emerged in a hunt that is more than a hunt, for the objects of the hunt are mostly to be found within myself, in the nature of my response and action. I am on a Parsifalian quest. I must be scientist, technician, athlete, perhaps even a queer sort of poet.

Nick Lyons, *Bright Rivers*, J.P. Lippincott and Co., Philadelphia and New York, 1977

Inch by difficult inch the river began to rise, spreading a film over dry rocks, turning trickles to rivulets and rivulets to cascades. In the pool below all was agitation. Excited by the taste of fresh water, the salmon were showing, jumping and swirling, making ready to go. Now the note of the fall had deepened and the pool was starting to fill, lessening the height a fish would have to jump, giving him greater depth from which to gain impetus. A curtain of water was arching over the lip of the rock and a salmon whose leap had not cleared the full height might yet by desperate swimming win through the last few inches. One got up, then another, then three at once. The water rose and rose, and soon there was a steady procession of writhing, splashing bodies, till at last the falls were drowned and the fish could go through unseen.

T.C. Kingsmill Moore, *A Man May Fish*, 1960; 2nd edn., Colin Smythe, 1979

Pale Watery A fly fisherman's description of some five or six species of ephemeral flies which are of a pale watery colour. The natural flies generally belong to the *Beätis* and *Centroptilum* species. The most common artificials in use when pale wateries are about are the Tups, Blue Quill, Blue Upright, Little Marryat and the Last Hope. This is a Skues's pattern:

Body: cream-coloured seal's fur
Whisks: cream dun cock
Hackle: the same, fairly full for the hackled pattern
Wings: young starling
Tying silk: cream
Hook: 15

Most of the dun patterns will do for the spent fly, providing they are made to lie low in the water.

Palmer Flies Trout flies with a long history, going back five hundred years or more. The style of dressing is a simple one: a hen or cock hackle wound the length of the hook, from eye to bend, producing a bushy appearance. The fly can be thinly or thickly palmered depending on how it is to be used.

The name is associated with the medieval Crusades: the knights and the travelling friars brought back palms from the Holy Land and the word 'palmer' was used in various contexts, in one case being applied to the travelling friars and in another to travelling woolly caterpillars or 'palmer worms'.

The Palmer Fly has the whole body covered with the buzz of hackle. Red or black palmers are the most usual. A good dressing for lake and sea trout is the Soldier Palmer:

Body: scarlet wool, the colour of a Guardsman's tunic
Rib: gold wire or tinsel
Hackle: bright red cock from head to tail, kept in place by the ribbing
Hook: 14 to 8

Palmer Nymph An adaption of the palmer principle of fly dressing to a wet fly, mainly for lake fishing. It is generally fished on hook size 14:

Underbody: two or three strips of lead foil on top of the hook
Tail: very short golden pheasant topping
Overbody: yellow seal's fur, finely dubbed
Rib: thin gold wire
Body hackle: an olive green hackle, very short in the fibre, wound from the neck about three turns towards the tail where it is secured by the gold wire which is then wound through the hackle to the head and tied off
Head hackle: about three turns of dark red cock hackle, short in the fibre

Parr Young trout and salmon of about three to six inches long, before the young salmon puts on its silvery coat, are difficult to tell apart, the markings are similar. The salmon parr, however, does not have a coloured adipose fin, which is the small stunted fin between the dorsal fin and tail. A young trout's adipose fin is either red or has a red-orange tinge. It is illegal to kill a salmon parr and they must be put back into the water unharmed.

Parton, Steve An informative book on boat fishing techniques on reservoirs such as Grafham and Rutland Water by Steve Parton, *Boatfishing for Trout* (Allen and Unwin, 1983) gives detailed information on the many ways that the fly can be fished from a boat, some indeed that will be new to most reservoir fishermen. Parton has a nice sense of humour:

The boat is really the refuge of free spirits among stillwater fishermen. It provides the chance for the enterprising to seek out their quarry without being unduly squeezed for elbow room.

Partridge and Orange A versatile and charming-looking trout fly of the spider type which has its home in the Borders and Yorkshire, a strong following in Wales and the West Country, and on the chalk streams:

Try bulging fish with a rough olive, or your favourite nymph or, what is best of all, an orange partridge. (J.W. Hills, *A Summer on the Test*, Bles, 1924, 3rd edn., 1946)

The partridge hackles should be fairly sparse. The body, when wet, takes on an attractive reddish-orange colour, very similar to the colour of both nymph and spinner bodies:

Body: orange floss silk
Hackle: partridge
Hook: 14–18, usually 16

There is another fly, the Yellow Partridge, with a yellow floss body, and this is said to be more use than the orange when fished upstream on spate rivers when pale wateries are about.

Pertwee, Roland Actor and dramatist, Roland Pertwee wrote one of the finest short stories about fly fishing ever written, *The River God*, published in *Faber's Best Fishing Stories* (1965) edited by John Moore.

Peter Ross A spectacular and deservedly popular wet fly for trout and sea trout, a variation of the Teal and Red, designed by Peter Ross (1873–1923) who kept the village shop at Killin in Perthshire:

Body: the abdomen of flat silver tinsel, the thorax red seal's fur, both ribbed fine silver wire
Whisks: golden pheasant tippet
Hackle: black
Wing: matching slips from the breast feathers of a teal
Hook: 14–8

Pheasant Tail A Devon trout fly which dates back something like a hundred years, if not more, which probably accounts for several variations in the dressing. This, so far as one can tell, is fairly close to the Devon patterns of 60 years ago:

Body: dark herl from the tail feather of a cock pheasant
Rib: four or five turns of fine gold wire
Whisks: two or three fibres from the cock pheasant tail
Hackle: red cock
Hook: 12–16

The main variations are: a blue hackle, and red cock fibres for the whisks.

Phillips, Ernest The author of *Trout in Lakes and Reservoirs* (1914) Ernest Phillips listed some 152 reservoirs in the British Isles which were then open for trout fishing, of which 134 allowed worming or bait fishing for the reason that:

. . . the vital principle of angling is to catch fish by any method. It does not matter whether you offer a Zulu, a real mayfly, a worm, a minnow, or a caddis grub . . .

The various types of reservoir fishing that were allowed varied considerably. At Ravensthorpe, for example, boat fishing was fly only, yet minnow fishing was allowed from the bank. The Elan Valley reservoirs allowed the worm, as well as other methods, yet at Thirlmere every method was allowed except the worm.

Mixed angling methods persisted in many reservoirs for another 40 or 50 years and some continue now in smaller reservoirs, particularly in Wales.

Piddle *See* Frome.

Piscatorial Society One of the oldest fly fishing clubs, the Piscatorial was founded in 1836. The society rents water on rivers such as the Wylye, and on the Avon, where it has a club house. It is largely a dry fly fisherman's club. The rule book is interesting for what one member has described as a 'modified Halford' rule:

The style of fishing required by the fishing regulations on these [waters] is dry fly and upstream nymph. There are two styles of nymph fishing on the chalk streams, one usually attributed to G.E.M. Skues, the other to Frank Sawyer and Oliver Kite.

Skues lightly dressed his nymphs with soft hackle and used a quill, herl, floss silk or dubbing for bodies. He fished them upstream, without drag, and just under the surface. He advocated size 15 hooks as the largest suitable for chalk stream fishing.

His style was intended to be used for trout which can be seen to be feeding at or near the surface yet not taking the dun or its imitation. It is a dry fly style to which Horace Brown, President of the Society includes this style in the term 'dry fly' on the Avon, Lambourn and Wylye; [and] . . . in the interest of giving all members a chance of the larger trout, which may surface only a few times a season, and of providing conditions for an increase in the number of these trout, the sunk or weighted nymph is not permitted.

The rules of behaviour include the following:

Members do not wish to be addressed whilst covering a fish. The practice on all Society waters is to give a wide berth and not to approach, nor to cut in less than an arbitrary fifty yards above a Member fishing, unless invited to do so. The aim is simple: to do all that is conducive to peaceable fishing; to be considerate (and rise more fish) by being slow moving, low-lying, quiet of foot; and when not fishing or walking downstream to walk as far from the water as paths or fences will allow.

Plunket Greene, Harry (1865–1936) 'Generous, warm-hearted, and full of humour, Plunket Greene will be mourned by all who came even into the slightest contact with him,' wrote *The Times*, when Plunket Greene's death was announced at the age of 71. Towards the end of the nineteenth, and in the early part of the twentieth century, he was a singer of world fame. He appeared

Harry Plunkett Green

at The Three Choirs Festival, and sang the bass parts in Elgar's *Dream of Gerontius* at the first performance in Birmingham in 1900. He created the popular song recitals of his time and travelled to many countries with the pianist Leonard Borwick to give memorable performances of Schumann's *Dichterliebe Cycle*, and songs by Parry and Stanforth. He married Gwendolin Maud, the younger daughter of Sir Hubert Parry, and there were two sons and one daughter of the marriage. He is buried at Hurstbourne Priors.

For practically all his life Plunket Greene was a devoted fly fisherman and all the character which *The Times* ascribed to him – generous, warm-hearted and full of humour – survives in his classic book on fly fishing, *Where The Bright Waters Meet*, first published in 1924, reissued by Witherby in 1969 with a foreword by Howard Marshall, and again as a paperback by André Deutsch in 1983, with a foreword by Anthony Atha. The title was taken from a poem by Tom Moore:

There is not in this wide world a valley so sweet
As that vale in whose bosom the bright waters meet.

Pollution: Acid Rain Evidence of the harmful effects on rivers and lakes of acid rain has been accumulating for the past thirty years. The rain – precipitation is a better description – comes from oil- and coal-burning power stations, smelters and factories. Sulphur and nitrous oxides are emitted in the smoke from fossil fuels and these turn to sulphuric and nitric acids in the atmosphere. Tall chimneys, designed to minimise ground level contamination, carry the pollutants on intercontinental air masses for many hundreds of miles to fall in rain, snow, fog, mist and cloud, especially on high ground and afforested areas.

From the mid-1950s to the early 1970s sulphur levels over Europe increased by 50 per cent, in the Scandinavian countries by 100 per cent. (*The Times*, 15 March, 1983). The rain falling in Norway in 1982 was between ten to 30 times more acid than normal rain.

Lakes in over 13,000 square kilometres of South Norway are now practically devoid of fish. In an additional 20,000 square kilometres the fish stocks are in the process of being depleted. A similar situation exists in Sweden. A number of studies have identified acid precipitation as the dominant cause of the decline in fish populations. It is estimated that 90 per cent of the sulphate depositions in Norway are caused by emissions from other countries (Erik Lykke, Director General, Norwegian Ministry of the Environment, August, 1982)

The Scandinavian countries were hard hit. Within a year there was more bad news, given at the first British conference on acid rain at Two Lakes in Hampshire:

Many salmon rivers in southern and south-western Norway are now barren. – Dr Rosseland, Norwegian Directorate of Wildlife.

Twenty thousand of Sweden's 90,000 lakes are now affected by increased acidity. Of that 20,000 some 5,000 are badly affected, some of them completely fishless, some with a few surviving fish. (Dr Bengtsson, Swedish National Board of Fisheries)

Towards the end of the 1970s similar reports of fish deaths from acidification were coming in from parts of America and especially from Canada.

In Britain, a BBC television programme on acid rain (BBC 2, *Horizon*, 25 October, 1982) caused concern. A question from Lord Thurso in the House of Lords was replied to for the government, by Lord Mansfield 21 December, 1982). Lord Mansfield said the problem was being studied, and continued:

The major Scottish salmon rivers lie in eastern Scotland where the underlying geology is such that a major impact by acid rain is less likely. Nevertheless I am concerned that there is some evidence of surface water acidification in the area of the headwater streams of the Dee and Spey catchment areas. It is recognised that salmonid fish are vulnerable to high concentrations of acidity and aluminium, particularly at the hatching and fry stages, and waters which frequently or continually have high acid levels are unlikely to support self-generating fish populations.

In spite of a statement by a spokesman of the Central Electricity Generating Board that no serious problem of acidification of English and Scottish rivers had been identified (C.E.G.B., January, 1983) evidence of some problems began to accrue.

In 1979, the North West Water Authority was carrying out studies into the death of sea trout in the Cumbrian Esk due to an increase in acidification. (N.W.W.A., February, 1983)

In the same period an official of the Forestry Commission confirmed that a number of hill lochs in Galloway, in south-west Scotland, which previously held trout, were now barren and sterile. They included Loch Grannoch, Loch Enoch, and Loch Dee – the latter being reclaimed by liming.

In 1982, 20,000 trout died at a fish farm in Galloway as a result of sudden increase in the acid content of a feeder stream. (Two Lakes conference, 9 October, 1983)

The Times reported (14 January, 1984) increased acidification of rivers and lakes in parts of Wales. These were in areas where there was hard bedrock, poor soil and big coniferous plantations. The senior fishery scientists of the Welsh Water Authority, Dr Alun Gee, was reported as saying that Llyn Berwyn, near Tregaron, which was a fine trout fishery some ten to 15 years ago was now fishless. Dr Gee went on:

If you look at a map of Wales you will see that the problem here is far more complex than you would glean from reading the popular press. It is really not so much a problem of acid rain, because the rain here is not particularly acid compared with Sweden and Germany, but we get a lot of rain and it is therefore cumulative in its effects.

Areas like Dyfed and Gwynedd which have a poor geology, are susceptible to dry and occult depositions of sulphur which are filtered from the air by coniferous forests. These plantations also increase the production of acids as a result of increased soil aeration due to drainage. This acid then leaches out aluminium from the soil into the streams and lakes, and that in itself can be lethal, possibly more of a problem than the acidity of the water itself.

The headwaters of some of the finest game fishing rivers in Wales are in the danger areas referred to by Dr Gee. They include the Conwy, Clwyd, Seiont and Dyfi (Dovey), the Teifi, Tywi, Rheidol, and the upper reaches of the Wye. Dr Gee continued:

Fish stocks at the top of the Tywi are now non-existent. Salmon and sea trout as well as trout are no longer there. We also suspect that at certain times of the year the acidity and aluminium content of other rivers become so critical that fish in them are also wiped out.

A report by the Government laboratory at Warren Springs for the Department of the Environment (10 January, 1984) said there was evidence of increased rainfall acidity in Britain and called for more long-term monitoring. The report said that lack of research precluded identification of the sources of the pollution.

An article in *The Field* (12 April, 1983) gave figures of the increase in the acidity of rainfall in Scotland:

Natural or normal rainfall is only slightly acid at pH 5.6. All rain monitored in Scotland was below that figure. In north-west Scotland it was slightly more acid at about pH 5. In most of Scotland it was more acid, at between 4.4 to 4.6, and in south-east Scotland more acid still, at pH readings of about 4 to 4.3. Newly-hatched salmon and trout were unlikely to survive in water where the pH reading was below 4.5. Some spawning burns in Scotland were believed to be below this figure.

Sources of information on acid rain include articles in the *National Geographical Magazine* (November, 1981) *Nature* (3 June, 1982), and *New Scientist* (August, 1982). Publications: *Acid Precipitation – The Effects on Forests and Fish*, Norwegian Government, 1980; *Acidification Today and Tomorrow*, Swedish Government, 1982; *Acid Rain* by R.H. and R.A. Boyle, Nick Lyons Books, New York, 1983.

The following organisations in Britain are carrying out research: Pitlochry Fisheries Laboratory, Freshwater Biological Association, Forestry Commission, Solway River Purification Board, North West Water Authority, Welsh Water Authority, Central Electricity Generating Board, National Coal Board, Warren Springs Laboratory, Meteorological Office, and two Government ministries – Environment and Agriculture and Fisheries.

Pollution: General Millions of tons of chemicals listed in the British Pharmacopia find their way into the rivers and lakes of Britain each year. Some are innocuous. Quite a few are not. Take one that is both. In 1983 the Royal Society published the result of a three-year survey of nitrogen usage. It concluded, among other things:

Only a tenth of nitrogen added to agricultural land ends up in food, most of the rest of it ends up in the environment, the air, the earth, and the rivers.

More than a third (150,000 tons) of nitrate added to arable land goes into rivers and ground water.

About 150,000 tons of nitrogen drains into fresh water every year from human sewage.

Nitrogen can be good for rivers. Up to a point. Beyond a certain point it becomes dangerous for animals, plants and humans. Other substances lack ambiguous qualities. They are killers from the start. Insecticides and pesticides drain into rivers and lakes in minute quantities, an imperceptible pollution that works itself into the bed of the stream. Over months, years, decades, the ecology alters, the insect population declines, struggles to live, at times dies out.

Sometimes the pollution of killer chemicals will block a whole river, prevent the runs of migratory fish, kill the smolts descending to the sea. The escape of dieldrin and aldrin from a sheep dip can kill a hundred thousand trout in minutes. So can farm slurry, factory effluent, a sudden flush of chemical waste.

By the end of the last century some 3,000 miles of rivers in England had been made sterile. A moderate estimate. Tees, Trent, Ouse, Tyne and Thames no longer held fish populations except in their upper reaches.

The cost, public and private, of a ten year clean up of just one river, the Thames, has been estimated as something like £250m. The cost of bringing in all the anti-pollution measures contained in the well-meaning Control of Pollution Act, 1974, would be far greater. By 1984, large sections of the Act were still not in force. **Sources include:** *Pesticides and Pollution*, Kenneth Mellanby, Collins, 1967; revised and reprinted 1970 and 1971.

Pollution: What To Do Nearly all river pollution has been illegal since the passing of the Rivers Pollution Prevention Act of 1876. The Act has not been effective but water authorities can take action under it in the courts. More important, from the fisherman's point of view is the common law. Under this every riparian owner or tenant is entitled to have water flowing past his land in a state of purity. (*See* A.C.A.) An owner of the water or those who have a legal and unexpired lease of the water can take action in the courts, generally with the assistance of the Anglers' Cooperative Association and obtain damages.

An A.C.A. leaflet, issued from Midland Bank Chambers, Westgate, Grantham, Lincolnshire, gives full information of procedure. In the case of a sudden pollution it is essential to obtain as soon as possible two quarts (three litres) of the polluted water. Then:

Take the samples of the polluted water as soon as possible to the Public Analyst. His address can be found in the Yellow Pages under 'Chemists: Analytical'.

Telephone the regional water authority.

Advise the A.C.A.

The A.C.A. gives the following advice on how to take water samples:

Use a clean baler or jug and pour water into bottles, or submerge the bottles a few inches below the surface and let them fill. Metal containers are not advised. Bottles should be completely filled.

When wading always take samples upstream of the wader's feet.

If solid or oily matter is present include this in the sample but not mud from the bottom.

Label each bottle with the time, date and exact place where the sample was taken.

Try to find the source of the pollution by moving upstream.

If it is too late to collect water samples collect half a dozen of the dead fish, different species if possible, and deep freeze them.

Polystickle A minnow fly designed by Richard Walker for reservoir fishing, which blossomed out into various colours and methods of tying. This seems to be one of the simplest but there must be at least a dozen variations:

Body: white floss ribbed with silver tinsel and over-wrapped with clear polythene strip
Back and tail: various dark feather fibres or imitation raffia, dark coloured, tied along the back and down above the hook bend where it is opened out to imitate a fish's tail. Dark coloured backs seem most popular but some fishermen use vivid yellow or orange
Hackle: a fluff of red wool at the throat, or coloured fibres
Head: built up with tying silk, varnished black or red, often with a fish's eye painted on

A most ingenious representation of a minnow, stickleback or small fry.

Poult Bloa A North Country trout fly. Poult is a young bird or young chicken, bloa is (probably) blue. The fly suggests a drowned dun or spinner and is fished upstream.

Body: yellow silk dubbed with red squirrel fur
Hackle: slate-blue feather from the underwing of the young grouse
Hook: 16

Pulman, G.P.R. Has the reputation, given to him by J. Waller Hills, of being 'the father of the dry fly'. It may well be so. George Pulman had a newsagents and fishing tackle business at Axminster, with branches at Dorchester and Totnes. He fished the River Axe from shortly after the end of the Napoleonic wars until he retired in the late 1840s. His best-selling book on fishing, which ran into several editions, is quite a small one which can easily fit into a pocket, called *The Vade Mecum of Fly Fishing for Trout*. (Vade Mecum: a handbook, a pocket-companion).

The first edition, 1841, had the basis of his description of the dry fly, elaborated in later editions. It was not a fly treated with floatant but one taken 'dry' from the fly box which would float for a while until it sank. Pulman was giving instructions how to fish to trout which were lying 'high in the water' when the angler's line and fly had become soaked:

So, as it is not in the nature of things that this soaked artificial fly can swim upon the surface like the natural ones do, it follows the alternative and sinks below the rising fish, the notice of which it entirely escapes, because they happen to be looking upwards for the materials of their meal. Let a dry fly be substituted for the wet one, the line switched a few times through the air to throw off the superabundant moisture, a judicious cast made just above the rising fish, and the fly allowed to float towards and over them, and the chances are ten to one it will be seized as readily as the living insect.

This dry fly, we must remark, must be an imitation of the natural fly on which the fish are feeding because if widely different the fish instead of being allured would most likely be surprised and startled at the novelty presented, and would suspend feeding until the appearance of their favourite and familiar prey. We mention this as an illustration of the importance of imitating action, and must not be understood to recommend the constantly substituting of a dry fly for a wet one over every rising fish. Better, as a general rule, when the angler after a few casts finds the fish over which he throws unwilling to be tempted, pass on in search of a more willing victim . . .

There, complete, was the theory and practice of fishing the floating fly, false casting, accurate presentation of an artificial resembling the natural, all excellently argued and set out. Waller Hills, writing more than half a century later, expressed astonishment that a Devon fisherman should know all this and thought that Pulman must have got his knowledge from Hampshire. However, it is clear from the text of the *Vade Mecum* that Pulman was not describing any new method of fishing which he had learnt from fishing Hampshire streams, merely a useful tactic to adopt on any river when trout were taking duns on the surface. There is a distinction between fishing a fly which floats for a time and the 'dry fly' method as we know it today. (See Dry Fly Origins on page 52)

Purism Dictionary definition: 'over fastidious insistence on purity'. Sometimes used as a term of abuse. Halford's definition which separated purists from ultra-purists, was given in *The Dry Fly Man's Handbook* (Routledge, 1913):

The dry fly is, as its name suggests, an artificial fly used dry, i.e. with no water in suspension between the fibres of the hackle, wings and other feathers etc., used in its construction. In this state it floats on the surface of the stream. Mayflies, duns or sedges should sail down cocked, i.e. the mayflies and duns with their wings erect and the sedges with their wings at an angle of about 30 degrees to the horizontal. The spent gnat or spinner which represents the female imago after it has voided its eggs, or the male imago when its share of the work of procreation is complete should float down in its natural position with wings laid flat and at right-angles to the line of the body . . .

When fishing dry the angler must in the first instance find a fish taking the winged insects on the surface, and it is essential that he should locate its position with the greatest precision . . .

If he should perchance catch sight of a fish near the surface which is evidently on the

look out for duns or other flies but not actually rising he may cast to this fish . . .
The artificial fly having been placed on the water lightly and accurately so that it will float down over the exact spot where the fish is feeding, the next essential is that it should follow precisely the same course and travel at precisely the same pace as the natural insects under similar conditions . . .
Those of us who will not in any circumstances cast except over rising fish are sometimes called ultra-purists and those who will occasionally try to tempt a fish in position, but not actually rising, are styled purists. The expressions are often used by angling authorities as a species of reproach or commiseration . . . [but] . . . I would urge that the first rule to be observed by every man who wishes to be deemed a dry fly fisher is to follow the example of these purists or ultra-purists.

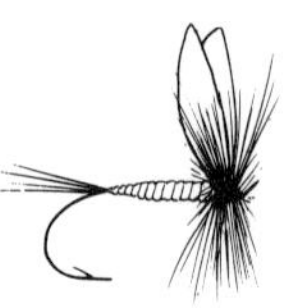

Contrasts

For him [Bob Church] there is no right or wrong way to catch trout; no unwritten laws to be observed which are within but different from the rules pinned up in the fishery office. He respects the rights of others to restrict themselves, if that is what they wish, but for him – and we believe this to be the majority view – the first object is to catch fish.

Colin Dyson, in a foreword to Bob Church, *Reservoir Trout Fishing* (2nd edn) A and C Black 1983

I know that trout can be caught with a worm, or a maggot, or by spinning, by wet-fly fishing, or by nymph fishing, and I know that at times these methods will catch more fish than any other. I have no objection to anglers practising these methods to their heart's content. As for myself, I am not particularly interested in killing trout. What does interest me immensely is catching trout by a method we call dry fly.

David Jacques, *Fisherman's Fly*, A and C Black, 1965

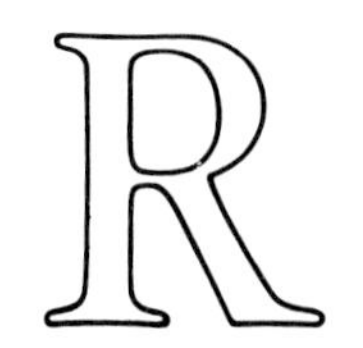

Rabley, Charles A. Rabley was a schoolmaster at Ashwater, West Devon, in the late 1800s and early 1900s who fished the Tamar and Carey for over 40 years and was the author of *Devonshire Trout Fishing*, published privately, undated, probably about 1910. The book is of interest because Rabley always fished the floating fly and was unaware that trout would take a sunk fly as well. He describes an incident on the Carey when the trout were rising but would not look at his fly. He then cast up and across and allowed the flies to sink. He drew them towards him. This time the trout took.

I now feel convinced that trout do feed freely below the surface on insects and can be caught with the artificial fly by touch as well as by sight. (*West Country Fly Fishing*, edited by Anne Voss Bark, Batsford, 1983)

This is probably the earliest description of an induced take with an upstream wet fly. Rabley called it 'drawing the water'.

Rainbow Trout (*Salmo gairdneri*) The scientific name covers two forms of rainbow, the steelhead, or migratory rainbow, and the non-migratory. At one time the non-migratory were given two names, *shasta* and *irrideus*, which are not now accepted scientifically but are still in use at times by fish breeders who call spring spawners *irideus* and autumn spawners *shasta*.

The first successful importation of rainbow eggs from the United States was in 1885 and fish were produced at the Delafield and Howietown hatcheries. By the early 1970s rainbows were stocked in more than 500 rivers, lakes and reservoirs in England, Scotland and Wales, but only in four of them – Blagdon Reservoir; the River Wye, Derbyshire; the River Misbourne, Buckinghamshire, and the River Wey, Surrey – did they breed naturally. In some of these they no longer breed. By the mid-1970s a tributary of the Derbyshire Wye, the Lathkill, was reported as having a population of self-perpetuating rainbows, and some rainbows were thought to be breeding in parts of the Chatsworth fisheries on the Derwent.

It is difficult to be certain about the distribution of self-perpetuating rainbow populations as in quite a number of rivers small rainbows escape from fish farms and give the impression that they are wild-bred fish.

The advantage of stocking with rainbow is that on average it costs about 20 per cent less than farm-bred brown trout, they grow more rapidly, and are liked both for their fighting and culinary qualities. **Sources:** Dr E.B. Worthington, articles, *Salmon and Trout Magazine*, 1940 and 1941; Dr Winifred E. Frost, *A Survey of the Rainbow Trout in Britain and Ireland*, a Salmon and Trout Association publication, undated, probably 1973 or 74.

Ransome, Arthur Journalist, foreign correspondent, essayist, children's story-teller. Arthur Ransome wrote a fishing column for the *Manchester Guardian*, as it then was, in the 1920s from which extracts have been quoted ever since:

Escaping from the Stone Age by the morning train from Manchester, the fisherman engages in an activity that allows him to shed the centuries as a dog shakes off water and to recapture not his own youth merely but the youth of the world.

The Guardian essays were first published by Jonathan Cape in 1929 and were reprinted as an Oxford University Press paperback in 1980. The title *Rod and Line* was used in a Granada Television production in 1982 in which Sir Michael Hordern, also a fisherman, played the part of Ransome. *The Times* wrote (24 November 1982):

The camera watches him climb rocks, duck under trees, get the hook caught in his mittens, sees his hat blown off, and hears him mutter 'sod it' beneath his breath as he bungles his backcast. This brings us near to the truth of things – an all-too-rare picture of what angling is all about.

It was particularly moving, said *The Times*, to see Hordern lost in thought beside the river and hear Ransome's farewell lines:

It is said that gardeners and fishermen make fine old men. That is not surprising. They have been caught up into Nature, grow old with a will and no hanging back, and are without misgivings about their own mortality.

Record Fish The official British record fish include the following:

Brown Trout	19lb 4oz 4drms	1978	J.A.F. Jackson, Loch Quoich, Inverness-shire
Rainbow Trout	19lb 8oz	1977	A. Pearson, Avington Fishery, Hampshire
Brook Trout	5lb 6oz	1979	A. Pearson, Avington Fishery, Hampshire
Salmon	64lb	1922	Miss G.W. Ballantyne, Glendelvine Water
Sea Trout	20lb	1983	G. Leavy, Castle Pool, River Tweed

The official records are not necessarily records of the biggest fish that are known to have been caught but those which have been identified and recognised by the British Record (rod-caught) Fish Committee which (in 1984) has its offices at 11 Cowgate, Peterborough. The secretary of the committee is P.H. Tombleson who describes its work:

Formed in 1956 the committee was launched at about the same time as the Irish Specimen Fish Committee. Its objects are to provide a record list nationally recognised by the sport and a procedure for claiming new records. Freshwater and sea fish records are included but no 'line class' records on the North American style as this system is unacceptable to the major British angling bodies.

Over the years the committee has established a network of identification stations throughout the country and works closely also with other record committees founded along the same lines, including Guernsey and Jersey committees. Membership of the committee includes members of the main angling media, newspapers and magazines, the national angling organisations and scientific advisers. Scottish and Welsh record committees are also involved and procedures now for claiming records established through the Welsh committee will be processed as a British claim if eligible. Continental committees – in Germany, Austria, Poland, Italy and Holland are based on the British Record (rod-caught) Fish Committee.

The committee issues annually a new list showing species of fish caught by fair angling on rod and line and outlining procedures. A mini-record list caters for sea fish under one pound in weight after which level they move on to the main sea list for boat caught or shore caught sea fish.

Generally fishing tackle shops or the angling press are contact points for record claimants who must then contact the committee secretary for advice on how to proceed. Fish for which claims are made need not be killed as arrangements can be made for them to be identified and weighed fairly quickly. Retain the body of the fish alive or dead as production of the body is the vital rule the committee follows for identification. Advice will be given on witnesses to capture and weighing and verification of the weighing instrument. The committee issues a signed certificate for all record holders.

There are many unofficial records. The biggest salmon ever seen on the bank was said to weigh 103lb, and was taken off the River Devon in Scotland, but details are missing – even of the year it was taken, which was either 1902 or 1903. Other big salmon include:

94lb	Eger	Norway	1867	
94lb	Tana	Norway	1878 or 79	
84lb	Netted in the Tay	Scotland	1869	
69½lb	Aaro	Norway	1921	caught on rod and line by J. Aarven
67lb	Nith	Scotland	1812	caught by a poacher, Jock Wallace
60lb	Eden	England	1888	length 54in., girth 27in., caught on a fly by Mr Lowther Bridger
59½lb	Wye	Wales	1923	caught on rod and line (? fly) by Miss Doreen Davy

The unofficial record British brown trout was 39½lb, caught on Loch Awe by Mr W. Muir in 1866. It was foul-hooked on a trout fly and took 2½ hours to land. Other big trout have been recorded, the next biggest a 29lb slob trout from Loch Stennes in 1889 on a hand line, which possibly might be listed as a semi-sea trout. Sea trout unofficial records are:

38lb	Tees	England	—	said to have been caught by James Teasdale in the early 1800s
28lb	—	Sweden	1930	caught by Mr W.H. Barrett
26½lb	—	Sweden	1929	also caught by Mr Barrett
22½lb	Loch Maree	Scotland	—	a cast of this fish in in the Loch Maree Hotel
21lb	Frome	England	1918	caught at Bindon by Mr R.C. Hardy Corfe

A grayling of 4½lb was caught by Dr T. Sanctuary on the Wylye at Bemerton in 1885 and one of 4¾lb was netted from the Avon at Longford in the same year by Dr Sanctuary and Mr G.S. Marryat and returned. **Sources include:** *The Fishing Gazette*; Braithwaite, *Fishing Vignettes*; Calderwood, *Salmon Rivers and Lochs of Scotland*, Jack Chance, *Salmon Stories*; A.H. Chaytor, *Letter to a Salmon Fisher's Sons*; Eric Taverner and John Moore, *The Angler's Week End Book*.

Red Quill An admirable dry fly and as much a favourite of many fishermen as the Pheasant Tail or the Greenwell.

Body: stripped peacock quill from the eye feather tied to give a well-marked banded appearance, dyed red optional
Whisks: a few fibres from a bright red cock hackle
Hackle: bright red cock
Wings: pale or medium starling primary
Hook: 14–16

Red Spinner Not so popular as a trout fly as it used to be, having been overtaken by the Pheasant Tail and the Tups, nevertheless a good pattern when spent olives are on the water:

Body: red wool or red floss silk
Rib: fine gold wire
Hackle: red cock
Wings: blue hackle points, tied spent
Hook: 14–16

Red Tag A grayling fly, sometimes confused with another North Country fly, the Treacle Parkin. The Red Tag has spread to Wales and the West Country.

Body: bright green peacock herl
Tag: bright red wool, cut short
Hackle: red cock
Hook: 14–18

Reed Smuts A small humpy-bodied black fly, very small, less than an eighth of an inch long, frequently known with other small black flies, as 'smut' or 'curse'. They are a river fly, so far as is known rarely or never hatching on still waters, but on rivers they sometimes appear in vast numbers. It is on record that fly fishermen have been infuriated by reed smuts ever since the first known artificial imitation was tied – by Scotcher around 1800. Practically every fly-dresser of repute has tied his own version since. This is a fairly simple one:

Body: dark brown tying silk, slightly bunched and humpy
Wings: blue dun or badger hackle points, tied spent
Hook: 18–22

The difficulty of taking trout with this fly, (J.C. Mottram pointed out), is that when trout are taking the natural there are so many of them on the water that the artificial has to be cast very accurately to drift precisely over the trout's nose.

Reservoir Fishing

In truth, reservoir trouting has gradually grown away from fly fishing as our fathers knew it and today can be considered a branch of angling in its own right. (*Fly Fishing Tactics on Still Water*, Geoffrey Bucknall, Frederic Muller, 1966)

No other participant sport has shown such an increase as reservoir trout fishing. In the 40 years since the end of World War Two, public water supply reservoirs have been stocked and opened for angling at a rate of not quite two a year. They include:

Chew Valley Lake, 1,200 acres, opened in 1957
Grafham Water, 1,670 acres, opened in 1966
Rutland Water, 3,100 acres, the biggest stocked trout fishery in Europe, opened in 1977

Taking into account that something like 30 to 35 per cent of anglers do not put in returns of trout caught, the average aggregate catch for those three reservoirs is of the order of 150,000 trout a season. The official, and therefore under-estimates, of trout caught in 1983, based on the returns that were made, were:

Chew Valley Lake	19,475
Grafham Water	41,752
Rutland Water	60,358

But Chew, Grafham and Rutland – the Big Three as the fishing magazines call them – provide only a proportion of the new fishing. According to an unofficial estimate in 1974, based on replies to a questionnaire, 75 reservoirs had been opened for angling in England and Wales over the 28 year period, 1945–1973. In 1974, 228 reservoirs were available for fishing, practically all for trout fishing, an increase compared with pre-war of 65 per cent. The reservoirs were in all areas:

Seven were opened in Yorkshire, five in Lancashire, 12 in the Glamorgan River Authority area, four in South West Wales, nine in the Dee and Clwyd area, three in Kent, six in Somerset, seven in Cornwall. (*Trout and Salmon* magazine, July, 1974)

A few reservoirs originally stocked with trout may have since reverted to coarse fishing. No account was taken of Scottish reservoirs.

In the last 20 years or so, reservoir trout fishing has attracted a number of coarse fishermen, enabling them to fish during their close season, and there has been a general increase in the number of fly fishermen on both rivers and stillwaters. The latest survey shows that there are about a million game fishermen out of a total of four million anglers in Britain. A very approximate comparison suggests that game fishermen have increased in number by about a quarter to a third in the last ten or 12 years (1970–1982). A large part of this increase must have been due to stillwater fishing. **Sources:** A survey commissioned by the Standing Conference on Countryside Sports from Cobham Resource Consultants, carried out in 1981–82, published 1983, estimated there were 947,750 game fishermen in Britain out of a total of 3,730,000 anglers.

The National Angling Survey carried out by NOP Market Research, published 1970, estimated that there were 614,000 game fishermen in England and Wales.

Estimates pre-1940 from various sources, not sampling, gave figures of between 150,000 to 200,000 game fishermen.

The post-war expansion of reservoir trout fishing (1946–1973) provided room for an additional 200,000 game fishermen, according to the unofficial survey of 1974. The survey did not attempt to estimate whether all those additional facilities had been taken up.

According to an article in *Trout Fisherman* (May, 1984) there may be some 300,000 stillwater fly fishermen.

Reservoirs: From Float to Fly

When one comes to think about it there is no reason at all why these public sheets of water should not be used for fishing . . . When we see £200 a year offered for a mile or so of a famous trout stream we can say goodbye to the possibility of it ever again being open to the rank and file . . . (Ernest Phillips, *Trout in Lakes and Reservoirs*, Longmans, 1914)

Reservoir fishing began in the 1870s when many rivers had become unfishable due to pollution. In Sheffield, 20,000 anglers were members of the local association whose river, the Don, was 'a mass of ink, stink, bubble and malarial gas'. Sheffield Corporation owned several public water supply reservoirs on the sides of the Pennines which had a natural stock of trout. To meet the need they opened these at 2s. 6d. for a day's fishing. Dam Flask, Rivelin, Redmires could be fished by any legal method with rod and line – fly, bait or spinner.

Manchester opened Thirlmere, Audenshaw and Gorton 'for fishing for the relaxation of the working class'. There were some trout but it was mostly coarse fishing. Fishing at Thirlmere was free. Liverpool opened Lake Vyrnwy in Wales with fly and minnow fishing at 2s. 6d. a day to hotel visitors, 5s. extra for a boat. Birmingham opened seven reservoirs that could be fished by 'all sporting methods'. Northampton opened Ravensthorpe for fly fishing from a boat, at 10s. a day, but the minnow could be fished by anglers at 5s. – an arrangement later to cause conflict.

One hundred and twenty-five reservoirs were opened for public fishing by the early 1900s, and of those only 11 were restricted to fly fishing only. All the rest opened for coarse fishing, predominantly bait – worm and minnow or the artificial minnow. Manchester was one of the few cities which lagged behind the others in providing fishing because they were 'determined to keep inviolate the purity of their domestic water supply'. Manchester's attitude in those days was understandable because maggots were in use as both hook and ground bait at reservoirs which had allowed 'all sporting methods'. Ground baiting and maggot fishing were soon to be excluded everywhere.

Arguments about the various methods of fishing developed.

> There are a good many anglers who consider it almost a sacrilege to tempt a trout with a common worm. I have met many fishermen who, having made a journey to fish for trout, have returned without putting up their rod because they found the water unsuited for the fly, and they could not bring themselves to the use of any other lure. This is very nice, to be sure, but it isn't fishing. The business of angling is to catch fish and though these purists may be satisfied that their conduct lifts them high above the common crowd of sportsmen, it is not sufficiently satisfying for those whose days at the waterside are only a few, and whose desire it is to enjoy the thrill and the pleasure of hooking and landing a basket of trout. (*Trout in Lakes and Reservoirs*, Ernest Phillips, Longmans Green, 1914)

It was not those who found bait fishing aesthetically unpleasant who forced the change that came in the next half century. The reasons were partly social, and partly economic.

Most reservoirs which had opened for fishing allowed a bag limit of eight or 12 fish. Many natural lakes were soon fished out and had to be stocked, often with the new import from America now bred widely at fish farms, the rainbow, which at first were almost universally disliked. But rainbows were cheaper and economic problems were acute. Permits had to cost more or else bag limits reduced. Arguments and ill-feeling grew.

At the same time anglers using one method found themselves in conflict with those using another. It was not uncommon for a fly fisherman, fishing the drift from a boat to see a spinner from a bank angler splashing directly in the path of his drift. Segregation was tried, in many cases unsuccessfully. New and more effective spinning rods brought angry protests from worm and float fishermen. According to the recollections of one fisherman of the time, fights often broke out.

The city corporation and water companies who had opened their reservoirs for public fishing with a high sense of social responsibility soon found they were involved in complex and intransigent problems of management. They had to discover ways in which they could keep the cost of running the fisheries within reasonable limits, for ratepayers were reluctant to subsidise them. They could not increase the cost of a day permit to a viable level without risking an unacceptable decline in revenue. It was difficult to reduce the over-generous bag limits which had worked well enough so long as the wild fish stocks lasted. Anglers expected the bag limits to continue.

The accountants and fishery managers who had to try and solve the problem were not long in finding out that the conflicts between the various methods of fishing were soon resolved if only one method was in force. The very few reservoirs where fishing was restricted to fly only – not more than about eight per cent of the total – provided the answer. Moreover, and this was the deciding factor, fly fishing was then thought not so efficient in taking reservoir trout as spinning and worming. There was no need to reduce the official bag limits as they would be reduced by smaller catches if fishing was restricted to the fly. The purists had little or no influence in the gradual change that took place over a period of something like 30 to 40 years. It was the economists, local government accountants, fishery managers, who were instrumental in persuading, and sometimes forcing, a large body of reluctant anglers to change.

If they start bringing in fly-only on Blagdon we'll get round it somehow. We'll fish fly spoon or fly minnow, something like that, and bugger Bristol Waterworks. (Willie Cox, scene-painter at the Bristol Theatre Royal, at some time in the 1930s)

Anglers adapted to the change by becoming more proficient in the use of the fly. The old habit of using salmon flies for surface fishing was abandoned. Deep-sunk fishing developed. New fly patterns were created which were far more efficient than the old. Fishery managers also helped by creating an atmosphere in which worming and spinning were to be deplored as unsporting:

It did me good to see from the fishing return that you and your Invictas did so well. I am sorry now we did not bar Spinning throughout the Season, but we have a number of Blagdon enthusiasts who are keen on Spinning and I feared that the result of such a ban might be disastrous from the financial point of view, because under War conditions we only just pay our way as it is; however, the good results obtained with the Fly only during the first 8 days encourages me to stop all Spinning next year.

I have just heard that 24 fish were killed by 4 rods, all Spinning, on Sunday last – sacrilege! Dr Bell was one of the culprits, he got 6, but a man named Rugg got his limit.

I am going to do my best to spend a few days at the Lake during August, and it would be a real pleasure to meet you again. (A letter from W.A.D. Alexander, general manager of Bristol Waterworks, to Colonel J.K.B. Crawford, a master at Clifton College, in the early part of the 1943 season)

When spinning at Blagdon was banned in 1944 there was a resistance movement among some of the regulars. This description of the way they tried to avoid the fly-only rule was given by one of the regulars – Willie Cox:

If you stripped off a good length of line from your reel you could cast a plug or fly-spinner a good distance by coiling the line on the grass and letting it shoot through the rings as the heavy bait pulled line after it. We said that was fly fishing for we were using a fly rod. We used rubber eels, and Halcyon flies which had a propellor at the head, and fly spoons, but we always had a bit of feather on them so that we could say they were a fly. Then there were imitation baits made out of ebonite or plaster, lifelike frogs and fish and tadpoles, and you could cast these like a spinner too. I think it was Hardy that produced what they called a Wake Lure which was a wooden body that skated over the surface and we called this a fly because it was covered with feathers. We had some fun, I can tell you, but we gave it up in the end.

Reservoir Fishing: Regulations Most fisheries like to keep their rules as simple as possible. Not many people read them. From time to time changes are made, generally as a result of pressure and lobbying in the case of complaints about the use of shooting heads, or for safety reasons, such as the banning of special drift-control apparatus and of wading in certain areas. The rules of Grafham (1983) are fairly typical:

Fishing only permitted by means of rod and line with artificial fly or feathered lure fished floating or sunken on an unweighted cast, except when dapping when a natural fly may be used
The use of any form of dead, live or groundbait is prohibited
Unauthorised tackle should not be taken into boats or round the bank
Trolling, which shall be interpreted as continuously pulling any fly or feathered lure through the water behind a boat is permitted only from a rowed boat and only in certain areas [defined and with an accompanying map]
With motor boats no fishing is permitted while the motor is running
Side casting, which for the purpose of this rule shall be the term used to describe the manner of fishing when one angler is slowly rowing the boat while the other angler(s) cast out over the boat shall be subject to the same restrictions as trolling
Anglers may fish with four hooks at any one time. These may be in combinations of singles, doubles or trebles at the discretion of the angler

Other rules are: no fishing without a permit, no fixed spool reels or bubble floats, no litter, or camping, breast waders forbidden, and no wading along the dam for safety reasons. A red flag is flown if the water is too rough for boats. Drogues are provided but anglers may use their own, subject to the fishery officer's approval. A recent addition to the rules concerned boat fishing:

Lee boards and/or special drift control rudders or any other attachments are not permitted

These attachments control the direction of a drift and in unskilled hands are said to be dangerous.

Grafham is controlled by the Anglian Water Authority which issues guidance to anglers about personal behaviour by publishing a code of practice drawn up by the Federation of Midland Fly Fishers:

Know the fishery regulations and keep to them
Keep clear of anglers already fishing
Know your boat and motor – if in doubt obtain advice before starting
Don't concentrate all the weight in the stern
Leave tackle behind which is prohibited from use
Avoid cutting across another boat's drift
Move your boat very slowly when near other anglers
Respect the right of other users of the water
Respect wild life – in particular, take away waste nylon
Co-operate with fishery staff
Close gates and use stiles and paths where provided
After fishing, leave a return of your catch

Most authorities ask for nil returns as well as returns of fish caught.

Reservoir Fishing: Methods The prohibition of bait fishing and spinning on reservoirs led to considerable experimentation and a surge of inventiveness. Fly rods and tackle, previously capable of putting a fly or lure only a few feet below the surface, were soon being developed in such a way that they could fill the gap that had been left. The fly rod, in effect, had to take over the functions of the bait caster. This was made possible by two main developments: the importation from America, of the shooting head and the lead-cored line.

Lead-cored lines can be used as shooting heads attached to a nylon backing or as full 100-yard lengths for trolling, reaching down to previously unheard of depths with large feathered lures 4in. to 5in. long. Their use is no longer particularly controversial though it was at one time:

I think my friends and I were the first to use this American import and for quite some time we had staggering success. Our catches were so conspicuously better than most other people's that we were practically accused of being on the fiddle. That, plus the fact that we were worried that the lead line might be banned, unless it came into more general use, persuaded us to reveal the big secret. Some of the tweedy types, who regarded any line which sank as some sort of devil's invention, were quite horrified. Others, however, could appreciate that there was certain problems in catching big trout from the bottom in up to 70ft of water were they to restrict themselves to dry fly chalk stream tactics. (Bob Church, *Reservoir Trout Fishing*, collated and written by Colin Dyson, 2nd edn., A and C Black, 1983)

The new deep-fishing methods were not universally popular, even among committed reservoir fishermen and many still preferred traditional techniques.

Reservoirs: Nymph Fishing This method has taken over and in many ways improved upon the bait fishing of the early 1900s. The term 'nymph fishing', derived from the chalk streams, is a convenient shorthand on the reservoirs for fishing a wide selection of imitation bait – pupae, bloodworms, snails, shrimps – all of which are understood by long usage to come under the term 'nymph'. The pioneer of this method is generally agreed to have been Dr Bell of Blagdon in the 1920s and 1930s. He spooned out the trout he caught and tied flies to imitate the insects he found in their stomachs. Some of his original patterns are illustrated in colour photograph 10(d).

Various ways have been devised for fishing the nymph on reservoirs. The problem is the area of water that has to be covered and in general the lack of any visible indication of fly life. Stillwater fishing books, by John Goddard, Peter Lapsley, and others, provide charts which show when various underwater creatures are likely to be active in sufficient numbers to attract the trout. Enquiries suggest that anglers are inclined to use a more pragmatic approach, putting on a favourite pattern, fishing it for a while, putting on another, fishing that, and so on, until something happens.

A survey at two reservoirs suggests that most nymph fishermen have one or two favourite patterns which they use most of the time and these are often general patterns that suggest a number of underwater creatures. Only in obvious cases of selective rises – such as to midge pupae – are specific patterns used.

Most midge fishermen are bank fishermen, using a floating line or a sink-tip floater, with a fairly long leader of about 10ft–12ft, sometimes a floating shooting head to reach for distance. The floating line or the unsubmerged part of the butt of the leader act as 'bite' indicators. An intermediate line, which sinks very slowly, is often useful in rough water conditions but the nymph generally has to be fished faster in order for the take to register.

Fishing a nymph on reservoirs is a highly sophisticated and fascinating technique, which has its addicts who will fish little else.

Reservoirs: Attractors and Deceivers A coherent philosophy for reservoir fishing was largely the result of the work of Midland fly fishers from about the 1930s to the 1950s, one of whom was T.C. Ivens who set out the principles in a book first published in 1952. Ivens divided fly patterns into two categories – attractors and deceivers. This sounds simple now but for many fishermen at the time it was a revelation. It resolved, or at least convinced them that it resolved, most of their problems. Ivens's confidence was infectious:

I have always attempted to elevate fishing to the plane of an exact science. The man who *thinks* 'fish and fishing' must ultimately succeed in catching more fish than the man who leaves it to luck. (*Still Water Fly Fishing*, André Deutsch, 1952)

The attractor or flasher patterns are fished when there is a lop on the water, when there is a wind of anything more than about fifteen miles an hour. At other times deceiver patterns are fished. These suggest but do not imitate various types of underwater creatures.

The Jersey Herd and the Alexandra are attractor patterns, to be fished fast. The Peacock Spider, the Green Nymph and the Green and Brown Nymph are deceiver patterns. Of these the Peacock Spider is the favourite. Deceivers are fished slowly or fairly slowly, and Ivens gives precise times for the retrieve.

He emphasised that reservoir fishing was quite distinct from any other kind on river or on loch:

. . . river tackle, in 95 per cent of cases, is hopelessly unsuited to use on reservoirs. Ashore or afloat, reservoir angling requires a special skill which can be achieved only with specialised tackle. Contrary to the general impression, long casting is frequently as necessary from a boat as from a bank and particularly is this so in calm weather. Except on rare occasions, the 'traditional' loch outfit is unsuitable . . .

Reservoirs: Fishing the Drift The scope and extent of reservoir fishing, the way it attracts so many different methods and seems to accommodate them all equally well has meant, in spite of Ivens, that traditional loch-style fishing has not only survived on the reservoirs but has actually increased in popularity. This is entirely, or very nearly entirely, due to competitions creating the interest.

The competitions, originating in Scotland, gain more adherents each year as teams from fishing clubs in England, Scotland, Ireland and Wales compete for national prizes given by commercial sponsors. They fish the drift from a boat in the traditional way, casting ahead and retrieving standard wet flies such as the Butcher, Greenwell, Peter Ross, and many others, and it is noticeable how many times quite small flies – down to # 16s – will often take big fish. **Sources include:** *Stillwater Fly Fishing*, T.C. Ivens (Deutsch, 1952, and subsequent editions); *Stillwater Flies – How and When to Fish Them*, ed. John Goddard, with contributions from Syd Brock, Bob Carnill, Bob Church, John Ketley and Dick Walker describing their methods (Benn, 1982); *The Pursuit of Stillwater Trout*, Brian Clarke (Black, 1975) an informative book about a fishermans' progress on stillwaters; *Competitive Fly Fishing* by Tony Pawson (Pelham Books 1982) the standard reference work on competitive fishing with descriptions from some 60 contributors on their winning methods; *Trout From Stillwaters*, by Peter Lapsley (Black 1982), an informed study of all kinds of stillwater fishing, from lakes and lochs to big reservoirs.

Sources also include the Travis Commission Report, *Angling in Britain, 1980*; *Reservoir Trout Fishing in England, 1976–1981*, published by the Water Space Amenity Commission; *Stillwater Trout Fisheries*, H.F. Wallis (Benn, 1976) and several articles in *Salmon and Trout* magazine.

The main historical information came from *Trout in Lakes and Reservoirs* by Ernest Phillips (Longmans, 1914); from private diaries and letters including interviews with Willie Cox, Lawrie Williamson, Donald Carr, Alick Newsom, Colonel Crawford, and others.

Reversed Flies A method of tying the dry fly with the hackle reversed; that is put on at the part of the body of the hook which lies at the bend, just above the point, the wings also, and the whisks or tails projecting under the hook eye. The whole fly is therefore reversed. This method of tying was first recommended by Alexander Macintosh, river keeper of the Driffield Beck, in his book, *The Driffield Angler* (1808), and has been revived occasionally since.

Ribble The Ribble and its companion river, the Hodder, come from the land of the broad acres, rising in the high moors of the Pennines, lovely small streams which are grand places for fishermen. There may be a worm here and there but the upstream wet fly should be paramount – the Partridge, Bloas and Watchets – and the wild brown trout take well and savagely. The closer the Ribble gets to Preston the fewer the trout, which is not surprising as pollution has been bad. The Royal Oak Hotel at Settle can provide tickets for association water. There is also good fly fishing at Malham Tarn, a famous nature reserve, a few miles away.

Ritz, Charles Hotelier, fly fisherman, designer of fly rods instructor in casting, Charles Ritz wrote a charming and readable autobiography, *A Fly Fisher's Life* (Max Reinhardt, 1959, reprinted and with a second edition). In this, Ritz gave a fascinating picture of fly fishing adventures in most of Europe, England and America together with an examination of the casting and fishing techniques of many leading fly fishermen. The book reveals Ritz as an exuberant man with strong opinions but he was warm-hearted and generous as well and had many fishermen, among them Frank Sawyer, as his guests at the Fario Club luncheons at the Ritz in Paris. He died, aged over 80, in 1976.

Charles Ritz was the son of César Ritz (1850–1918) the thirteenth child of a Swiss peasant who worked his way up in the hotel industry and founded the Ritz in Paris and later, the Ritz in London. His son Charles was on the board of Ritz Hotels but as someone once said he was more of a fisherman than an hotelier.

Rods The sophistication of fly fishing came with advancing technology. Individual handcraftsmanship gave way to mass production. Space age composite materials have replaced natural fibres. L.U. Borenius writes:

The development of the fly rod gradually became differentiated from rods required for other forms of fishing since progressive flexibility (action) became an essential requirement of what was essentially a casting instrument.

The flexing and unflexing inherent in casting a fly placed a much greater strain on the rod and the traditional materials of which fishing rods were originally made. Hazel, willow and ash were replaced by rods of denser and much stronger materials greenheart and hickory, both imported from abroad.

The all-important change in design of fishing rod from instrument of placement to casting instrument took place during the last century and the fly rod became a comparatively heavy rod throwing a silk line. The normal method of joining the rod pieces together was by binding with leather thongs which were wetted before binding. As the thongs dried, the leather contracted and the pieces were held firmly in position. Normally a knob was carved into the ends of the rods to prevent the thongs from slipping.

The greatly increased range achieved by casting made the use of much longer lines necessary and a mechanism for carrying the line, i.e. the reel, came into common use. Previously fish were 'played' by a tight line with the flex in the rod tip being the only buffer between fisherman and fish. If all else failed the fisherman would throw the rod into the water with the hope that eventually when the fish had exhausted itself, by pulling the rod through the water, rod and fish could be recovered.

The joining of the different pieces of a rod by thongs ('splicing') was both cumbrous and not entirely reliable. In the case of coarse fishing rods of whole cane it was possible to join the pieces simply by inserting the pieces inside each other. By a natural process of adaptation, this technique was extended to rods made of other non-tubular materials by using metal 'ferrules' for joining the pieces.

Thus there was completed, by the turn of the century, the fundamental design which today constitutes modern fly tackle – a flexible rod, a line heavy enough to throw and a reel large enough to store the whole length of line which could be thrown, together with 'backing' i.e. a reserve of line for enabling a strong fish to swim a considerable distance from the angler without breaking the line.

All subsequent developments in the design and construction of the fly rod were founded upon the discovery and application of new materials to the fundamental requirements of throwing the fly line with optimum facility.

At the end of the nineteenth century split cane rods were introduced. They were in fact longitudinally split pieces of bamboo glued together. The hard outer bark of the bamboo was utilised so that in a well manufactured rod the tapering effect was achieved by reducing the thickness of the pieces in the inner pulpy sides of the bamboo. In order to give greater stiffness to the sections without increase in weight the technique of heating the sections (before gluing and binding) was introduced. Since it was virtually impossible to provide a handle of sufficient thickness from split bamboo the modern cork handle (made of rings of cork sandpapered to the required shape) was introduced. This method was subsequently applied to all fishing rods, including greenheart rods the handles of which had originally been made of the same materials as the rest of the rod.

The introduction of the split cane rod had a dramatic effect on fly tackle and ultimately on casting techniques. Trout rods, instead of weighing 15 or 16oz weighed less than 8oz and by 1920 were normally between 5½ and 6½oz in weight.

By 1930 the refinement in manufacturing methods (notably the introduction of hollow built butts) and the introduction of light weight aluminium rod fittings made possible the production of powerful 8ft rods weighing as little as 4oz. The lightness of these modern rods made it possible to impart much greater speed to the tip of the rod in making the forward (or power) cast. The result was that maximum casting distance achievable with ordinary tackle increased very substantially, since governed almost entirely by the speed with which the tip of the rod can be made to move during the forward cast. The lighter the rod the faster the tip can be moved through the air.

By 1930 split cane was the major material for all fly rods; only in Scotland were the old two handed greenheart salmon fly rods widely used for Spey casting (largely because of their better resistence to 'torque' in executing the Spey cast and also because of their comparative cheapness).

The extreme lightness of split cane combined with its virtual immunity from sudden fracture was the determining factor in securing its ascendancy in fly rod manufacture. If a greenheart rod dried out (by being kept in a warm atmosphere) it would fracture without warning. A split cane rod which is weakened will almost invariably fail gradually thus giving warning to the owner that a replacement of the affected section is necessary.

One marked feature of the split cane was the individuality of each rod. Since the degree of relative stiffness and resilience of a fly rod depended largely upon the characteristic of the individual pieces of cane from which the pieces had been cut, no two split cane rods, however identical in taper they might be, ever had exactly the same 'action'.

The source of all split cane of quality was a district in north-west China (Tonkin) and the climatic conditions affecting each individual crop of cane would have an effect on the quality of the ultimate product. This individuality gave each fly rod its own inimitable 'feel' comparable to the difference between finely made violins.

From 1930 to 1950 split cane ruled supreme. In the 50s, however, the worsening diplomatic relationship between China and the U.S. (and a consequent embargo on purchase of further stocks of Tonkin by American tackle manufacturers) made it necessary for the Americans to develop an alternative synthetic material – 'Fibre' Glass. This material consisted of manmade artificial glass fibre cloth wrapped round a metal mandril impregnated with plastic and baked in an oven. The method of manufacture lent itself to mass production and once the teething troubles were ironed out the resulting product was almost unbreakable, highly flexible and extremely light in weight. It was also possible to reproduce rods in large batches with identical 'actions'. By 1960 glass rods were a substantial threat to split cane. The growth of fly-fishing in reservoirs greatly increased the market for mass produced cheap light and powerful rods since reservoir fishing required powerful light single-handed rods capable of casting long distances all day without tiring the users. Significantly, almost all trout and salmon distance tournament casters adopted the new material because of its extreme lightness. Increases in wages made split cane rod manufacture increasingly costly. Glass fibre manufacture, on the other hand, cost progressively less as sales increased and the manufacturers benefitted by the resultant economics of scale.

Tubular glass rods, however, suffered from certain disadvantages. Although light and resilient they were inclined to cause a tiring vibration in prolonged use. Also, being tubular in construction they would not readily bend beyond a certain point without inwards 'collapse' of the whole tube. By the mid 1970s the long dominance of split cane was ended – fibre glass and split cane rods were equally popular.

During the last decade the introduction of a completely new material (carbon fibre) has had a dramatic effect on the development of fly rods. This new material was developed in space technology to combine extreme lightness with extreme strength. It reproduces almost all the qualities of hollow built split cane in terms of responsiveness and 'steely' action but with enormously reduced weight. For long rods (over 9½ft) there can be no doubt that carbon fibre is in course of completely replacing the traditional materials, as a visit to any tackle shop will show.

There will always remain a specialist market for cane fly rods of up to 8½ft individually designed and built for special application (especially for dry fly work on rivers). Whether any new materials will replace carbon fibre remains to be seen. The introduction of quantities if boron into the carbon material of carbon fly rods has produced rods with an action similar to that of cane. The methods of manufacture for all carbon fibre or boron rods is similar to that used for glass fibre rods i.e. the initial design and making of a steel mandril (tapered exactly to reproduce the desired configuration) and the subsequent wrapping of carbon fibre cloth round the mandril followed by impregnation of epoxy resin and baking. This technique makes 'one off' manufacture entirely uneconomic because the cost of the mandril cannot be recovered until several dozen rods have been produced on it. It seems certain therefore that the individually split cane fly rod will remain as a craft built alternative to the mass produced carbon fibre products. Where extremes of lightness and strength are required, however, carbon fibre would appear to be irreplaceable by any other material, however much the devotees of split cane may appreciate the undoubted individuality of their beautifully finished traditional products.

Rogan, Michael A famous Irish fly-dresser with many English admirers, Michael Rogan was born in Ballyshannon in 1834. He specialised in tying mixed-wing salmon flies with special dyes which he kept secret (one of the dyes was said to come from a donkey's urine) and won a gold medal and diploma at the London Fisheries Exhibition of 1883. The business has been carried on by his son and grandson, also Michael Rogan. All their flies are tied by hand without the use of a vice.

Rough Olive A trout fly which suggests the large dark olive, popular in Ireland and in many rivers in England and Wales:

Body: originally heron herl dyed a dark green-brown but wool is often used as a substitute

Wings: starling primary
Hackle: brown-green cock
Whisks: the same
Hook: 14–12

The fly is often tied for wet-fly fishing as well as dry.

Royal Family Many members of the Royal Family have been keen fly fishers, including Queen Elizabeth the Queen Mother and Prince Charles. George IV was also a keen fisherman. The best story about a Royal fisherman, was about George V, told by Sir George Aston in *Mostly About Trout* (George Allen and Unwin, 1921).

At the time of the Anglo-French 'entente cordiale' it was customary for journalists to write flattering articles about heads of state of the other country. These were 'vetted' by the respective diplomatic representatives before publication. Here is the literal translation of an article by a French journalist about King George V written as a compliment to that monarch during World War 1:

'He is an angler of the first force, the King of Britain. Behold him there as he sits motionless under his umbrella, patiently regarding his many-coloured floats. How obstinately he contends with the elements! It is a summer day in Britain, that is to say a day of sleet and fog and tempest. But, what would you? It is as they love it, those who follow the sport.

'Presently the King's float begins to descend. My God! But how he strikes! That hook is implanted in the very bowels of the salmon. The King rises. He spurns aside his footstool. He strides strongly and swiftly towards the rear. In good time the salmon comes to approach himself to the bank. Aha! The King has cast aside his rod. He hurls himself flat on the ground on his victim. They splash and struggle in the icy water. Name of a dog! But it is a 'braw laddie'!

'The ghillie, a kind of outdoor domestic, administers the coup de grace with his pistol. The King cries with a very shrill voice 'Hip, Hip. Hoorah!'. On these red-letter days His Majesty King George dines on a haggis and a whisky grog. Like a true Scotsman he wears only a kilt.'

Rusty Spinner A useful chalk stream dressing of the Sherry Spinner devised by G.E.M. Skues:

Body: chestnut-coloured seals fur
Rib: fine gold wire
Hackle: rusty dun cock
Whisks: three fibres of the same-coloured spade feather
Tying silk: orange
Hook: 14–16

Rutland Water The largest water storage reservoir in Europe and also the largest stocked public trout fishery, Rutland Water, 20 miles from Peterborough, was opened in May, 1977. It covers some 3,100 acres and was originally stocked with half a million trout in the ratio of two to one in favour of rainbow. Some 70,000 to 80,000 fish were stocked annually in the first few years. Bank anglers are able to drive round a perimeter road – about 24 miles – and there is a sailing centre, club, café, fishing lodge, nature reserve, and parking for 3,000 cars.

Rutland Water is twice the size of any other trout-stocked reservoir in England and the water area is roughly the same as Lake Windermere. Planning for a viable trout fishery was begun in 1972 by Roland Field, divisional scientist, Welland and Nene area, Anglian Water Authority, and Peter Tombleson, chairman of the region's fishery committee. The hatchery attached to the reservoir has the capacity to produce 3m trout fry a year. The reservoir has 50 power boats for anglers and 17 miles of its shores are available for bank fishing.

The reservoir was originally intended to be called Empingham but residents of the former small county of Rutland – part of which the reservoir covers – started a resistence movement with banners, T-shirts, and a great deal of local publicity, asking for the water to be named Rutland to commemorate the county of Rutland, which had been merged in local government reorganisation. The Anglian Water Authority wisely bowed to public opinion.

All this area of England, the Midlands too, are well-served with reservoir trout fishing. Fishery officers and committees are rightly proud of the quality they provide. There is Ladybower, 500 acres, near Sheffield; Draycote, 600 acres, near Rugby; Eyebrook, 400 acres, near Uppingham; Pitsford and Ravensthorpe, two smaller reservoirs close together between Northampton and Coventry; Tittesworth, near Leek; and of course the 1,600 acres of Grafham just off the A1 near Huntingdon. For smaller waters there are the private fisheries, the best known Packington, near Meriden.

Colour

For the choice of a salmon fly . . . the old rule is: bright day, bright fly; dull day, dull fly. This is sound doctrine. I always used to think it should be the other way round; for it seemed to me that a bright fly would show up better on a dull day, whereas on a bright day a dull fly would be good enough. The fact is that a brightly-coloured fly is out of place on a dull day. A salmon presumably thinks that the fly is something alive and the live things of the stream do not flash or glitter on dull days. Conversely, on a bright day, when everything below water is a mass of moving beams and shadows, a dull black-looking object would be quite out of place.

Antony Bridges, *Modern Salmon Fishing*, Black, 1939

In bright weather some fishermen prefer to use a bright fly. Experience has taught me that, with a greased line, that is a mistake. You may, of course, catch fish with a bright fly, but I am certain you will catch more with a sombre one. In fact, the brighter and more glaring the day, the duller and darker should be the fly.

G.P.R. Balfour-Kinner, *Catching Salmon and Sea Trout*, Nelson, 1958

I could easily give a list of flies likely to take salmon . . . but of what use would it be when we don't see two on the same river use the same kind of flies?

Andrew Young, *Angler's Guide to the Rivers and Lochs of the North of Scotland*, 1857

Safety Fly fishing can be dangerous, particularly when wading fast rivers (*see* p 219). There can be other hazards:

An American ambassador, Lewis Douglas, was blinded in one eye while salmon fishing. The short rod he was using was not able to give sufficient velocity to a large single-hook fly he had just put on to replace a smaller one. The fly lagged because of the extra weight and swerved in flight.

If a fly is snagged and you have to pull hard to break, turn your face well away. In 1981, several anglers suffered severe facial injuries, one was blinded by pulling on flies or spinners.

Two fly fishermen were electrocuted in the early days of carbon fibre (graphite) rods by casting too near power lines. Carbon fibre is an excellent conductor of electricity.

When casting a fly in high winds make sure that the fly is travelling on the sheltered side of the body. If on the other side wind pressure can blow the fly into neck or face.

If line speed is lost during a cast, do not try to recover it in mid-air. Let the line drop and start again.

Night fishing can be hazardous. Carry a torch and reconnoitre the banks and the pools beforehand in daylight. Preferably go night fishing with a companion. If fishing alone, let someone know where you are.

Salmon

The number of salmon caught in Iceland's streams and rivers has doubled in just over a decade. The ever-increasing stock of this fine game fish is attributed to three main factors: an extensive breeding programme, a fishing ban in coastal waters, and inland waters that are pollution free. (The official publication, *News From Iceland*, July, 1983, quoted by Sir Andrew Gilchrist in a letter to *The Times*)

The salmon is an anadromous fish – an adjective taken from the Greek which means that it is a fish which runs up rivers to spawn. The name of the Greek goddess, Aphrodite, comes from a similar word that meant emerging from the sea.

From the time that the young salmon hatch from their gravel cots, or redds, in the spawning grounds of the rivers where their parents mated some 14 weeks earlier, the tiny fingerlings (alevins) are in constant danger. When they shed their yolk sacs they are known as parr, and look more or less like small wild brown trout.

A parr can be distinguished from a trout by several markings. The easiest to remember is that if the adipose fin (on the back, nearest the tail) is coloured red or orange it is a trout, if colourless it is a parr.

After one to three years in the river, depending on conditions, the parr puts on a silvery colour when it is known as a smolt. It is preparing to cross the salt barrier of the estuary. This takes time, a year, perhaps two. Only one in ten of the fish which hatched are likely to have survived by the time they reach the sea. Only about four or five in a hundred of these survivors will return.

After spending anything from a year to several years in their deep sea feeding grounds the salmon and the grilse – the young salmon – feel the urge to make the long journey of several thousand sea miles to return to the rivers of their birth.

How do they find their way home? It is a problem that puzzles scientists as well as fishermen. It was once thought they followed ocean currents. It is almost certainly more complex:

While the full answer is not yet clear, a number of mechanisms are known to guide salmon at sea. These include guidance by the stars as well as the use of receptors [a receptor is an organ adapted to receive certain stimuli] which are attuned to the weak electrical impulses of the earth's magnetic field. Ocean currents may also play an important role. Near the coast and in the rivers, salmon are guided by a chemical memory which apparently allows them to identify and home to as yet unidentified substances in the water. (The *Atlantic Salmon Facts*, a booklet published in 1983 by The Atlantic Salmon Trust, Moulin, Perthshire, based on a research booklet issued by the International Atlantic Salmon Foundation in Canada)

Grilse are young (one-sea-winter) salmon that have spent anything from a few months to a year or 18 months at sea. Fishermen are inclined to call any salmon under about 10lb a grilse. The origin of the word grilse is unknown. Old prints spell it grisle, which means grey (Middle English) which might suggest that it was a description originally taken from the colour of the young fish compared with the bright silver of a 'springer', a mature salmon.

When they return to the rivers, salmon do not need to feed. Their journey up river to the redds may last several months. After spawning, many die; some start their journey downstream, weak, emaciated, with protruding vents and ragged fins. These fish, now known as kelts, may be fortunate and mend, put on a silver coat again and find the sanctuary of the sea. Many do not.

Salmon: Conservation Rod and line fishermen have been concerned about the salmon resource for more than 150 years. As long ago as 1828 Sir Humphrey Davy was complaining about the deterioration of the catches on Tay and Tweed:

The net fishing which is constantly going on, except on Sundays and in close time, suffers very few fish to escape; and a Sunday's flood offers the sole chance of a good day's sport, and this only in particular parts of these rivers. (Sir Humphrey Davy, *Salmonia*, John Murray, 1828)

Salmon in those days were looked upon as God's gift to man, an illimitable resource. Netsmen were active in the estuaries, and in weir pools for miles upstream. Millions of fish were taken, nor did the smolts escape on their journey down river:

The millers take them in traps by the thousand and dispose of them by the gallon to neighbours; indeed at times they are taken in such vast quantities that pigs are regaled upon their delicate flesh. (G.W. Saltau, Little Efford, Devon, in 1847, quoted in *West Country Fly Fishing*, edited by Anne Voss Bark, 1983)

A hundred years later the deep sea feeding grounds of the salmon were discovered off the coast of Greenland; and Greenland trawlermen were not slow in exploiting this new discovery. A few years later Faroese long-liners found the salmon migration routes not far from their coasts.

The Americans made the first moves to limit the killing. Britain and Europe followed. By the 1960s catch quotas had been agreed with both the

Greenlanders and the Faroese. At the same time there was an increase in illegal netting on the high seas by boats using new nylon monofilament nets.

It was not until the mid-1970s that the fishery scientists of Western governments were able to give a factual warning that the world stocks of salmon were diminishing. The private fishery organisations kept up the pressure for a salmon conservation policy to be brought in. The decline in the spring runs of Scottish salmon from 1980 onwards prompted an estimate in *The Times* (24 August, 1982) that the runs were about 20 to 30 per cent down compared with the 1950s.

A gloomier picture was reported a year later, based on studies by scientists belonging to a subsidiary body of the United Nations Food and Agriculture Organisation. They estimated that the world catch of salmon in 1982 showed a decline of 41 per cent in 15 years.

By 1982 the warnings had made an impact. Catch restrictions, of various kinds, had been brought into force in Canada, Iceland, Scotland and France. In 1983 restrictions on coastal netting were proposed by the Norwegians. They also warned of the damage to salmon rivers in south-west Norway caused by acid rain.

In London, the Salmon and Trout Association and the Atlantic Salmon Trust sent a joint letter (13 July, 1981) to the British government asking for the adoption of a national salmon policy. They recommended:

A complete ban on all drift netting throughout the United Kingdom and the phasing out of existing drift netting licences (in Scotland drift netting had already been banned).
A complete ban on the use of monofilament nets for the taking of salmon.
Sales control of salmon throughout the United Kingdom, either by a system of licensed dealers or by tagging, or both.
Compulsory rod licences and annual catch returns for all salmon fishermen throughout the United Kingdom (bringing Scotland into line with England and Wales).

There was little response. Additional pressure came from the National Water Council who urged a system of tagging based on Canadian practice. The Atlantic Salmon Trust urged in October, 1983, that there should be strictly controlled salmon fishing, by net and rod, on a river-by-river basis, as they believed that only in this way could it be certain that each river had 'an annual escapement of the optimum breeding stock' – in other words neither too few nor too many fish on the spawning grounds.

Three years intensive lobbying in Whitehall and Westminster for a national salmon policy had, by mid-1984, produced no result. Progress came from an international initiative.

As a result of conservation pressure from American and British organisations, notably the Atlantic Salmon Trust, a North Atlantic Salmon Convention was ratified in 1983 by the United States, Canada, Iceland, Denmark for the Faroes, and the E.E.C. for its member states, which include Britain, Ireland, France and Denmark. Norway and Sweden have yet (1984) to ratify.

On 18 July, 1984, the West Greenland commission of NASCO, meeting in

Edinburgh, recommended to member governments that the West Greenland catch should be reduced in 1984 from 1190 tons to 870 tons. Recommendations come into force if there are no objections within 30 days.

On 18 July, 1984, on the recommendation of NASCO, the Greenland catch was reduced from 1190 tons to 870 tons.

The Salmon Bill was introduced by the Government in the House of Lords in January 1986. The Bill would create a new offence in Scotland, England and Wales of possessing salmon, believing or having reasonable grounds for believing the salmon to have been illegally taken. After debate, the Government agreed to bring in dealer licensing in England and Wales as well as Scotland. The Bill also proposed reforms in the Scottish District Fishery Boards. It was also announced that further restrictions were to be placed on the Northumbrian netsmen. The Government did not accept the concept of a national salmon conservation policy.

Salmon: World Catches The following chart was published by an American conservation and research organisation – the Restoration of Atlantic Salmon in America – from its headquarters in Hancock, New Hampshire, in October, 1983. The chart was prepared from figures supplied by the International Council for Exploration of the Seas, a scientific body which is part of the Food and Agriculture Organisation (FAO) of the United Nations. The figures show the catches of salmon in home waters from 1967 to 1982, excluding the catches of the West Greenland, Faroese and Norwegian sea fisheries. The figures cover commercial and sport fishing of salmon, including grilse.

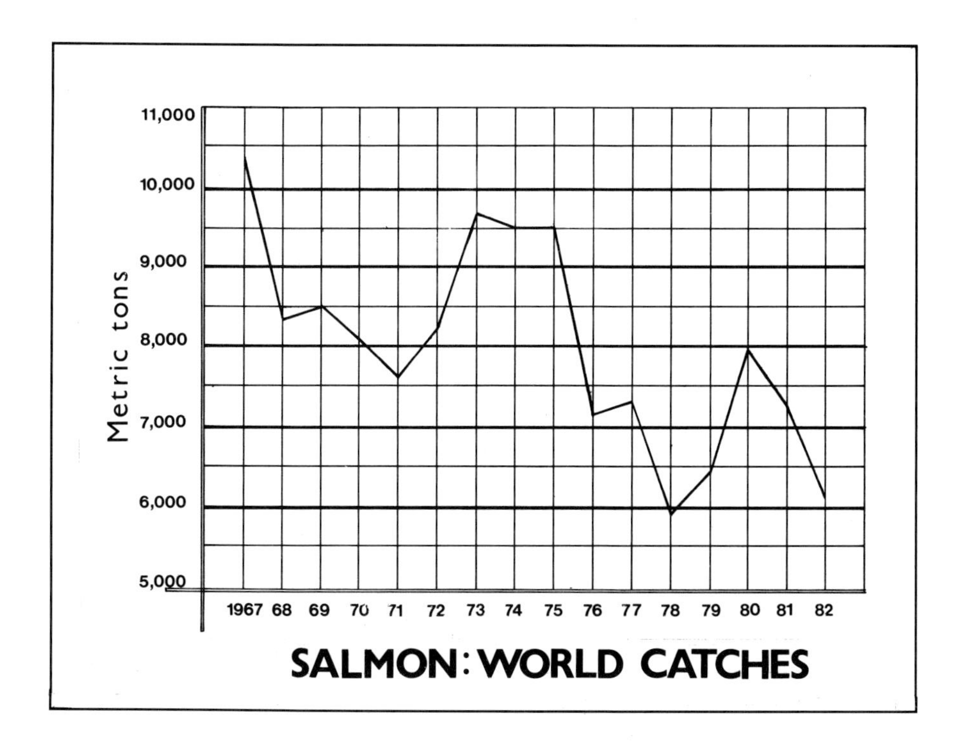

The 1982 figures are provisional. Figures were not available from the USSR for 1976–8, nor from Iceland for 1982.

The legal catches of the West Greenland, Faroese, and Norwegian sea fisheries, for the three years 1980–2, were as follows (figures in metric tons):

1980	West Greenland	1194	Faroese	718	Norwegian Sea	155
1981	West Greenland	1264	Faroese	1027	Norwegian Sea	213
1982	West Greenland	1077	Faroese	939	Norwegian Sea	334

The main point to make about all these figures, as in the chart as well, is that they are incomplete. They take no account of the catch of salmon as a 'by-catch' of other species, or of illegal netting, or of poaching in rivers. Estimates of all these additional illegal catches may well be between 50 to 100 per cent of the legal harvest.

Salmon Farming *Atlantic Salmon Facts*, published by the Atlantic Salmon Trust, shows the progress of salmon farming. The figures, supplied by the Fishmongers' Company, record the number of 'packages' of cage-reared salmon delivered to Billingsgate Market:

	Producing Country	
Year	Scotland	Norway
1975	140	128
1976	56	162
1977	46	53
1978	332	66
1979	1106	4870
1980	2122	1612
1981	3843	5809

The Scottish Salmon Grower's Association says that production of farm salmon in Scotland in 1985 was of the order of 6,000 tons.

Salmon: Pacific In addition to the growth of cage-reared Atlantic salmon, fishery scientists at Lowestoft, a government laboratory, have been examining the possibility of adding another type of salmon to British waters for commercial development. A working group was set up by the Department of Agriculture and Fisheries in 1982 to make further studies and report on the possibilities of importing Pacific salmon.

Salmon Fishing

If a woman wade through the one fresh river in Lewis there shall be no salmon seen there for a twelvemonth after. (Hollinshed's *Scottish Chronicle*, 1577)

Hollinshed was wrong. But only partly. Salmon can pick up the taste or smell of their home river many miles out to sea. In the river itself a man knocking his pipe out or throwing a cigarette end into the streamy water above a pool can be certain that the salmon in the pool will be aware of it. Whether the smell of rubber coming from wading above their lies or the taste of tobacco in the water will put a salmon off the take is impossible to say. There have been fairly well-authenticated stories of salmon reacting strongly to a sudden pollution even though it has been an exceptionally faint one.

Fly fishing for salmon is first recorded in the *Treatyse of Fysshynge* (1496), without any details. In 1651 Thomas Barker gave an inadequate description of a salmon fly which had 'six wings or four at least'. This is not of much help. Nor is the Scottish ghillie's story that the first salmon fly was a long red feather which was tied to the hook when they were unable to dig worms from the frozen byre. The Roman historian, Aelian, talks of fishing a plume on a hook. The Romans used feathers to troll for sea fish, as we do now for mackerel, and it is likely that they brought this technique to their colonies, including Britain.

The recorded history of the salmon fly can be said to begin with early guide books to Scottish lochs and rivers around the 1820s and 1830s. When Andrew Young published his *Angler's Guide* in Edinburgh in 1857 the salmon fly was already a fairly sophisticated creation.

Ever since the first railway services had been opened in the 1830s the North Eastern and the Caledonian railway companies had been pushing to the north, to Edinburgh, Perth, Forfar and finally Inverness. The speed of those early trains was not very great – an average of 30 to 40 miles an hour – but they opened up a country rich in fish and game to the outside world.

The owners of the large estates with hundreds of thousands of acres for shooting and many miles of rivers for the fishing were not slow to take advantage of adventurous young men who were coming north in increasing numbers with their rods and guns. Salmon fishing became fashionable, and like most fashionable occupations developed a mystique: the elaborate multi-coloured salmon fly.

It was called a fly; but no fly like it ever swam in air or flew through water. Its tag, which had glinted, was of silver from Nevada and silk of a moth from Formosa; its tail, from the feather of an Indian crow; its butt, black herl of an African ostrich; its body, yellow floss silk veiled with orange breast feathers of the South American toucan, and black Macclesfield silk ribbed with silver tinsel. This fly was given the additional attraction of wings for water-flight, made of strips of feathers from many birds: turkey from Canada, peahen and peacock from Japan, swan from Ireland, bustard from Arabia, golden pheasant from China, teal and wild duck and mallard from the Hebrides. Its throat was made of the neck feathers of an English speckled hen, its side of Bengal jungle cock's neck feathers, its cheeks came from a French kingfisher, its horns from the tail of an Amazonian macaw. Wax, varnish and enamel secured the 'marriage' of the feathers. It was one of hundreds of charms, or materialised riverside incantations, made by men to persuade sleepy or depressed salmon to rise and take. Invented after a bout of seasickness by a Celt as he sailed the German ocean between England and Norway, for nearly a hundred years this fly had borne his name, Jock Scott. (Henry Williamson, *Salar the Salmon*, Faber edn., 1972)

By the end of the nineteenth century, the feather-winged salmon fly had become a cult. The high priest was George M. Kelson. In his book, *The Salmon Fly*, privately printed in 1895, Kelson put forward a system under which the choice of fly was made on 'well-ascertained principles'. Judged by such influences, amongst others, as the bed of the river, the flow of water, sunlight or the lack of it, Kelson urged that the angler could decide on the proper pattern for each particular occasion:

Supposing the bed of the river to be of a slaty nature and the day dull, dark blue, dark claret, or even dark orange with seals' fur at the throat will form the best body materials. And where the fish will stand it, a few or more strands of peacock herl should be added to any built wing. Spey fish object to herl; Usk fish adore it . . .

Kelson's book was illustrated with coloured drawings of some 60 salmon flies. Only about four or five of them are now in use, the best known being the Thunder and Lightning. He also gave the dressings of 300 flies, all feather-wing traditional patterns, all founded on 'well-ascertained principles', though in putting them forward to his readers he admitted that 'I may seem now and then over-didactic'.

Kelson's flies, from the Ackroyd to the Yellow Parson, the Fairy King to the Bronze Pirate, were charming and colourful. But the belief that they could be fitted into 'a system of salmon fishing with indestructible principles' did not survive.

The flies which took over – the hairwing double and trebles and the tube with a detachable treble – have considerable advantages.

Presentation – wet fly downstream – remains the same, with regional variations.

Salmon: Dry Fly Mainly an American technique, the dry fly has made little progress on British waters, though a few fish have been taken on the Dee and the Naver in recent years. Antony Bridges described the method in *Modern Salmon Fishing* (Black, 1939) and in America E.R. Hewitt in *Secrete of the Salmon* (Scribners, New York 1922) claimed to be the pioneer. There were reports of salmon being taken on a dry hackled mayfly on the Tyne in 1896 and on a dry fly (not named) on the Test by Major R.G. Fraser in 1906. Hugh Falkus gives further information in *Salmon Fishing* (Witherby, 1984).

Salmon in Norway and Iceland Beats on the Norwegian rivers are generally booked for a week by two or three fishermen and their wives with accommodation in Scottish-type lodges. Strutt and Parker, the London agents, handle a number of lettings. The minimum charge (1985) for a fisherman for a week, covering fishing, food and accommodation is about £900; for a non-fishing guest, food and accommodation is about £300. On top of the charges for fishing, food and accommodation, a ghillie and boat for a week will probably come to something like £200 to £250 extra. Charges in Iceland are considerably more.

Salmon: Put and Take Fishing Suitable freshwater lochs and lakes can be stocked with cage reared grilse as put-and-take fisheries. The first of these was at Cardney Loch in Perthshire in 1980. In 1984 another was opened at Upton Bishop near Ross-on-Wye, Herefordshire. The grilse are transported in sea-water filled tanks, oxygen aerated, and placed into freshwater without harm. The price for a day rod at Upton Bishop (1984) was £23 with a bag limit of two fish. The fish weigh between 4lb to 10lb. **Sources include:** Publications of the Atlantic Salmon Trust; The Restoration of Atlantic Salmon in America Organisation; The Salmon and Trout Association; *The Atlantic Salmon*, A.

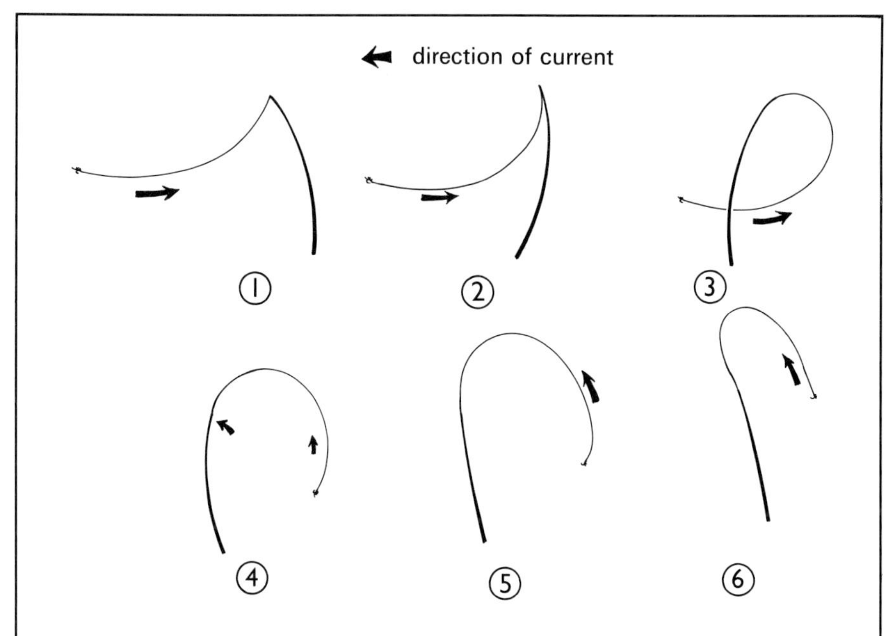

The Spey Cast. When the fly is dangling downstream of the angler, he faces it, one foot pointing towards the fly, the other in the direction across the river where he intends the fly to go. Then these movemens are made: *1.* The rod begins to move the fly upstream. *2.* The fly accelerates and . . . *3.* . . . passes in front of the angler. *4.* A forward stroke is made by the rod. *5.* The fly changes direction and . . . *6.* . . . follows the line as the power stroke ends

Netboy, Faber and Faber 1968; *Salar The Salmon*, H. Williamson, Faber and Faber, 1936; *Salmon Fishing*, Hugh Falkus, Witherby, 1984, *A Line on Salmon*, John Ashley-Cooper, Witherby, 1983; and various books and pamphlets in The Flyfishers' Club library.

Salmon: Spey Casting Salmon fishermen have a special cast with a double-handed rod which is particularly useful, often essential, when there is a high bank or a growth of trees behind the fisherman which prevent the orthodox overhead cast.

Partly switch, partly roll, when the Spey is well done the swirling rhythm of the moving line around the head of the fisherman is beautiful to watch; when it is badly done it is dangerous.

Salmon: Line Control Salmon fishermen often allow the loose line they gather during the retrieve to fall at their feet, either when they are wading or bank fishing. If they are wading, the line will lose speed on the forward cast through water friction, if on the bank the loose line can snag on sticks and grass and bracken and the forward cast is restricted.

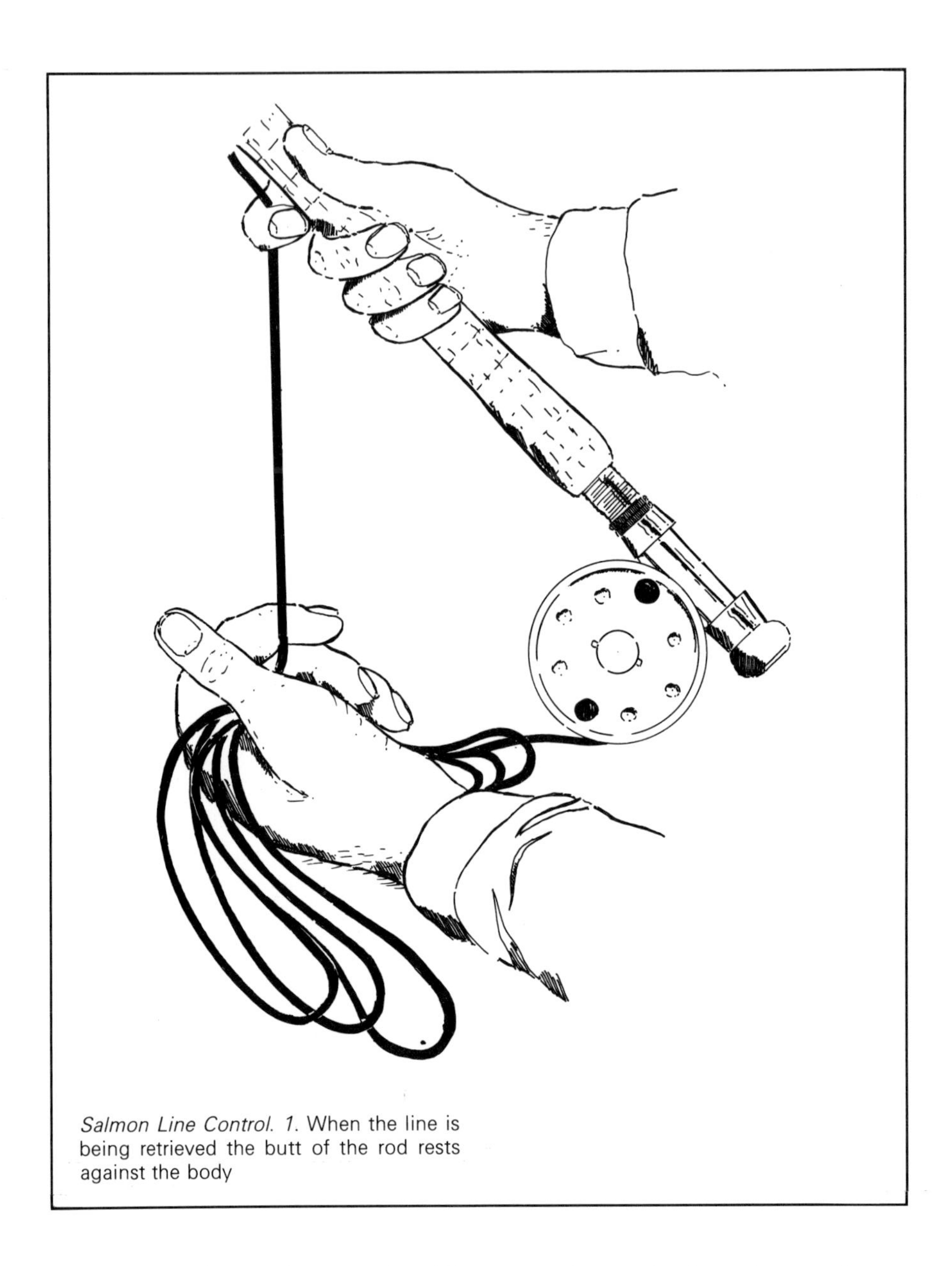

Salmon Line Control. 1. When the line is being retrieved the butt of the rod rests against the body

Salmon and Trout Association The national organisation of game fishermen, the S.A.T.A. has headquarters in Fishmongers' Hall, London, and branches throughout the country. The former Director, T.D. Thompson, summarised its work and history:

Founded in 1903 by a group of riparian owners, the association currently (1984) has some 8,000 direct members of various categories throughout the United Kingdom and beyond. Many of these, however, represent game fishing clubs, associations and federations so that the Salmon and Trout Association is supported by many more than 8,000 anglers and its work is of direct or indirect benefit to anyone who fishes for salmon and trout in the United Kingdom. Its objectives are:

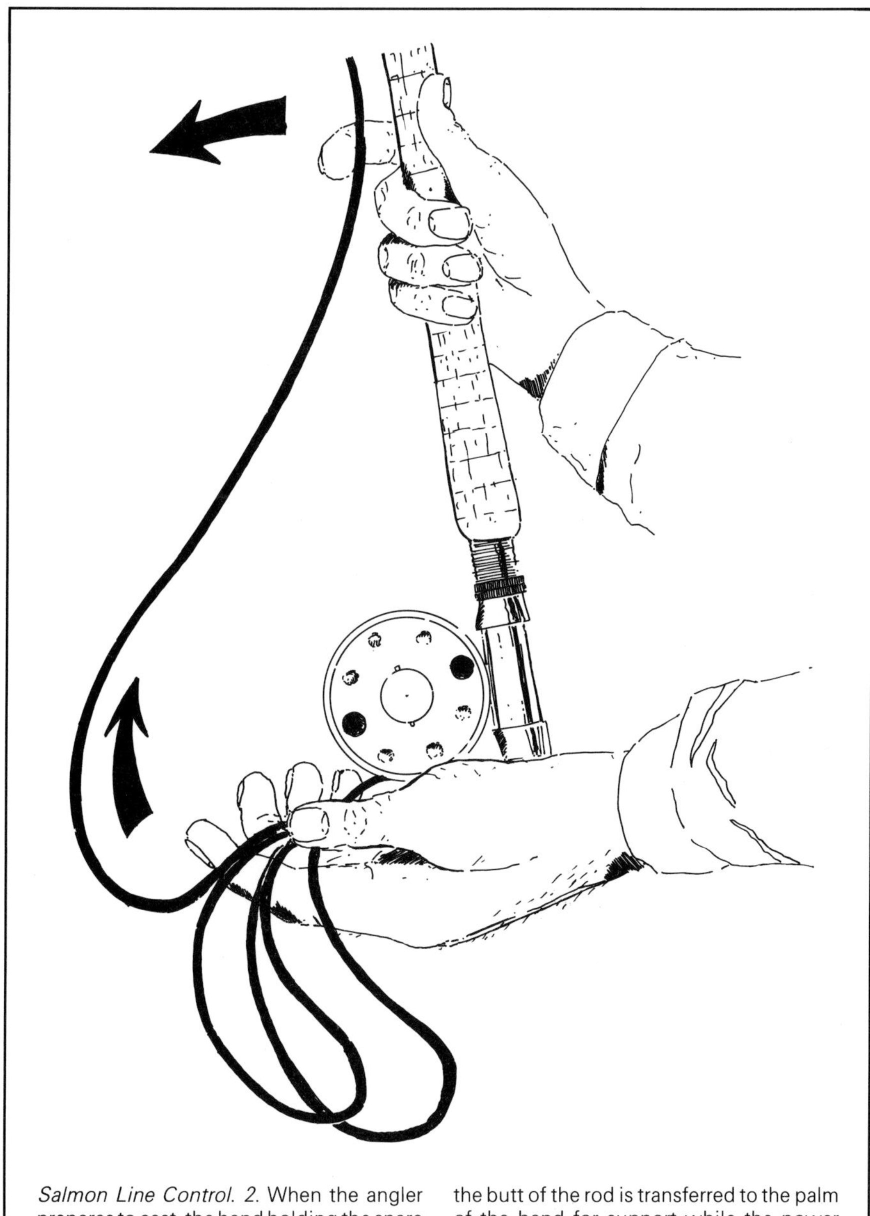

Salmon Line Control. 2. When the angler prepares to cast, the hand holding the spare line opens to allow the line to be shot and the butt of the rod is transferred to the palm of the hand for support while the power stroke is made

To safeguard and improve the salmon and trout and other salmonid stocks and fisheries of the United Kingdom and their environment and to ensure the maintenance of adequate supplies of clean water for these fisheries.

To protect and further the interests of all who fish for salmon and trout within the United Kingdom with rod and line by fair and legal methods.

As a founder member of the National Anglers' Council, and otherwise, to conduct and encourage any lawful activities in furtherance of these objects, including the promotion of or opposition to legislation, sponsorship or research and development, dissemination of information and the provision of education and advice.

The Association has some 60 branches throughout the country and its headquarters is situated within Fishmongers' Hall, the home of the ancient Fishmongers Company on London Bridge. Its affairs and activities are controlled by a full-time director responsible to a council elected from various game-fishery interests including the Association's regional organisations. There are three standing committees charged with responsibility for policy on Migratory Fish, Stillwaters and Conservation and, out of these, two action groups have been formed to deal with matters affecting national water resources and privately-owned stillwater game fisheries.

A part-time field secretary is responsible for liaison with the branches and represents the Association at the more important game fairs and shows throughout the country; a part-time editor produces the Association's excellent twice-yearly magazine and scientific advice is provided by highly qualified experts in fish and freshwater biology, hydrography and water engineering and the law. All of these very valuable expert advisers give their services free to the association.

The Association's main activities are conducted on three fronts:

a) In Parliament, where our supporters among both the main political parties and in both Houses raise questions, support us in discussions with ministers and help us to initiate or oppose legislation which will affect game fisheries.

b) In Whitehall, where we have contacts with and are recognised by the Ministries of Agriculture, Food and Fisheries; Sport and the Environment as well as the Scottish Office.

c) In the water authorities, where the Association has members on many of the fisheries, recreation and resources bodies.

The Salmon and Trout Magazine The official journal of the Salmon and Trout Association, contains authoritative articles on the Association's work, on fishery science, and on all matters connected with trout and salmon. The headquarters of the Association and the journal are at Fishmongers' Hall, London, EC4.

Sandison, Bruce In *Trout Lochs of Scotland* (Allen and Unwin, 1983) Sandison records the fishing at some 700 of the best trout lochs from the Borders right through to the Highlands and the Hebrides. He gives a most detailed assessment, the size and type of trout, the best flies to use, where, when and how to fish them, and the places to obtain permits. There are useful maps and a tourist guide.

Samuel, William William Samuel's book, *The Arte of Angling* (1577), is said to be the model on which Izaak Walton based his *Compleat Angler*. The main characters are Piscator and Viator, one the tutor, the other the pupil, as in Walton. The main difference, however, is that Samuel gave Piscator a nagging wife – 'Good Lord, Husband, where have you been all this day!' – and lacks the charm of Walton. Not many people have seen *The Arte of Angling* which was bought at a London auction by the late Otto Keinbusch and is now in the rare books and special collections department of Princeton University Library in the United States. This was believed to be the only known copy that has survived. Not much is known about Samuel except that he fished the Ouse and was vicar of St Mary's, Godmanchester. **Source:** article in the *American Fly Fisher* magazine (Fall, 1983 by Dr Anne Imbrie, Assistant Professor of English at Vassar College, New York.

Sawyer, Frank (1907–1980) The modern method of nymph fishing is largely due to the work of Frank Sawyer. His Pheasant Tail Nymph is now fished world-wide in more than 60 countries. Sawyer was born at Bulford, Wiltshire. The River Avon, close to his home, occupied all his working life and most of his spare time for more than 60 years. He became keeper on the Officers' Fly Fishing Association water in 1928 – later the Services' Fly Fishing Association water – which was then dry fly only.

By sheer persistence, skill, and an almost unique knowledge of trout and insect life, acquired by long observation of the river, Sawyer began to spread the doctrine of fishing a weighted nymph to subaqueously-feeding trout. Originally he used the weighted nymph to remove unwanted grayling from the water and achieved remarkable results. His phenomenal underwater vision helped him to see a trout take a tiny nymph many feet below the surface.

Encouraged by Sir Grimwood Mears and by G.E.M. Skues, he wrote articles on his method and in 1958 his book, *Nymphs and the Trout*, brought him world acclaim. He had also published, in 1953, the charming *Keeper of the Stream*. Anglers in many countries honoured him. He received the Fario Club medal in France, given by Charles Ritz, and at the Game Fair at Bowood in 1979 the Prince of Wales presented him with long-service award of the Country Landowners' Association. He had been made M.B.E. in the Prime Minister's Honours List the previous year.

An assessment of his influence on nymph fishing is on page 142.

Major John Walker, for many years chairman of the Wiltshire Fishery Association, gives this personal picture of Frank Sawyer as he knew him:

A placid and contented life, one would think – contented certainly in fulfilling what he liked doing best, but in some of his keepering theories he was inclined towards extremes. For a period he reared rainbow trout for the Services water, then suddenly, as it were overnight, he took against them and they were reared no more; he actively disliked them and considered them a greater detriment to his river than pike or flannel weed. In his report of the season's fishing, one might find his prediction of the future so gloomy, with a forecast of ten years for the river to recover, that it was sometimes slightly surprising to read that the following season was a record one. If it was, it was his keepering skill that had helped to make it so, and he had no lack of that.

He was a great observer of everything that happened on the river, not only of what the trout were doing but fly-life, weed, water currents and particularly the state of the river bed itself; this led him to form scientific theories to fit the facts of what he saw. He had an idea that rivers needed chalk and if they became mudded or in poor condition it was through lack of it; consequently, at any unsightly part, he would dump a ton or so of powdered chalk to be incorporated in the river flow. Very often that procedure

Frank Sawyer – photo courtesy Dan Callaghan

worked, the action of the flow of chalk eroding the bank of mud; the idea caught on and as the then chairman of the Wiltshire Fishery Association, I was asked if there was any scientific reason for this, which naturally neither the committee nor I were qualified to answer. The ball, in the shape of a well-prepared paper by Sir John Paskin, was thrown to the Freshwater Biological Association with an invitation to give their opinion on it; in due course it returned, after great trouble had been taken over it by Mr. Le Cren, as another paper, the gist of which was that he could find no scientific reason to support the theory and in fact about 22 tons of dissolved chalk passed through Netheravon every day and 78 tons down the Wylye at Wilton. It was not easy to pass on this information to Frank Sawyer without hurting his feelings.

If this side of him was a weakness in his mental make-up, it was certainly a very minor one and so far from detracting from his character, somehow made it more endearing. His devotion to the river, his management of it, patience in coaching fishermen, young and old, and his skill in describing it, will ensure that his name long lives on. When his time for passing came, this gentle giant of the Avon, was found lying in the sun on the bank of his favourite beat near Netheravon church.

Frank Sawyer, Man of the Riverside (George Allen and Unwin, 1984) by Sidney Vines contains much of Sawyer's unpublished writings and notes of his observations of trout and insect behaviour.

Scrope, William *Days and Nights of Salmon Fishing on The Tweed*, by William Scrope, was first published in 1843 and contains many good fishing stories. The last reprint was in 1921. Quaintly written, a little discursive, but full of interest.

'Scott, Jock' Probably the best book on salmon fishing for beginners ever written is 'Jock Scott's' *The Art of Salmon Fishing* (Witherby, 1933) but unfortunately all his advice about lines and rods is so outdated now that large parts of it are of little interest, but when he comes to tactics, and how a fly should be presented, 'Jock Scott' is unbeatable. His description of A.H.E. Wood's method of fishing the floating line – the greased line cult, he calls it – was approved by Wood himself.

Sea Trout

In Scottish law, sea trout are salmon; in English law they are distinct. Scientifically they belong to the single species of trout found in Europe. Ecologically they show a broad pattern of behaviour spanning the clear-cut distinction between the sea-going salmon and the riverine brown trout. (Gilbert Hartley, former Inspector of Salmon and Freshwater Fisheries, in an article in *Salmon and Sea Trout Fishing*, edited by Alan Wrangles, Davis Poynter, 1979)

Not a great deal is known of the life of a sea trout. The young spend two or three years in the river of their birth before going down to the estuary. Some remain there and come back within a few months. If they retain a habit of estuary feeding they are often called slob trout. Their sea-going is almost as uncertain as their return for spawning. Hartley records that some sea trout from South Devon have been found in the Tweed. On the other hand, sea trout in the Fowey in Cornwall have been found to stray very little from the river of their birth.

Although scientifically they are a brown trout (*Salmo trutta*) the silvery fish that ascend our rivers are so like salmon in appearance and so unlike brown trout that many anglers think of them as a different fish. It is not known whether sea trout breed true or whether some offspring can remain in the rivers and give up migratory habits forced on them by their environment. There is some evidence that male sea trout can at times remain in a river and become sexually mature and indistinguishable from brown trout in appearance.

Identification Even experienced anglers make mistakes. In one embarrassing case, only laboratory tests proved that one of the fish hailed as a Thames salmon in 1983 was a large estuarine trout. The problem is complicated by variations in the appearance of salmon and by occasional cases of hybrids. The simplest tests are shown on page 192.

Feeding Sea trout do feed in fresh water, especially in their first few days in a river or loch, but the habit of feeding diminishes fairly quickly, probably less quickly in a freshwater loch than in a river, but this is not proven. Like salmon, they do not need to feed on their spawning run. The situation is well put in Falkus and Buller's *Freshwater Fishing* (Macdonald and Jane's, 1975):

> . . . there is a very great difference between the taking of occasional food items and feeding. If feeding is defined as the taking of nourishment in order to sustain life, then the sea trout, like the salmon, is a non-feeder in fresh water.

Sea Trout: River Fishing

Over a period the fly will catch more fish than any other method. (Hugh Falkus, *Sea Trout Fishing*, Witherby, 1971)

Night fishing is the best way of taking sea trout and the deadliest method is with the fly. (Roy Buckingham, in an article in *West Country Fly Fishing*, edited by Anne Voss Bark, Batsford, 1983)

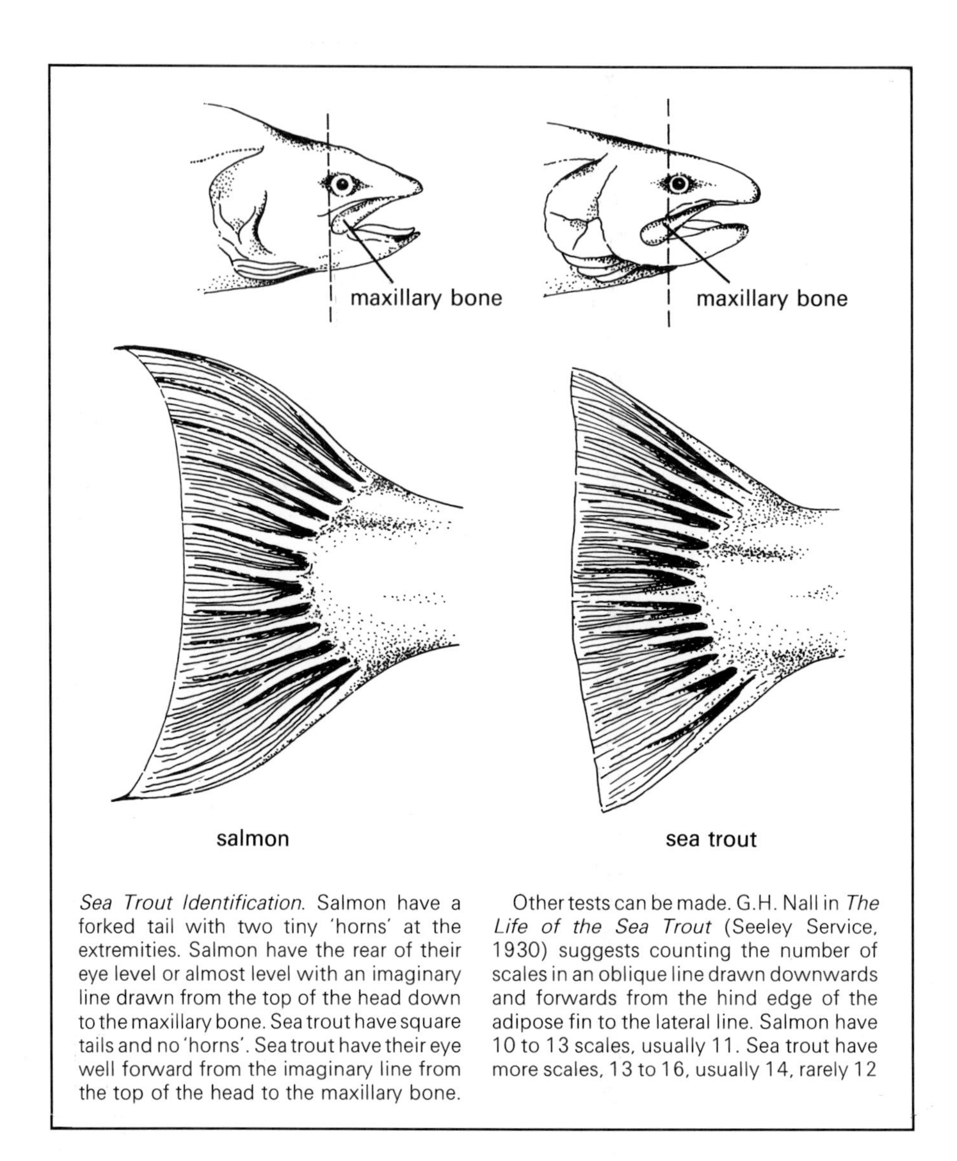

Sea Trout Identification. Salmon have a forked tail with two tiny 'horns' at the extremities. Salmon have the rear of their eye level or almost level with an imaginary line drawn from the top of the head down to the maxillary bone. Sea trout have square tails and no 'horns'. Sea trout have their eye well forward from the imaginary line from the top of the head to the maxillary bone.

Other tests can be made. G.H. Nall in *The Life of the Sea Trout* (Seeley Service, 1930) suggests counting the number of scales in an oblique line drawn downwards and forwards from the hind edge of the adipose fin to the lateral line. Salmon have 10 to 13 scales, usually 11. Sea trout have more scales, 13 to 16, usually 14, rarely 12

Night fishing is generally the best time to take sea trout in rivers but many sea trout are caught during the day on big rivers like the Tweed and on big Scottish lochs. Kingsmill Moore recalls that in Ireland the rivers in Connemara are generally fished during the day while the Slaney is fished at night. In sea pools in the west of Scotland sea trout will rise readily to a fly during the day. In general, however, night fishing, especially on the smaller rivers, is most productive.

Flies and fishing methods vary. In some rivers long thin lures are effective, in others less so. On the Torridge, in North Devon, some of the most effective flies are small ones, about size 12, while only a few miles away on the Tamar no one fishes anything smaller than a 10 and mostly big bushy flies on 8, 6 and 4 low water salmon hooks. On the Spey and Tweed many sea trout are taken by salmon fishermen on large salmon flies, singles, doubles and tubes, during the day. On the Conway and Dovey big tandem lures, demons and terrors, will take sea trout at night but alarm them in daytime.

The best kind of fly and the best ways of fishing are subject to argument. In *Sea Trout Fishing* (Witherby, 1971) Hugh Falkus sought a compromise, a formula for success, involving a frequent change of the various methods: floating lines, sunk lines, small lures, long ones, surface flies fished with a drag, fly-maggot, and bait fishing. The important thing was to have confidence:

There is great truth in the saying that the best fly to use is the one you believe in.

Many modern reservoir lures – the Muddler Minnow, Ace of Spades, Whisky Fly, Black Lure, to mention a few – are also effective sea trout flies. The traditional Scottish sea trout flies, such as Peter Ross, are widely used in sizes from 10 to 8.

Practically all sea trout fishing on rivers is wet fly downstream with a single fly, a strong leader, and a flexible single-handed rod.

Daytime reconnaisance of the water to be fished at night is essential. The angler must take into account not only where the sea trout shoal is, or is likely to be, but must know in advance where to stand, how far and where to put his cast, how far he need wade, the rock or gravel formations underwater, the type of wading, the dangers from potholes or other obstructions.

Fly fishing at night is difficult. Most good casters are inclined to speed up the rhythm of casting. There has to be a deliberate effort to keep the slow rhythm which comes naturally during the day. A slack line on the water cannot be seen and is often the cause of a lost fish – a trout will pluck at the slack fly and because of the lack of tension will not be hooked.

Night fly fishing can be alarming to those who have been brought up in cities. Strange sounds, rustles in the undergrowth, heavy breathing, can be frightening, even terrifying, to those who do not recognise country sounds. Many sea trout fishermen at night go out in pairs, arrange where they are going to be, carry whistles or communicate by flashing a torch. In real wilderness country it is best to let someone know where the angler is likely to be if he goes fishing alone.

Upstream wet fly, dry fly and nymph fishing can take sea trout during the day but the sea trout is easily scared. Small flies on fine long leaders are needed.

Sea Trout: Loch Fishing In Scotland, the great way of taking a sea trout in one of the big lochs is dapping. A 15ft rod is best, either a light salmon rod or a telescopic dapping rod. Anything shorter is unlikely to fish the dap properly. The rod must have height. A special reel is not needed. To the ordinary fly line is attached a good length of nylon monofilament of about 15 to 20lb breaking strain and about 20 to 30ft long, depending on conditions. To the end of the nylon monofilament is attached about 15ft of nylon floss. This is the line that will float out in the breeze over the water. At the end of this line is about 3ft of 10 or 15lb nylon monofilament to which is attached the big dapping fly. The fly must be bushy, a big black or blue Zulu, on a fine-wire salmon hook, size 8 or

6. Each loch and each fishing hotel have their own favourite dapping flies, among them the Loch Ordie and the Willie Ross.

Dapping must take place in a reasonable wind. One or two fishermen in a boat, controlled by a ghillie at the oars, take up position at the head of a drift, hold their rods high, and allow the fly to dance on and close to the water surface, moving the rod from side to side as they do so in order that the fly covers as wide an area as possible.

If the wind is unfavourable then the standard wet fly practice of fishing the drift is adopted, using two flies, a point and a dropper.

Sea Trout: Sea Pools The west coast of Scotland, the Western Isles, and smaller rivers on the north and east, provide wonderful sea pool fishing for sea trout. The trout take a fly during the day; generally, though not always, for about two hours either side of high water. Small sea pools are best, for the whole of the pool can be covered and the trout lie in particular places, hidden in seaweed, and though the pool may look empty a fish will suddenly flash out of the weed, rise to the surface and take the fly at astonishing speed.

Salt and brackish water can corrode reels and rod fittings which must be cleaned in fresh water as soon as possible after use, the reel taken apart, washed and oiled and dried. Small flies or streamers are the most popular – a Butcher, Black Pennell, Peter Ross, Teal, Blue and Silver in standard sizes – or some of the long thin streamers, fished on floating lines.

Sea Trout: Big Fish Sea trout over 10lb are exceptional. The official British record is a 20-pounder taken in 1983 from the Tweed. A bigger fish, 22½lb, is in a glass case at the Loch Maree Hotel. Norway and Sweden have produced far bigger fish of 26 and 28lb (Nall).

Sea Trout: Young Fish It is mostly young sea trout which have regional names (peal in Devon, herling in Scotland) but not always. In Wales a sewin and in Ireland a white trout can be both young and old sea trout. Sea trout – said Kingsmill Moore – have as many names as royalty. **Sources include:** H. Sambrook, *Report to the Third British Freshwater Fisheries Conference*, Liverpool University, March 1983; 'Hybridisation on the River Wear', *The Field*, November 13, 1982; Hugh Falkus, *Sea Trout Fishing*, 2nd Edn., Witherby 1975; Roy Buckingham in an article in *West Country Fly Fishing*, Ed. Anne Voss Bark, Batsford, 1983; T.C. Kingsmill Moore, *A Man May Fish*, 2nd Edn., Colin Smythe, 1979; Falkus and Buller, *Freshwater Fishing*, Macdonald and Jane's, 1975; *Salmon and Sea Trout Fishing*, Ed. Alan Wrangles, Davis Poynter, 1979; *Sea Trout Studies*, J.C. Mottram, The Field Press, undated; *River Fishing for Sea Trout*, F.W. Holiday, Jenkins, 1960; *The Life of the Sea Trout*, G.H. Nall, Seeley Service, 1960; *The Book of the Sea Trout*, Hamish Stuart, Martin Secker, undated.

Sedge Flies There are some 200 varieties of sedge flies (*Trichoptera*) including very big ones and very small ones and most of the few which are of interest to fishermen look like moths and some are semi-nocturnal.

Artificial patterns of the sedge are often localised. In the northern rivers of England a large sedge which hatches in the evening is known as the Bustard, which has several dressings, but can also be suggested by a large Red Palmer. Lunn's Caperer is a good pattern for some of the sedges often found on the chalk streams. The grannom is a medium-size sedge which often hatches in vast numbers (*see* page 79), so do the grouse-wing on lakes and the little red sedge on rivers.

Hatching from an egg in the bottom of the river, the larvae protect themselves by making cases from an extruded fluid which they cover with microscopic particles of detritus, mud and sand. The cases are anchored on stones, the ends closed. The larva pupates, bites its way through the end of the case, and rises to the surface of the water or crawls along the bottom and climbs to a resting place to hatch into the mature fly.

Trout take the fly on hatching and again when the females lay their eggs in the water. A sedge can be distinguished from a stone fly (*Plecoptera*) by looking at the wings. The sedge wings are slightly hairy and, at rest, are carried in the shape of a roof over the insect's body. The stone fly has hard shiny wings, without hairs, carried flat over the body. **Sources:** Goddard's *Trout Fly Recognition* and J.R. Harris's *An Angler's Entomology.*

Sedge Pupae The pupae of sedge (*Trichoptera*), are often called caddis flies, from their case-building habits. In the seventeenth and eighteenth centuries the grubs were known as cods or cod-bait. The artificial sedge pupae are mostly stillwater flies, generally fished just below the surface. The best known pattern is the Amber Nymph. Others that will take fish during a sedge hatch include the Invicta, Alder, Chompers and Palmer Nymph.

Senior, William A former Editor and fishing columnist for *The Field* who wrote under the name of Red Spinner. Senior gave valuable encouragement to Halford and Marryat in their researches into fly life on the Kennet and the Test and wrote the introduction to Halford's autobiography.

Shadow Flies An interesting development in dry-fly fishing, the shadow dressing (*see* page 134) is designed to give the illusion of a natural fly instead of making an attempt at a copy.

The first conscious efforts at impressionism were made by a chalk stream fisherman, Dr J.C. Mottram, in the late 1890s and early 1900s, published in book form by *The Field* in 1915 – *Fly Fishing: Some New Arts and Mysteries.*

Another pioneer of shadow flies was P.D. Malloch of Perth with his parachute dressings. Howard Marshall records that Richard Threlfall, who fished the Kennet and the Lambourne, tied a fly which he used when duns were on the water which had no body, no whisks, merely a hackle palmered from eye to bend. This must have been a cousin to J. Arthur Palethorpe's dressing of a shadow mayfly which he showed to Peter Deane in 1950 and which Deane has since improved and developed.

The theory behind the dressing is that the imprint of the hackles on the water surface before the fly arrives in the trout's window, followed by the first direct sight of the fly as it appears as 'a buzz of hackle' gives an impression of reality: moving legs and buzzing wings and the shadows from the wings.

The theory could well be confirmed by the publication of the first photographs of artificial flies as they approach, and appear in, the trout's window, taken from a trout's eye view in the Goddard-Clarke book, *The Trout and the Fly* (Benn, 1981). These showed a strange flare of wings as the fly entered the window – something that Goddard was able to show to fishermen for the first time and in colour. Goddard's interpretation, however, was to return to the principle of the parachute dressing though this time with the body of the hook turned uppermost instead of in the usual position.

Sheringham, H.T. (1876–1930) Son of a vicar of Tewkesbury, where he fished as a boy, H.T. Sheringham was angling editor of *The Field* for many years in the early 1900s. He wrote a number of country books and one, *Syllabub Farm*, was a considerable success, so too was *Trout Fishing*, published in 1920 by Hodder and Stoughton. Sheringham, a witty and thoughtful essayist, was one of the first to praise Blagdon fishing, and wrote with perception on both the spate rivers and chalk streams.

Sherry Spinner Originally an artificial to suggest the female spinner of the blue-winged olive (*Ephemerella ignita*) the anglers' name seems to cover a large number of olives. Trout will also take other patterns – Pheasant Tail, Orange Quill, Rusty Spinner – when spent blue-winged olives are about. Goddard gives Woolley's dressing of the Sherry Spinner:

Body: pale gold quill or gold-coloured floss
Whisks and hackle: pale ginger cock
Wings: glassy blue cock hackle fibres, or two pale blue cock hackle tips, in both cases tied spent at right-angles to the hook
Hook: 14

Skues dressing was:

Body: amber seals' fur slightly mixed with orange and green and a little hares' fur
Rib: fine gold wire
Whisks and hackle: pale honey dun cock
Wings: none
Hook: 13 or 14

Shipley, William A fisherman on the Dove who kept a fishing diary from about 1780 onwards which was edited and published by his son, also William, together with Edward Fitzgibbon, in 1838. Shipley's description of fishing the floating fly on the Dove is frequently quoted:

> Let your flies float gently down the water, working them gradually towards you, making a fresh cast every two or three yards you fish. We distinctly recommend frequent casting, for . . . the quick repetition of casting whisks the water out of the flies and line and consequently keeps them drier and lighter than if they were left to float a longer time in the water.

Shrimp (*Gammarus pulex*) An important trout food, shrimps are found in rivers and lakes, among stones and weed, in most cases fairly close to the bottom. Early patterns (Horsfall-Turner and Skues) were unweighted but most of those tied in the past few decades have been heavily weighted for fast sinking, sometimes on hooks with curved shanks. The artificial shrimp is useful on lakes and reservoirs and on many spate rivers. On most of the chalk streams weighted shrimps are banned as being imitation bait. There are various dressings:

Under-body: lead wire or lead strip
Body: pale orange or yellow-brown seals' fur mixed with olive seals fur
Rib: fine gold wire
Hackle: grey or olive palmered over the body from head to bend
Back: a speckled dark feather laid over the back of the fly from head to bend, sometimes varnished
Hook: 14–10

Silver Doctor A salmon fly dating from the mid-1850s, the modern version simplified:

Body: flat silver tinsel
Rib: oval silver
Tail: golden pheasant tippet
Hackle: bright blue hen, dressed beard
Wings: strips of goose or swan, dyed green, yellow and red, flanked by grey mallard or teal

Silver Wilkinson A salmon fly designed by the Rev. P.S. Wilkinson in 1859 for fishing the Tweed:

Tag: silver tinsel
Tail: golden pheasant crest
Butt: scarlet wool
Body: silver tinsel wound silver wire
Throat hackle: guinea fowl fibres dyed blue
Wings: a mix of red and yellow swan with teal and jungle cock
Wing topping: golden pheasant crest
Cheeks: jungle cock

This is an approximation of the original design.

Sink-Mix A substance to make nylon leaders sink quickly, made of mixing fullers' earth and glycerine to the consistency of putty. It should be kept in a sealed container.

Skues, G.E.M. (1858–1949) A London solicitor, with offices in Essex Street, off the Strand, George Edward MacKenzie Skues had a profound influence on his own and subsequent generations of fly fishermen. He was the first to challenge the 'dry fly only' code of the chalk streams, the first to urge chalk stream fishermen to return to the upstream wet-fly technique when trout were feeding underwater, and the first to tie imitations of the ascending nymphs on which the trout were feeding.

From the early 1900s for some 30 to 40 years Skues was always in the centre

G.E.M. Skues

of controversy with the purists, and it was their antagonism and resentment of the man who was rightly called 'the father of nymph fishing' which ultimately was the cause of his resignation from the Itchen fishery at Abbots Barton, just above Winchester, where he had fished for 56 years.

It took many years for Skues to formulate the theory of nymph fishing. He was, at first, a devotee of Halford but doubts began when one of Skues' dry flies sank and was taken by a trout which had previously refused to take it on the surface. From this followed a series of articles in *The Field*, the *Fishing Gazette*, and the *Flyfishers' Club Journal* in which he advocated the return of the upstream wet fly to the chalk streams when trout were feeding on the ascending nymphs.

By the end of 1909, H.T. Sheringham, angling editor of *The Field*, urged Skues to publish his articles in book form, with some extra material, and from this, *Minor Tactics of the Chalk Stream*, (1910) followed *The Way of a Trout with a Fly* (1921) *Nymph Fishing for Chalk Stream Trout* (1939), and, posthumously, *Itchen Memories* (1951). His angling letters, edited by C.F. Walker, were published in 1956, and a biography and many unpublished essays were skilfully put together by Donald Overfield in *G.E.M. Skues, The Way of a Man with a Trout* (Benn, 1977).

Nymph fishing was defined in the 1939 book with considerable precision. It followed an acrimonious debate in The Flyfishers' Club a year earlier which was given in full in Overfield's book. This is Skues' decription:

Nymph fishing means to me the practice of presenting to a subaqueously feeding trout, in position, an artificial nymph representing as closely as possible the natural nymph he may be expected to be feeding on at the moment.

The artificial nymph, if properly selected, more nearly represents the bulk of the trout's food than does any winged or hackled fly. I claim that the use of the artificial for subaqueously feeding fish is a definite advance in the chalk stream angler's technique of fishing for trout which are letting the hatched fly go by.

Skues' influence stretched far wider than the chalk streams. At Blagdon Lake, Dr Bell scooped out the trout he caught with a marrow spoon, as Skues recommended, and from this developed stillwater nymph fishing.

In time, in spite of much opposition, many chalk stream dry fly purists gave way. In 1938 a Piscatorial Society report had condemned nymph fishing because it took 'so many undersized trout'. Twenty years or so later the society recanted. It allowed the use of unweighted Skues nymphs, fished upstream, without drag, just under the surface, as being 'included in the term dry fly' on the Avon, Lambourn and Wylye. Sophistry it may have been, but it was a useful compromise.

With his back to the wall, facing the purists of the 1920s and 1930s, unaware of his approaching triumphs, Skues was hurt and lonely. He never married. He died at 23 Kelsey Park Road, Beckenham, Kent, in 1949 at the age of 91. Thirty years later, as a result of an appeal by Roy Darlington, who was renting the Abbots Barton fishery, and was an admirer of Skues, a memorial stone seat was erected near the place where Skues' ashes were scattered. The lower half of the Abbots Barton fishery was taken over by Winchester Council in 1975 for town planning purposes.

Dry fly purists came to have a somewhat guilty feeling about their intolerance, and of their treatment of Skues. They tried to make amends:

> When . . . Mr Skues wrote *Minor Tactics of the Chalk Stream* he effected a revolution. The dry fly was at the height of an intolerant dictatorship, and the other method was discarded and ridiculed to such an extent that enthusiasts of the school of Halford regarded Mr Skues as a dangerous heresiarch. Much water has flowed under the bridge since then, and in that water many trout were caught on a sunk fly which would not have fallen to the dry. More and more each year does nymph fishing become a part of the modern angler's equipment and he who does not possess the art is gravely handicapped. And at the same time has come the realisation that it is both difficult and delightful; and . . . upon my word, I find trout harder to catch under water than on the top. (J. Waller Hills, *A Summer on the Test*, 1924)

Slob Trout An unpleasant word, slob, which could mean slobbery or slovenly, but in this instance it comes from the Irish, slab, meaning mud, ooze, mudflats, reclaimed alleuvial land, so that a slob trout is one that lives in muddy or tidal estuaries. They are a mix, if you like to put it that way, of brown trout and migratory brown trout and often have a mix of colouring, some retaining their brown trout markings, up to a point, some fading from the brown trout markings to the silvery appearance of the fully migratory fish, the sea trout. One taken in the Thames in 1982 was first wrongly identified as a salmon. In the Hebrides, slob trout are said to grow to 20lb or more. In Yorkshire, on the Esk, they have the name of bull trout.

Smell Trout and salmon have a highly-developed sense of smell. In an article in *The Field* (14 May, 1983) Dr Andrew Allen quoted experiments carried out at the University Pierre et Marie Curie in Paris. From these it was concluded that trout had a sense of smell a million times more keen than a human's, about the same as a tracker dog's, but nowhere near as keen as an eel's. Dr Allen wrote:

Like most gamefish, trout use smell to detect prey from hundreds of yards away. Smell and hearing are used as they home in, and then vision – a very subsidiary sense – for the final attack.

So now we have a good idea what a trout is doing when it puts its nose to a dry fly and follows it downstream before turning away. Frank Sawyer always used beef fat or mutton fat as a floatant because he was convinced that chemical floatants put trout off the take. The findings also confirm the value of fly-maggot in sea trout fishing.

Snipe and Purple An invaluable pattern for fishing wet fly upstream, traditional, probably dating back 200 years or more, highly commended by Pritt and very simple to dress:

Body: purple floss silk
Hackle: small dark feather from the outside of a snipe's wing
Hook: 14 or 16

The Snipe and Purple is often fished as a middle fly in a team of three. Pritt also dressed it with a yellow silk body when it became Snipe and Yellow, but purple seems to retain its popularity as the number one choice.

Soldier Palmer A palmer fly which takes its name from the scarlet and gold of British soldiers of the line – the Redcoats – of the eighteenth and nineteenth centuries. The body is wool, the colour of a Guardsman's tunic, a bright scarlet, wrapped around with gold twist, allowing both the scarlet and gold to show through the brown hackle from head to bend.

Somerset Reservoirs The famous ones are Blagdon and Chew but there are several delightful smaller ones, well stocked with trout, that make up for the county's lack of good trout streams. Not much bigger than 100–150 acres, all are in peaceful unspoilt countryside:

Clatworthy, near Taunton, in the Brendon Hills
Durleigh, near Bridgwater
Sutton Bingham, near Yeovil

The big one in the south is Wimbleball, north-east of Dulverton, which is nearly 400 acres and produced something like 16,000 trout in 1983. There is boat and bank fishing at Wimbleball. For boat fishing, take cushions and a drogue. Good advice on fishing Somerset reservoirs is given by Brian Clarke in *The Pursuit of Stillwater Trout* (Black, 1975).

Spencer, Sidney The Welsh lakes and the Scottish and Irish lochs were well covered by Sidney Spencer in a series of books, notably *The Art of Lake Fishing* (Witherby, 1934) in which the angler is urged never to fish the drift with a rod shorter than 12ft as it will not work the bob fly properly. Spencer must have been a fairly tough character as he urged fishermen not to use boat cushions but to harden themselves to sitting on the wooden seats when drift fishing. The book has excellent diagrams about drift fishing and casting and much good practical advice.

Spey

The Spey is perhaps the most magnificent of Scottish rivers. It is not the largest, yielding place to both Tay and Tweed in this respect, but it is certainly the strongest and fastest, as anyone who has seen it in spate will confirm. It flows through a wonderful countryside of unforgettable surroundings and provides fishing for salmon and sea trout which is second to none. (John Ashley-Cooper, *A Salmon Fisher's Odyssey*, Witherby, 1982)

No one has ever written a better description of the Spey than that except perhaps one might add that it is among the most expensive of rivers to fish; and yet at the same time is also the cheapest, with many miles of association water at Grantown-on-Spey available for visitors. Private beats, often with lodges, are let by Seafield Estate office at Grantown; the Tulchan Estate office at Advie; the Ballindalloch and Pitchroy Estates at Ballindalloch, Grampian; the Gordon Castle Estate at Fochabers; and the Carron Estate at Carron. The Tulchan Lodge Hotel has good water for guests. Graigellachie Hotel water is now time-share but rods are occasionally available. Other fishing hotels are The Boat Hotel, Boat of Garten; the Dowans Hotel, Aberlour; Blairfindy Lodge, Glenlivet; and Tulchan Lodge.

In recent years there have been petitions against over-netting in the estuary and the best fishing is when the nets are off in the autumn, but there can be a good grilse run as well as a fine flush of big sea trout in July. The river is very broad and fast. Deep wading and long casting are essential.

In bright low water salmon will take quite small flies, down to # 10 or 12 doubles such as Stoat's Tail and the Munro Killer, a local fly from Aberlour. When the water rises heavy tubes are needed and at certain marks only spinning is possible.

Spiders Lightly dressed trout flies for upstream wet-fly fishing, generally in a team of three flies fished on a short line in the true Border and Yorkshire style. They suggest drowned duns and spinners or, occasionally, nymphs. They are generally fished without movement so that the soft hackle in the water gives the impression of outspread wings. W.C. Stewart (*The Practical Angler*, 1857) gave three dressings:

Black Spider: body of brown silk, hackle made from the small feather of the cock starling
Red Spider: body of yellow silk, the hackle from the small feather taken from the outside wing of the landrail
Dun Spider: body of light brown or tawny silk, the hackle made from the small feather taken from the inside of the wing of a starling – the original dressing used a dotterel wing
Hook sizes: 14–16

Stewart always dressed his flies very lightly. His Black Spider is now more frequently dressed with a black body and a black hen hackle and has been taken over by some reservoir fishermen as a better imitation of the midge than the standard reservoir patterns. The spider type of dressing is fairly common and applies to such well-known patterns as Partridge and Orange and Snipe and Purple.

Stoddart, Thomas Tod (1810–1880) The poet-angler of Teviotdale, Stoddart was a friend of Sir Walter Scott and of James Hogg, the Ettrick Shepherd, another angler-poet. Famous in his time, a memoir by his daughter, Anna, was published with some of his poems as *Angling Songs* (Blackwood, 1889):

All joy be with our hearts' kin bold
May care's nets ne'er entangle,
Nor woe nor poverty depress
A brother of the angle!

Stoddart was born in a house in Argyle Square, Edinburgh, the son of a Royal Navy Captain, Pringle Stoddart, and his wife, Frances (nee Sprot), lived for a large part of his life at Bellevue Cottage, Kelso, and is buried in Kelso churchyard. Teviot and Tweed were his loves:

Let ither anglers chuse their ain,
An'ither waters tak' the lead;
O' Hielan' streams we covet nane,
But gie to us the bonnie Tweed.

Stewart, W.C. An Edinburgh lawyer who fished the Borders, W.C. Stewart wrote one of the most popular fly fishing books of the latter half of the nineteenth century. The *Practical Angler* was first published in 1857, with the second and third editions coming out the same year, half a dozen reprints in subsequent years and a final revised edition 62 years after the first, in 1919, with a foreword by W. Earl Hodgson. Only the works of Halford and Skues can equal that record. See Wet-Fly Fishing, page 223: Spiders, page 20.

Stinchar An Ayrshire river with a good run of salmon in September and October and probably one of the best of the Ayrshire rivers for the fly. The Bardrochat and Knockdolian Estates have occasional lettings.

Stoat's Tail One of the best of the hairwing flies of this or any time, first tied by Wright of Sprouston on Tweed sometime in the 1870s and 1880s. There are a number of variations but the best dressing is Veniard's:

Body: black floss
Rib: silver or gold tinsel, preferably silver
Beard hackle: black cock or hen
Wing: the black tips from a stoat's tail, or squirrel dyed black
Hook: with the stoat's tail wing, not much larger than 6 or 4, but larger if need be with black squirrel

The variations can be tinsel tag, or dark claret floss, or blue or guinea fowl beard hackle. Quite a few black flies – the Connemara and the Munro among them – make obeisance to the Stoat's Tail which is also an excellent sea trout fly.

Stone Fly (*Plecoptera*) A fly of the uplands, the moorland streams, the becks, the spate rivers. In the north of England the big stonefly (*perla*) is called the mayfly and is just as important to a Yorkshireman as a true mayfly (*E. danica*) is to the fishermen of Hampshire.

The nymphs of the big stone fly, about an inch long, are often used as bait. They creep to the shore, hatch out of the water, and the adult flies return to the water to lay their eggs. The smaller stone flies are thin and narrow (needle fly, willow fly, yellow sally) and because they have the same habits as the big flies the trout feed mostly on the spent fly as it drifts downstream after egg-laying. Anglers generally find that it is not worthwhile to tie imitations of the small stoneflies and if there are any on the water the trout will most likely rise to a spider pattern, a Partridge and Orange, or a Grey Duster.

Stuart, Hamish Anyone who thinks that reservoir fishermen are sometimes a little unkind to the dry fly men of the chalk streams with their condemnation of purism had better read Hamish Stuart's *Lochs and Loch Fishing*, which Chapman and Hall published in 1899. Stuart was far more vindictive:

> Certain Purists have formed themselves into an exclusive society, in which mutual admiration, hypocrisy, sophistry, pharisaicism, and dispraise of the barbarian are strongly blended . . .

He goes on like that for several pages, becoming, if possible even more vituperative. When Stuart does get around to loch fishing he is sound, though discursive, and the book is now a little difficult to read. There are, however, some interesting passages, such as the one dealing with the hotel water at Loch Boisdale in South Uist.

Sutherland A good guide to fishing in Sutherland is published by the Sutherland Tourist Office, The Square, Dornoch, including details of rivers, lochs, and accommodation. Sutherland has many salmon and sea trout rivers and about 2,000 lochs, all of which are fly fishing only.

Sutherland, Douglas A photograph of the 70lb salmon taken from the Tay is in *The Salmon Book* by Douglas Sutherland (Collins, 1982).

Sweeny Todd Named presumably because of a crimson throat, the Sweeny is an effective reservoir lure designed by Richard Walker:

Body: black floss silk with a 'collar' of neon magenta fluorescent wool just behind the roots of the wing
Rib: fine silver wire
Beard hackle: crimson feather fibres
Wing: dyed black squirrel hair
Hook: down-eye longshank 14 to 6

Without the neon magenta wool it is a variation of the Stoat's Tail (or Black Squirrel Tail), another effective stillwater pattern.

Progress

The things which made the dry fly generally possible were the coming of the heavy American braided oiled silk line and the split-cane rod. I remember buying my first length of oiled silk line in 1877 but I knew so little of its purpose I used it for sea fishing, and it was I think in the eighties that, stimulated by American progress in the building of split-canes our makers began to build split canes suitable for carrying these heavy lines. The heavy line was needed to deliver the fly dry and to put it into the wind; the split-cane, or wood rod on the same lines, was necessary to deliver the heavy line. With the hour came the men, Mr H.S. Hall, Mr G.S. Marryat, and Mr F.M. Halford who evolved from the poor feeble types of dry flies of the seventies the efficient dry fly of the eighties and the present day.

G.E.M. Skues, *The Way of a Trout With a Fly*, A and C Black, 1921, 4th edn., reprinted 1961

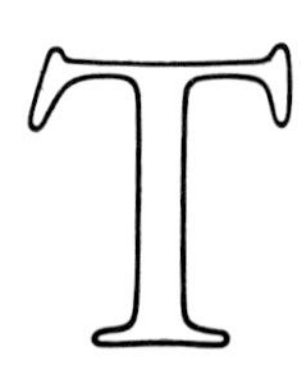

A Burden of Trout – The Reverend Hartwell James with about 50 trout taken in one day's fishing on the Tamar (*c.* 1920–1930) which he would then distribute to the poor and needy of his parish near Bridgwater, Somerset. His record catch on the Tamar was 152 trout in one day from 300 yards of river, all on the fly – photograph by John Tarlton in the collection of the late Gerald Fox-Edwards

Tamar The boundary river between Devon and Cornwall, rising in the north a few miles from the coast and entering the sea at Plymouth in the south, the Tamar has a good run of salmon and sea trout. In the upper reaches and feeder streams – Ottery, Carey, Kensey, Lynher, Lyd, Wolf and Thrussel – there is also some brown trout fishing. There are two good fishing hotels, The Arundell Arms at Lifton and Endsleigh House at Milton Abbot, both with their own private salmon fishing for guests. Tackle shops at Bude, Holsworthy and Launceston have permits for association water.

The Tamar flows through rich agricultural land and generally has a touch of colour so salmon flies must be slightly larger and more visible than on the clear waters of the Exe. The Yellow Torrish single on a 1 or 1/0 hook, or a 1-inch or 1½-inch Garry Dog tube are the most popular flies on the lower river, fished either with a sink-tip or sinking line, stripped in fairly fast. Doubles, by local tradition, are not popular.

Taw and Torridge Sister rivers in North Devon, badly polluted at one time, hopefully being cleaned up. There are good runs of salmon and sea trout and several good hotels with private fishing for residents – The Rising Sun, Umberleigh; The Half Moon, Sheepwash; The Woodford Bridge, Milton Damerel.

Salmon and sea trout run early on in the season on both rivers and some large sea trout are taken on quite small flies. A favourite sea trout fly is Peter Ross # 12 and the salmon flies are not all that big – # 10, 8 and 6 will do nicely with a Stoat's Tail type dressing.

Tay One of the three great major salmon rivers of Scotland, the Tay has many fine salmon beats which at times and in the right conditions can be highly productive. About 120 miles long, the Tay covers a huge catchment area, and is fed by tributaries and lochs which in their own right are great salmon waters – Almond and Dochert, Faskally, Garry, Isla, Lochy, Lyon and Tummel.

The British record salmon was caught on the Tay – a 64-pounder taken in 1922 on a spinner from a boat by Miss G. Ballantyne, daughter of the ghillie at Caputh. Ashley-Cooper records that two other fish over 60lb have been taken and many over 50lb, which makes it possible to compare the Tay with some of the big Norwegian rivers. If Miss Ballantyne's record is ever to be broken it is most likely to happen on these fast deep waters. On many beats, particularly below Dunkeld, the pools are so big and the river so wide that boat fishing is more or less essential to cover all the lies satisfactorally. In low water they should be waded deep and carefully, with breast waders and a wading staff.

Fly fishing in the middle and upper reaches is best from about May onwards but is entirely dependent on the water. In 1983 one beat produced around 100 salmon in a week for three rods and the next week one fish only was taken in five days.

There is good hotel water at Killin, Kenmore, Grandtully and Dunkeld. John D. Wood and Strutt and Parker, London; J.D. Malloch and Renton Finlayson, Perth; and Bell-Ingram, Edinburgh, have lettings. The best flies are in the range # 6 to 10 with Hairy Mary, Blue Charm, Tosh, Stoat's Tail and Munro Killer the most popular, either singles or doubles, but for deep pools one needs a fast sinking line and a big tube, a 2½ to 3-inch Garry Dog or Black and Silver. The Perthshire Tourist Board, PO Box 33, Perth, publishes a booklet on fishing which includes details of hotel and club water on the Tay for salmon and trout.

Teal, Blue and Silver The most popular of teal-dressed trout and sea trout flies, the standard dressing is:

Body: flat silver tinsel, ribbed fine oval
Whisks: a few strands of golden pheasant tippet
Beard hackle: bright blue feather fibres
Wings: two matching slips of teal breast, or failing teal a light mallard
Hook: from 14 upwards for brown trout; low water salmon hooks 8, 6 or 4 for big sea trout

The Teal, Blue and Silver is only one in a series. The Teal and Red is another and was the basis for the Peter Ross. The Teal and Green is always worth a try on the loch:

Body: apple green wool, ribbed oval gold
Beard hackle: red feather fibres

The whisks and wings are the same as the Teal, Blue and Silver. Hook sizes depend where one is fishing. On the drift on a loch it can be as small as 14 for brown trout; for salmon and sea trout a little larger, up to about 8 or 6.

Teifi A great Welsh river for sea trout with ample association water and permits for visitors. The sea trout (*sewin* in Wales) start to run from late June, early July, and there are some salmon about but not as many as there were. Around Newcastle, Emlyn and Llandyssel there is good association water but visitors should avoid weekends when there is still a good deal of worming. The Cawdor Estate at Broad Oak, Dyfed, has good fly water. Most local hotels will arrange permits for visitors on association water.

Teign A Devon river of great charm with small wild brown trout and a good run of sea trout. The upper Teign between Chagford and Steps Bridge provides fine dry fly fishing. The well-named Angler's Rest Inn at Fingle Bridge, Drewsteignton, can supply permits for association water but it is best to avoid holiday weekends.

Terrestrials A fisherman's name for land-bred insects which at times fall on the water in sufficient numbers to provoke a rise. They include flying ants, mostly in August; crane flies (daddy-longlegs) in late August and September; the hawthorn fly in April-May; beetles at any time; and an occasional odd drop of caterpillars and grasshoppers. Whether it is worth tying patterns of all these must depend on the angler's inclinations. It is possible that substitutions can be made – a Black Palmer for the hawthorn, a large mayfly trimmed with scissors can pass for a crane fly, a Black and Peacock Spider or a Coachman for a beetle. (For ants, *see* page 13.)

Terry's Terror A beetle-like pattern of trout fly, generally fished dry or in the surface film, designed by Dr Cecil Terry of Bath who fished the Hungerford Town Water of the Kennet for many years in the 1920s and 1930s:

Body: one strand of bronze peacock herl twisted with yellow tying silk
Rib: very fine flat copper tinsel
Tail: a stubby one, consisting of equal parts of orange and yellow bucktail hair
Hackle: medium red cock
Hook: 12–16

Test and Itchen Fishing Association Unique in several ways, the association has almost a hundred per cent membership of the riparian owners and lessees of the Itchen and the Test. A high proportion of members also consist of those who fish the rivers as guests or paying rods. It is almost certainly the most powerful and influential angling organisation of its kind in any part of the country, and it has in its care two of our most beautiful and famous rivers. It is an organisation to preserve and if possible improve the fisheries on both these rivers and to maintain the scenery and amenities of the river valleys as the secretary, Mrs M.F. Baring writes:

The Association helped to defeat Lady Brecknock's application to extract gravel in the Test valley. It has been represented at all the enquiries into the route of the new M3 motorway which cuts across these valleys. It has fought all applications for water abstractions and in many cases has had the amount of abstraction reduced. In 1983 it instructed Mr Allan, a former Inspector of Fisheries at the Ministry of Agriculture and Fisheries, to undertake a survey of fish farms on both rivers and has given advice to a House of Lords committee examining ways of controlling fish farms.

The Association gives advice to members on legal matters, rating, abstraction, pollution, and general problems of running a fishery, provides an annual report, and has close links with the Southern Water Authority and the Hampshire Anglers' Consultative Association, which is an association for game and coarse fishing clubs with a membership of over 7,000.

The Association was founded on April 6, 1907 at a meeting of riparian owners and lessees convened by Sir William Portal of Laverstoke. In June 1946 it was incorporated under the Companies Act as a company limited by guarantee, not having a share capital. There is a guarantee fund as an insurance against any major threat to the Test or Itchen. A register of guarantors is kept of those who have agreed to produce a stated sum should a call be made on this fund.

Test

A wonderful day truely. Five trout, the smallest 2lb exactly and the biggest 3lb 4oz. Was there ever such a sport as fishing, or such a river as the Test? (J.W. Hills, *A Summer on the Test*, 1924)

Those who fish and love the Test and who have not read J.W. Hills' book have a treat to come. The latest edition was published by André Deutsch in 1983, with a foreword by Anthony Atha, in which he rightly said that Hills had a magic way with words as well as giving good practical advice which was as good today as it was 50 years ago.

The Test is unique. Here was born the dry fly, as we now know it, here were set standards for fly fishing that have spread world-wide, here fishermen come on pilgrimage.

The Test is beautiful, broad in its lower reaches, fed by prolific springs from the chalk hills, and yet all the river lies within the one small county of Hampshire. Many famous men have fished the Test. Many famous men have cared for it, among them three generations of the Lunn family at the Houghton Club. This is Mick Lunn's description of his river:

A spring bubbles from the chalk below the little village of Ashe, near Overton, and from this comes the Test. The infant stream makes its way to Laverstoke, where Portals make the banknote paper, and then, fed by many more springs, on to Whitchurch, Tufton, Longparish and Chilbolton.

Before you get to Stockbridge the river is fed by three lovely little tributaries – the Bourne, made famous by Plunket Greene in *Where The Bright Waters Meet*, the Dever and the Anton. Just above Stockbridge is the Leckford water, owned by the John Lewis Partnership, and below that is the Houghton Club water. The club was formed in 1822 and we have a continuous record of every fish caught on the club water from that date up to the present.

Past Stockbridge – under the bridge over the main A30 road – the river comes to the village of Houghton, from which the club takes its name. Then, at Barrington, it is joined by the wonderful little Wallop Brook, broadening the river even more, through now to Compton, Mottisfont and Kimbridge. Then the last real tributary comes in, the Dun, and on the river curves through the broad green valley to Timsbury and Romsey where, at Broadlands, it also becomes famous for the salmon fishing.

What a wonderful river it is – fed all the way by pure crystal clear spring water, filtered from the chalk, extremely alkaline, creating a prolific growth of weed and all the right food insects – olives, iron blues, pale wateries, blue-winged olives, the big mayfly and a host of sedges. The fish feed well on these and on a profusion of shrimps and snail and all those many creatures that fall by chance on the water, the beetles and hawthorn flies and ants.

River weed is all-important for the fishery, a sanctuary and feeding ground, and the river keeper by selective weed cutting can control the height of his water as well as creating lies for the trout. The weeds I call good are ranuculous, water celery and water carrot; the bad are starwort and Canadian pondweed which collect silt and are not easy to cut.

The upper Test is shallow and provides a good breeding ground and there is a fair survival rate from the spawning redds. I have always thought of the upper river as being upstream from Leckford, the middle from Leckford to and including Kimbridge, the lower downstream from Kimbridge. The upper has probably less fly life than the middle or lower and fly life is reasonably localised, the one exception being the mayfly (*E. danica*) for they have been known to fly miles upriver before egg-laying. These extraordinary migrations of the big mayfly probably only happen once or twice in a lifetime.

May brings the first olives and iron blues, then the fall of hawthorn and of course the mayfly in the so-called 'duffer's fortnight' which is generally at its best between May 18 and June 8. June is less hectic but towards the end of the month comes the evening fishing with blue-winged olive, pale watery, and the fall of spinner. July and August see some of the best evening fishing but during the day there are black gnat and ants to bring the fish up; and I can remember some Augusts when the black gnat has created more rises than the mayfly. September is a law unto itself for by then the fish that survive are more accustomed to the sight of feathers on a hook and can recognise a clumsy cast. You will then need a finer nylon point, a smaller fly, and a greater attention paid to concealment. Fishing can be difficult in September but isn't that part of its charm?

Membership of clubs and syndicates on the Test is largely by invitation. Some rods are occasionally available for a day or a week through agencies, such as John D. Wood in London. The Rod Box, a tackle shop at Winchester, also can arrange fishing. The Greyhound Inn at Stockbridge has water available for guests. The Leckford Estate and one or two other estates occasionally let rods for a short period.

Thames The first salmon to be caught by an angler in the Thames for 150 years was taken in Chertsey Weir Pool in August 1983, a symbol not so much of the return of the Thames as a salmon river but of its freedom from pollution.

Some 50,000 salmon parr were released into the Thames in 1979. If they survived and returned as adult fish then the tremendous efforts made to clean up the Thames over many years by the Thames Water Authority would have a tangible reward. A stocking programme was started in 1979 and was intended to last seven years at a cost of some £20,000 a year (1979 prices). The overall cost of cleaning up the Thames and treating its effluent, for the TWA and for private organisations, is difficult to estimate. The TWA must have spent something of the order of £200m in 15 to 20 years.

Any serious effort to make the Thames into a salmon river again would cost far more than is now being spent. Fish passes would have to be built at some 30 weirs, a big hatchery built and there would have to be a large annual expenditure on staff and works. Such a programme would be strongly opposed by the many coarse fishermen and clubs now using the Thames.

There are not many trout in the Thames though there are in its tributaries, such as the Kennet, but those that are haunt the weir pools and run big. The best places are said to be the weir pools at Bray, Marlow and Molesey, and upstream above Oxford.

According to a letter in the *Flyfishers' Journal* (Winter number, 1975) a Mr Lowndes caught a brown trout on a mayfly at Sonning Lock around the year 1888 which weighed over 21lb. The Piscatorial Society has, or had, a 14lb specimen in a glass case. In an article in the *Flyfishers' Journal* (Spring number, 1975) David Martin recorded the catches of a dedicated Thames trout fisherman, A.E. Hobbs, who fished the weir pools for 66 years, from 1880 to 1946. He caught 878 trout over 3lb; 56 between 6lb and 8lb; and his top ten fish averaged 9¼lb.

Most Thames trout in past days were taken by spinning a dead bleak or dace. Today spinning a Rapala, or fishing a big salmon fly, especially in the pools at Chertsey or Teddington, might well do. Particular attention should be paid to fishing the white water below the sill and the eddy flows.

Thunder and Lightning Whether its name has anything to do with the survival of this traditional salmon fly is not a matter on which to have strong opinions; survive it has, from the late nineteenth century, when it was first dressed by James Wright of Sprouston on Tweed. Some feathers, such as jungle cock, are no longer obtainable but there are substitutes.

Tag: two turns of flat gold tinsel followed by one of yellow floss
Tail: golden pheasant crest, up turned
Butt: black ostrich herl
Body: black floss silk
Rib: flat gold tinsel
Hackle: orange feather fibre, tied beard, with blue jay or blue guinea fowl in front
Wings: brown mallard topped by golden pheasant crest
Side wings (cheeks): jungle cock
Head: black
Hooks: any size, singles or doubles

Thurso A salmon river in Caithness that is notable for the amount of water available to the public through Thurso Fishery estate office. There is a waiting list and early application is advised. Fishermen have to stay at the Ulbster Arms Hotel at Halkirk. Summer and autumn fishing is best with small dark flies on floating or sink tip lines.

Till A small and picturesque stream which enters the Wylye near Great Wishford and is mostly private but local enquiries may produce a rod. The water has a good head of wild brown trout which rise readily to the fly.

Towy There is plenty of trout fishing for visitors on this lovely river and salmon and sea trout permits can generally be had at Dyfed hotels. The sea trout (*sewin*) are best in June and July. Large flies, including tandems, are invaluable for night fishing, with hair wings and black, blue and silver dressings. Tube flies are becoming popular. Some of the best pools are heavily wormed.

Treacle Parkin In Yorkshire a treacle parkin is a biscuit made of oatmeal and treacle, but why the name has also been given to a trout fly which has the same dressing as the Red Tag we do not know. Courtney Williams has a long history of it as a grayling fly which emigrated from Wales to the north of England somewhere in the mid-1800s. Anyway, here is the Red Tag/Treacle Parkin dressing:

Body: bright green peacock herl
Hackle: bright red cock
Tag: a nice thick stub of bright red wool
Hook: 14 or 16

Sometimes a turn of gold or silver tinsel is added between the tag and the herl.

Trout Fisherman A magazine first published in 1978, originally intended to cater for the stillwater fly fisherman, but from about 1982 onwards a fair proportion of articles were on trout fishing in rivers and this was likely to increase. The editorial policy is based on how-to-do-it, with attractive typography and colour illustrations, intended also to introduce other anglers to fly fishing. For June/July 1983 the ABC circulation was 31,044 which was expected to increase by something like 5,000 by 1984. Editor: Chris Dawn. Address: Bretton Court, Bretton, Peterborough, PE3 8DZ. Publishers: East Midland Allied Press.

Trout and Salmon Founded by Howard Marshall, Bernard Venables and R.P. Winfry, then chairman of East Midland Allied Press, its publishers. The first issue appeared in July, 1955, price one shilling and sixpence. Editor was Scotsman, Ian Wood, who remained in the chair until retirement in June, 1969. He was succeeded by Jack Thorndike, previously editor of *Angling Times*, who relinquished the editorship of *Trout and Salmon* in August, 1976, prior to retirement. Roy Eaton, his deputy, took over and in 1985, John Wilshaw. *Trout and Salmon*, which changed from a black and white front cover to a full four-colour photograph in January, 1963, has risen in size and stature ever since its inception 29 years ago. Over that period its pages have increased from an initial 36 to a record 140 in April, 1984. Average monthly sale is over 42,000. Address: Bretton Court, Bretton, Peterborough, PE3 8DZ.

Tup's Indispensible R.S. Austin, tobacconist and fly dresser of Tiverton, tied a fly in the 1890s which was probably an imitation of the spinner of the pale watery. Skues tried it out, sang its praises in *The Field*, and Austin and his daughter were overwhelmed with orders. Skues gave it the name tups because part of the wool used in the dressing came from the genitals of a tup, one of the names for a male sheep or ram, and indispensible because he could not be without it when trout were rising to pale watery spinners on the Itchen. The original dressing was fished on the Exe, close to Tiverton, and has not changed a great deal since, apart from modifications to the mix of body materials:

Body: a mixture of rams' wool, cream coloured seals' fur, lemon spaniels' fur, and a few pinches of crimson seals' fur
Hackle: light blue cock freckled with gold
Tying silk: bright yellow, two turns exposed at the tail
Whisks: light blue cock spade feather, rather long
Hook: 16

Fly dressers who do not have access to rams or lemon-coloured spaniels can make up a mixture of wool which is slightly pink.

Tweed

Although the Tweed is the second largest river in Scotland (the Tay is the largest) it is for me the most fascinating of all I have fished. (Bill (Rogie) Brown, in *The Haig Guide to Salmon Fishing* in Scotland, Queen Anne Press, 1981)

There is no salmon fisherman worthy of the name who has not heard of the great beats of the Tweed – Kelso, Sprouston, Birgham, Floors, one could go on and on – and in the right water conditions, catches can be remarkable. The Tweed suffers the usual afflications of many Scottish rivers these days, abstraction, pollution, heavy spates which fall away too fast, and a great cause of bitterness – the amount of netting of Tweed fish that takes place off the Northumberland coast.

All being well, however, the Tweed can give some perfect fly fishing. Tweed men like big heavy tubes, some up to three inches long, especially towards the autumn. The fishing closes the last day in November and the last four weeks are on average much the best. In 1983 the best catches were made in October.

'Rogie' Brown tells how he defied tradition – the big long brass tube – in the autumn at the Mertoun beat at St Boswells. He used a 2-inch tube on a sinking line and – against all advice – worked the fly with his left hand during the retrieve. In two days he took 21 fish. That was his first experience of the greatness of autumn salmon on the Tweed.

Waiting lists for the famous private beats are long but – a sign of the times – one or two have been advertised in recent years. Bell-Ingram, Edinburgh, and Strutt and Parker, London, handle lettings. There are fishing hotels at Cornhill, Melrose and Kelso. The Ednam House Hotel at Kelso does not own water but can advise on the right contacts with private beats – such as Douglas and Angus Estates, The Hirsel, Coldstream, the Carham Estate at Cornhill, and others. The famous Junction Pool at Kelso is let through Strutt and Parker and is almost opposite Ednam House grounds.

The Tweed has largely recovered from the disease which began in 1966–67. Springers have declined in 1979–1983 but the autumn runs have been good. Salmon are found in many tributaries and there are good runs of sea trout. Dry fly for wild brown trout can be very good indeed. Splendid fishing can be found in the Tweed's feeders – Whiteadder, Teviot, Leader, Gala, Ettrick and Yarrow.

The Scottish Borders Tourist Board, High Street, Selkirk, issues a good guide to the Tweed and Border fishings.

Two Lakes (*See* Hampshire Lakes page 89; and Alex Behrendt, page 20).

Night

The value of night fishing is as a sedative to fretted nerves and a tired brain. A sedative, yet something more, a portal of escape from the instancy of the present. As the night deepens the river takes command. Its voice mounts, filling the valley, rising to the rim of the hills, no longer one voice but a hundred. Time and place are dissolved; the centuries have lost their meaning; timelessness is all. One foot is crossing the invisible frontier which bounds the land of the old gods. Then comes the whistle of an otter, the bark of a fox – and you are back in the world of sentiency. Almost you fear to turn least, black upon the moon-blanched sand, there should be the hoof marks of a goat.

T.C. Kingsmill Moore, *A Man May Fish*, 1960

In the Night usually the best Trouts bite and will rise ordinarilly in the still deeps; but not so well in the Streams. And although the best and largest Trouts bite in the Night (being afraid to stir, or range about in the Day time), yet I account this Angling both unwholesome, unpleasant, and very ungentiel and to be used by none but Idle pouching Fellows.

James Chetham, *The Angler's Vade Mecum*, 1681

UDN In the early 1960s, ghillies on an Irish river saw a salmon swimming about in an aimless fashion, its head covered with white fungus. It was blind. Within a few days there were more blind fish with their heads and backs covered with white patches. Like the first fish, they too swam blindly around for a while and then drifted ashore to die. Soon the banks of the river for miles up and down stream were fouled with dead and decomposing salmon. It did not happen in one river only. It happened all over Ireland. Soon the plague spread to Wales, to Scotland, then to England. Ghillies on the Tweed piled up dead fish in huge heaps all along the banks and made funeral pyres.

Scientists named the disease Ulcerative Dermal Necrosis, which in ordinary words means the death of part of a living body, but they were unable to find a cause or a cure. Gradually, as with myxamatosis, the disease lessened. Rivers began to recover. By 1984 the epidemic was no longer of plague proportions and some rivers were clear.

Was it an infection? In 1981, two Scottish scientists, Dr A.M. Bullock of the Scottish Marine Biological Association, and Professor R.J. Roberts, of the aquaculture department of Stirling University, suggested it could be a form of sunburn. Their tests showed that certain marine worms contained a substance known as porphyrin. If there was a population explosion of these worms and if salmon ate large quantities the porphyrin would enter the blood stream. When salmon came into the rivers and were exposed to strong sunlight in shallow water the porphyrin would cause the skin to become over-sensitive. The lesions which this created would be attacked by fungus.

Uist Remote islands off the west coast of Scotland have some wonderful fishing. The Uist Community Press, Benbecula, publish John Kennedy's *70 Lochs, A Guide to Trout Fishing in South Uist* (1983), a comprehensive guide with close and detailed advice. Wild brown trout of 2 to 3lb are by no means uncommon. Mr Kennedy suggests a rod of between 9½ to 10½ft for bank or boat, a point fly and two droppers on not less than 6lb nylon, with fly sizes from 12 to 8, with 10 being the most useful. Standard wet-fly patterns are used: Pennell, Zulu, Ross, Invicta, Grouse and Claret, and Butcher. Lochboisdale Hotel can reserve trout fishing for visitors. Salmon and sea trout fishing are also available from the hotel.

Usk Skues was among many visitors who have paid tribute to the fishing on the Usk, as well he might. It is one of the most charming of the Welsh rivers and to fish the March Brown in spring when the naturals are hatching can be a great experience. The late Lionel Sweet, British casting champion, was the doyen of the Usk and his tackle business in Usk town is carried on (1986) by Mrs Jean Williams. (*See* March Brown on page 132.) Permits for trout fishing on the town water can be had from the shop. The salmon fishing is preserved but can be had at Gliffaes Hotel, Crickhowell, a country house fishing hotel with two miles of its own water.

Usk Grub One of Lionel Sweet's salmon flies for the Usk water and for many other salmon rivers too:

Usk Grub

Body: lower half black floss; nearest the eye, yellow or orange seals' fur
Tail: golden pheasant breast feather wound as hackle
Tag: flat silver tinsel
Rib: round silver tinsel
Centre body hackle: light furnace or grizzle cock
Front hackle: same as centre body, but longer in the fibres
Wings: two long jungle cock feathers
Head: black varnish
Hook: generally about 8 or 6, singles, but larger in heavy water

Wading – I

The current caught at my extended boot foot and literally snatched me out of the protective patch of relatively calm water, picked me up bodily and began rolling me downstream in the torrent, handling me as if I were a small piece of gravel. I must have been upended and turned completely over somewhere between ten to twenty times in the course of being tossed and carried downstream about the length of a football field before I was finally plastered on to a large rock . . . After a few minutes of coughing and spluttering I cleared my head and regained my breath, enough to notice for the first time that I was still clutching my new two-piece rod, but that it was now neatly strung out along its line in seven splintered pieces.

Arnold Gingrich, *The Well-Tempered Angler*, Alfred A Knopf, New York, 1959

In order to enjoy a feeling of security on or beside water – whether river or lake – you should be able to paddle about fully clothed. If you can't, practice until you can, paying particular attention to the back-stroke.

Hugh Falkus, *Sea Trout Fishing*, 2nd edn., Witherby, 1975

Venables, Bernard Painter, sculptor, author, journalist, Bernard Venables has fished many countries for many kinds of fish but is convinced that fly fishing for trout and sea trout is without rival. He began to write about fishing while working on the *Daily Express*. In 1946 he left to become angling correspondent of the *Daily Mirror*, creating the Mr Crabtree fishing strip. He left the *Mirror* to become, with Howard Marshall, co-founder of the *Angling Times* and later the *Trout and Salmon* magazine. Then Venables founded *Creel* magazine which he edited for 18 months. He has broadcast regularly on television and radio on fishing, including the series of 13 programmes, *Angler's Corner*, for BBC Television. His publications include: *Mr Crabtree Goes Fishing*, *A Fisherman's Testament*, *Angling Waters*, *Fish and Fishing*, *The Gentle Art of Angling*, *Fishing Past and Present*, *The Angler's Companion*, *Fishing For Trout*, *The Piccolo Fishing Book*.

Venables, Colonel Robert (1612/13–1687) One of Cromwell's commanders, Robert Venables took part in battles in the Civil War at Chester and in Ireland. An expedition which he led to the West Indies failed and Venables was disgraced and for a time imprisoned in the Tower of London. He found time to write a useful and practical book on fishing, part of it on fly fishing, *The Experienced Angler* (1662), to which Izaak Walton wrote the foreword. The book was reproduced in facsimile by the Antrobus Press in 1969 with a biographical sketch of Venables by C.G.A. Parker. The book contains a soundly-based fly fishing philosophy:

> . . . the fish will sometimes take the fly much better at the top of the water, and at another time a little better under the superficies of the water; and in this your own observation must be your constant and daily instructor; for if they will not rise to the top try them under . . .

Sometimes it was right to fish upstream, sometimes down.

On salmon fishing he wrote:

> The salmon takes the artificial fly very well; but you must use a troll, as for Pike, or he, being a strong fish, will hazzard your line, except you give him length; his flies must be much larger than you use for other fish, the wings very long, two or four, behind one another, with very long tails; his chiefest ground-bait is a great garden or lob worm.

By ground-bait he meant fishing the worm along the ground – the bottom – of the river.

Wading – II

Avoid standing upon rocking stones, for obvious reasons; and never go into water deeper than the fifth button of your waistcoat; even this does not always agree with tender constitutions in frosty weather. As you are likely not to take a just estimate of the cold in the excitement of the sport, should you be of a delicate temperament, and be wading in the month of February, when it may chance to freeze very hard, pull down your stockings and examine your legs. Should they be black or even purple, it might, perhaps, be as well to get on dry land; but if they only rubicond, you may continue to enjoy the water, if it so pleases you.

William Scrope, *Days and Nights of Salmon Fishing in the Tweed*, 1843

Now let us wade in. You will find that the river is much stronger than you thought it would be and that it pulls at your legs in a most disconcerting fashion; but you will soon become acclimatised. Use your gaff handle as a staff and feel your way step by step – gently does it! Beware of gravel that slopes towards the deeps, being loose it will give beneath your feet and you may get a ducking. If you do go under, do not try to struggle back to the bank; drop downstream *with* the current, gradually edging your way inshore.

Jock Scott, *The Art of Salmon Fishing*, Witherby, 1933

Wading The deeper the wading in fast water, the more strange it feels, the more uncertain the balance, the more clumsy the legs and feet until a point is reached where the river takes command, lifts the angler up and carries him downstream. Water is an alien element. No wading is safe.

The safest wading boots are, marginally, those with felt soles. These are more or less unobtainable in Britain but are in common use in the United States where latex stocking waders and felt-soled wading boots are more popular than rubber chest waders. Cleated and studded sole waders are dangerous on certain surfaces. Studded soles give practically no grip at all on sloping wet rocks, cleated soles little or none on mud.

Some basic rules to follow when wading:

Use a wading staff on a lanyard, wade into the river with your back to the current. Put the wading stick at an angle in front of you and lean on it to make a tripod. Use it as a third leg.
Move out slowly, shuffling the feet.
Move out sideways to the stream, always with your back to the current.
Never turn round to face the current as you will lose the security – the tripod effect – of the third leg.
When you reach the place you want to be, place both feet carefully before giving up the tripod and putting the staff behind you.
When moving downstream to cover a pool, a step at a time, use the tripod and shuffle, keeping the feet well down, feeling the way with your feet, never hurrying or making uncontrolled steps.
When coming out of the water, shuffle out sideways, always with the current coming from behind.

When using the staff as your third leg, always waggle your staff a little to make sure it has a firm grip, then shuffle one foot, then the other. Remember that the normal walking balance of your body does not exist in water.

When a salmon takes and the angler is in deep water he must not move until the salmon is tiring and under some sort of control. Then, and only then, holding the rod lightly in one hand, the wading staff firmly in the other, the angler can shuffle out towards the bank. If the salmon takes off, stand still until it is under control again.

Many big salmon rivers have hazards caused by gravel banks and sudden deep holes. Some gravel banks on the bend of a river are highly unstable. The gravel will slide away under the least pressure. 'Whalebacks' are another hazard. The gravel is piled up facing downstream in a long ridge, shaped like the back of a whale. An angler wades down but finds the current too strong to wade back again. Scours, shifting gravel, sudden potholes – all can cause accidents.

If the angler is carried away by the current:
As soon as possible, turn on your back.
Do not try and swim, keep floating.
There will be enough air in your waders and clothes to allow you to float for a long time providing you don't struggle or try to swim.
Let the current take you, feet first, downstream. Sooner or later you will drift

towards a bank, help yourself to do so by paddling with the hands.
Do not try and climb a high bank, pull yourself along until you come to a shallow flat.
Crawl out, lie on your back, drain the water out of your waders, stand up and get home or to a fishing lodge as soon as possible.
You will be shocked, bitterly cold, but alive. If you panicked and shouted for help, struggled and tried to swim you might not be.

On a television programme, Hugh Falkus showed how to do all this by jumping in a river and demonstrating how to get out again. Within 18 months eight men wrote to him saying that seeing the way to do it had saved their lives.

There are hazards for trout fishermen on peaceful-looking rivers and lakes. On one stretch of the Itchen, for example, it is fatal to wade and a fisherman would sink quickly in soft mud.

On one of the Hampshire lakes a man wearing knee boots waded in to net a fish. He went into mud over both ankles. He had to be pulled out, leaving his boots behind. They gradually sank out of sight.

Walker, C.F. A chalk stream fisherman, C.F. Walker made an important contribution to the knowledge of lake fishing with the publication in 1960 of *Lake Flies and Their Imitation* (Herbert Jenkins). Based on studies which he and Alex Behrendt carried out at Two Lakes, Hampshire, C.F. Walker designed a new series of flies for stillwater fishing, based on 26 patterns, of which the midge and sedge pupae are the best known. His midge pupa dressing has been widely copied and adapted:

Abdomen: gut or nylon in various thicknesses and shades
Thorax: ostrich, condor or peacock herl
Wings and legs: a short hen hackle with the top fibres clipped off, or none
Hook: 12–16

Walker's other works include *Fly Tying as an Art*, *Chalk Stream Flies*, and *An Angler's Odyssey*.

Walker, Richard Angling columnist for more than 30 years for the *Angling Times*, Richard Walker is probably best known for his capture in 1955 of the record British carp, 44lb, which he presented to the London Aquarium. Born in 1918, he was educated at The Friends School, Saffron Walden, St Christophers, Letchworth, and at Caius College, Cambridge, where he took an engineering degree. During the Second World War he played an important part in radar research, returning afterwards to the family business of lawn-mower manufacturing. Some of his articles on fly fishing are in *Dick Walker's Trout Fishing*, edited by Peter Maskell, with a foreword by Peter Lapsley (David and Charles, 1982).

Walton, Izaak (1593–1683) No other fishing book anywhere or at any time has had the success of Walton's *The Compleat Angler*. It was first published in 1653. In Britain alone, since then, it has been republished more than a hundred times, world wide there have been some 400 editions in 60 languages. The second part of the book, on fly fishing, written by Charles Cotton, first appeared in the fifth edition of 1676.

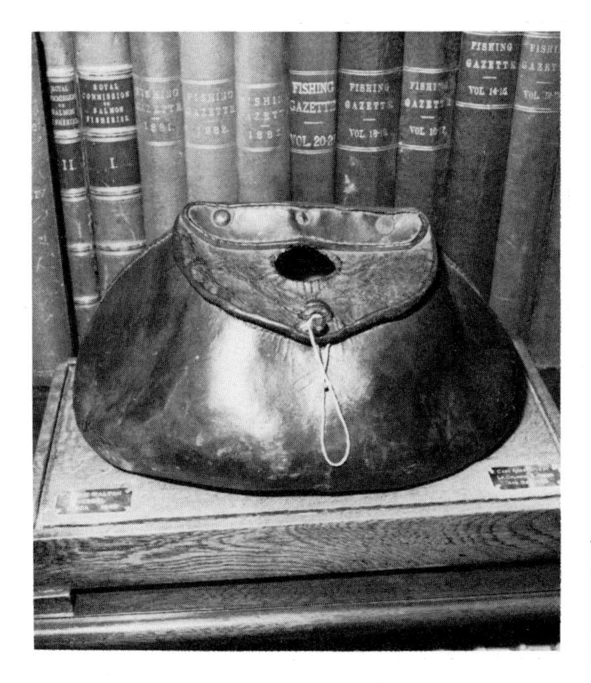

Walton's Creel – A tackle pouch or creel believed to have belonged to Izaak Walton, now in the museum of the Flyfishers' Club in London – photo courtesy of John Tarlton

Walton was born at Stafford and became an ironmonger in Fleet Street, London, close to St Dunstan's church. He cultivated literary men – Michael Drayton, Henry Wotton, Ben Johnson and John Donne. He wrote a number of books, including the lives of Donne and Wotton. In his later years he retired and lived with George Morley, Bishop of Winchester, and with his son-in-law Dr W. Hawkins, Prebend of Winchester, at 7 The Close, Winchester, a house which still stands.

He is buried in the cathedral's south aisle. There is a memorial window to him in the cathedral and a service to commemorate the centenary of his death was held there in July 1983.

Walton had a hazardous life. He was a Royalist, who managed to escape the purges carried out under Cromwell. He had more than his share of grief. When he wrote *The Compleat Angler* – which he always regarded as one of his less important books – he was nearing 60 and had outlived two wives and seven of their eight children. His two close friends and fishing companions were dead. It is more than likely that he wrote to escape from loneliness, for he had little to do, having retired from his business which had been 'on the north side of Fleet Street two doors west of Chancery Lane'.

Perhaps that is partly the reason for the charm of the book, its singing milkmaids and shepherds, friendly inns and good companions. Through it all moves Walton himself (Piscator), dispensing good advice, gossip, and queer tales of distant parts and strange happenings. To say, as some fishermen have, that a good deal of the fishing part of the book is nonsense, is to miss the point: it is a picture of Arcady, of a world of romance, a world in which Piscator could escape from the drab and ugly and dangerous times in which he lived. Whether, as Walton said, pike are born from the pickerel weed or flies from drops of dew, is of no real consequence. What comes shining through all the pages of the book is the quality of the man himself:

I will walk the meadows by some gliding stream, and there contemplate the lilies that take no care, and those very many other various little living creatures that are not only created, but fed, man knows not how, by the goodness of the god of nature, and therefore trust in him. This is my purpose; and so let everything that hath breath praise the Lord.

A fishing charity, The Izaak Walton Foundation, was set up as part of the tercentenary celebrations in 1983. Apart from its activity in collecting money to restore 7, The Close, Winchester, where Walton died, its main purpose is educational – the advancement of education in the prevention of pollution of all fishing waters and to support other organisations with like aims. The Honorary Secretary (1985) is Tony Pawson, fishing correspondent of *The Observer* newspaper.

Welshman's Button Courtney Williams is quite right to say that the true Welshman's Button is a beetle, the word button being a distortion of butty, meaning friend. Applied, as it was by Halford, to a sedge, a Welshman's Button is out of context. For the sedge, try Caperer. Williams gives Taverner's dressing for the friendly beetle:

Body: greenish-bronze peacock herl
Hackle: black cock
Wing cases: red feather from a partridge tail
Hook: 13

The wing cases should be a shining dark red, a beetle red, and if partridge tail is unavailable other red feather fibres, varnished, would be reasonable. A Coch-y-Bondhu is a useful substitute.

West, Leonard A first edition of *The Natural Trout Fly and Its Imitation* by Leonard West, privately printed in 1913, is valuable. A second edition, revised and enlarged, was published in 1921. West was among the first fly dressers to call attention to the importance of midge patterns. His book gives drawings and coloured plates of something like 100 trout flies, side by side with the natural insects they represent, together with coloured plates of all the main hackle feathers used in fly dressing.

Welsh Partridge A general pattern trout fly recommended by Courtney Williams for limestone and spate rivers and stillwaters, fished wet or dry. One suspects it might be quite a good pattern to use during a hatch of March Brown.

Body: claret seals' fur ribbed with fine gold wire
Head hackle: two, one being a short stiff claret hackle, the one in front a snipe rump feather or one from the back of a partridge
Whisks: two strands from a partridge tail
Hook: 14–12

Wet-Fly Fishing

The whole art of the upstream wet fly is to give the flies as long a natural drift as possible, while covering as much water as possible. Just a little drag doesn't matter too much. It may even help to give the flies an extra bit of life. But a long pronounced drag just won't do. (Reg Righyni, *Trout and Salmon* magazine, October, 1983)

Upstream wet-fly fishing for trout was developed to a peak of perfection in the Borders and North Country by the early 1800s. It is difficult to give a precise date and it may well have been earlier. By the mid-1850s it had reached a sophistication which has never been surpassed, though modern rods and lines have made for easier presentation.

The Border and North Country streams are fairly fast, with a good deal of broken water and riffles. The fly patterns, sometimes one on the point, sometimes two or three – point, middle and bob – are cast upstream and float down without drag. They are hackle patterns which suggest drowned winged insects. The angler wades upstream, fishing the water or the rise with his one fly or team of flies, using a fairly long rod, casting a short line, delicately, so that the trout is unaware of his approach.

That is the classic method of upstream wet-fly which Skues revived for the chalk streams, in the form, ultimately, of fishing the inert unweighted nymph just below the surface.

For the Border and North Country upstream wet-fly fishermen it does not matter whether his flies float or sink but he likes to prevent them from sinking too deep and will frequently grease the upper part of his leader to prevent this.

A variation of this method involves working the fly. In most cases different patterns are used, types that suggest water beetles, larvae, pupae or nymphs, as with weighted nymph fishing. These are often used in pools between riffles, allowed to sink deep, and retrieved fast or slow or in jerks.

The great exponent of the upstream wet-fly in the classic style was an Edinburgh lawyer, W.C. Stewart, who fished the Border rivers from about 1800 until shortly before his death in 1872. His book, *The Practical Angler*, published in 1857, had great influence and was reprinted many times in the next 50 years. He was the first to emphasise in print the importance of fishing upstream:

The angler is less likely to be seen by the trout, is able to hook the fish better, does not disturb the water over which he is to fish, and is able to present his flies to the trout in a more natural manner.

Stewart, very much the practical angler, had no idea what his hackle flies represented. He called them spiders. He fished these with several droppers using a 12ft greenheart rod. The flies should 'fall first upon the water' and as little of the line as possible, so that the rod must be kept well up.

After your flies alight, allow them to float gently downstream for a yard or two, taking care that neither they nor the lines ripple the surface. There is no occasion for keeping them on the surface, they will be quite as attractive a few inches under the water. As the flies come downstream, raise the point of your rod so as to keep the line straight, and as little of it in the water as possible; and when they have traversed a few yards of water, throw again about a yard or two higher up than where your flies alighted the previous cast, and so on.

Unless the spot looks extremely promising you need not cast twice in one place if you do not get a rise, but if there is any quick turn in the water where there is likely to be a good trout, we frequently cast over it six or seven times in succession, just allowing the flies to alight when we cast again. Where the current is strong the trout may not see the flies at first, and so we cast repeatedly to make sure; and we have frequently, after casting unsuccessfully half a dozen times over the same place caught a good trout at last.

Move up the pool as quickly as you can, first taking a cast or two straight up on the side you are on, and then fishing the opposite side, and so on, until you finish the pool. Although it is about the edges of the pool you will generally get most trout, the main current must by no means be neglected; indeed in it you will frequently capture the best fish . . .

Streams should be fished in exactly the same manner as pools . . . In fishing still water with no breeze on it you should wait until the motion of the line falling on it has subsided and then draw the flies slowly towards you, as, if they were allowed to remain stationary, the trout would at once detect their artificial nature.

The fly must be large enough to ensure it being seen, but not so large as to enable the trout to detect its artificial character.

Stewart's flies – the hackled or spider patterns – had been in use on Border rivers long before his time and he pays tribute to a James Baillie, generally regarded as the most able fly fisherman in Scotland, who fished the Border rivers in the early 1800s; possibly the late 1700s. These were Baillie's and Stewart's patterns:

Black Spider: James Baillie's favourite, the hook covered with brown silk, the head hackle being 'the small feather of the cock starling'
Red Spider: a yellow silk body and the hackle from 'the small feather from the outside wing of the landrail'
Dun Spider: dun silk body and the hackle from 'the soft dun or ash-coloured feather from the outside wing of the dotterel', or the small feather from the inside of the starling

The main North Country methods were codified in 1885 by T.E. Pritt, angling editor of *The Yorkshire Post*. Pritt's *Yorkshire Trout Flies* contained some 65 patterns which he had collected from anglers in the Dales. They included such classic flies as the Orange Partridge, Poult Bloa and Dark Watchet. Perhaps the best book ever published on North Country fly fishing was *Brook and River Trouting* by Edmonds and Lee in 1916.

In Devon, a good account was given of upstream wet-fly fishing on the Mole and the Bray by H.C. Cutcliffe, a surgeon in India for many years. He used hackle flies, with body dubbings of fur.

West Country Fly Fishing, edited by Anne Voss Bark (Batsford, 1983) has an informative article by David Pilkington on the upstream wet fly.

Variations of the classic method – the inert drift – were suggested in an article in *The Field* (25 August, 1982). On fast rivers like the Wharfe the olives hatch rapidly and do not ride the water as on the slower chalk streams.

The trout will often be seen rising but are taking the ascending nymphs and not the surface fly. In such cases a traditional pattern – such as a winged Dark Watchet – cast above a rise and stripped back fast will often be effective.

The wet fly fished downstream – the lure – is the basic method of fishing for salmon and sea trout where the lies are uncertain and the whole river has to be covered. The flies are cast towards the opposite bank and allowed to swing round in the current until well below the angler who then retrieves the fly, takes a step or so downstream, and casts again. The method is sometimes varied by drawing in the fly as it sweeps across the stream, giving it life.

For trout fishing the upstream wet fly is more accurate and more effective for it suggests the habits and movements of the natural insects on which the trout are feeding or can be expected to feed.

Wharfe The Wharfe is one of the finest, many would say *the* finest, of the Yorkshire trout streams, a lovely clear-water river flowing through some 50 or 60 miles of the Dales, past Bolton Abbey to join the Ouse near Cawood. A correspondent writes:

Yorkshire anglers know how to fish the Wharfe from the manner born but the southerner who comes from the chalk streams has to learn. For one thing the river can be fast and the wading over the gravel difficult. For another, the southerner will not find the duns riding the stream as they do on Test or Itchen. There are plenty of nymphs about – iron blue, several olives in places and the big mayfly, yellow may duns and little sky blues – but they come up and hatch like lightning, no sooner getting their backs out of water than the wings are up and away they go. Therefore, you will understand why your dry fly is pretty useless. Instead, fish the wet fly upstream, one if you like, no more than three on a cast, and cast to and above any rise you see, and if there is no take to a drifting sunk fly strip it in fast as though it were one of the river's fast moving nymphs. Most anglers seem to fish a point fly and a dropper but no harm in using three flies if you like or alternatively just one on the point. It is a prerequisite of fishing a Yorkshire river, especially the Wharfe, that you use the Yorkshire patterns that have been tried and tested for a couple of hundred years at least and most likely far longer than that. They include Dark Watchet, Poult Bloa, Partridge and Orange, and Snipe and Purple.

The fly fishing is best in the middle and upper river, the closer to the Ouse the less interesting it becomes. Visitors can fish the Bolton Abbey estate water (avoiding bank holidays and hot summer weekends). The Devonshire Arms at Bolton Abbey has tickets. There are also good hotels at Burnsall, Ilkley and Grassington which issue permits for association water where there are some very good stretches and the occasional big trout.

Whip Finish Sometimes called a wrap knot, the whip finish or whipping is used to attach line guides to a rod or to finish of the head of a fly. Several strands of thread are wrapped over and round the end of the thread which is then pulled back underneath them and varnished.

Whisky Fly A popular reservoir lure, designed in the 1970s by Albert Whillock:

Body: silver tinsel
Tail: red or orange nylon fibres
Hackle: long red or orange fibres, well spread
Hook: longshank 10, 8 or 6

As with most reservoir lures this is a very useful fly for sea trout fishing at night.

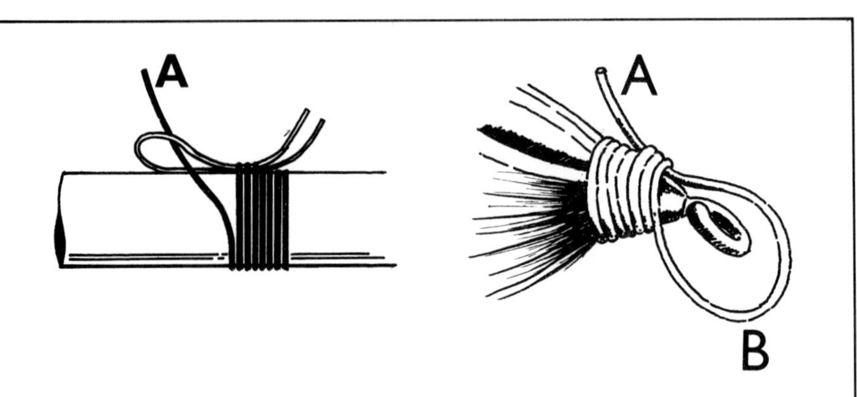

Rod Whipping. A loop of thread is placed on the rod, several turns of whipping taken round the loop, the end of the whipping (A) is put through the loop which is then pulled tight, pulling the end of the whipping back under the turns

Whip Finish or Wrap Knot. The strongest way to finish off the head of a fly, tricky to do, easier when seen. The end (A) goes under several turns of tying silk (B) and is then pulled tight and the knot varnished

Wickham's Fancy A trout fly designed about 100 years ago, either by a Captain Wickham or a Dr T.C. Wickham. There is some confusion about the names. Both fished the chalk streams of Hampshire and the Wickham is often used during a sedge hatch, either wet or dry:

Body: flat gold tinsel, sometimes ribbed gold wire, palmer dressed from head to toe with ginger or ginger-red cock hackle
Whisks: red cock
Wings: starling primary, sometimes upright, but mostly sloping back in sedge fly style
Shoulder hackle: red cock, a few turns longer than the body hackle tied in front of the wings
Hook: 12, 14 or 16

Wiggin, Maurice *The Angler's Bedside Book* (Batsford, 1965), edited by Maurice Wiggin, was one of the best anthologies about fishing for years, all the contributions specially written by fishermen of the quality of Bernard Venables, Howard Marshall, Macdonald Hastings and many others. It was excellently produced with many black and white photographs and line drawings.

Williams, A. Courtney (1892–1951) Introduced a classification of flies with commentaries and their appropriate dressings in his *Dictionary of Trout Flies*, first published in 1949, the fifth edition published posthumously in 1980. Williams saw service in the First World War in the Royal Field Artillery as a lieutenant and was wounded and invalided out in 1917. He later wrote a book about his experiences in France but it is for his invaluable Dictionary that he is remembered. It was produced while he was with the well-established tackle

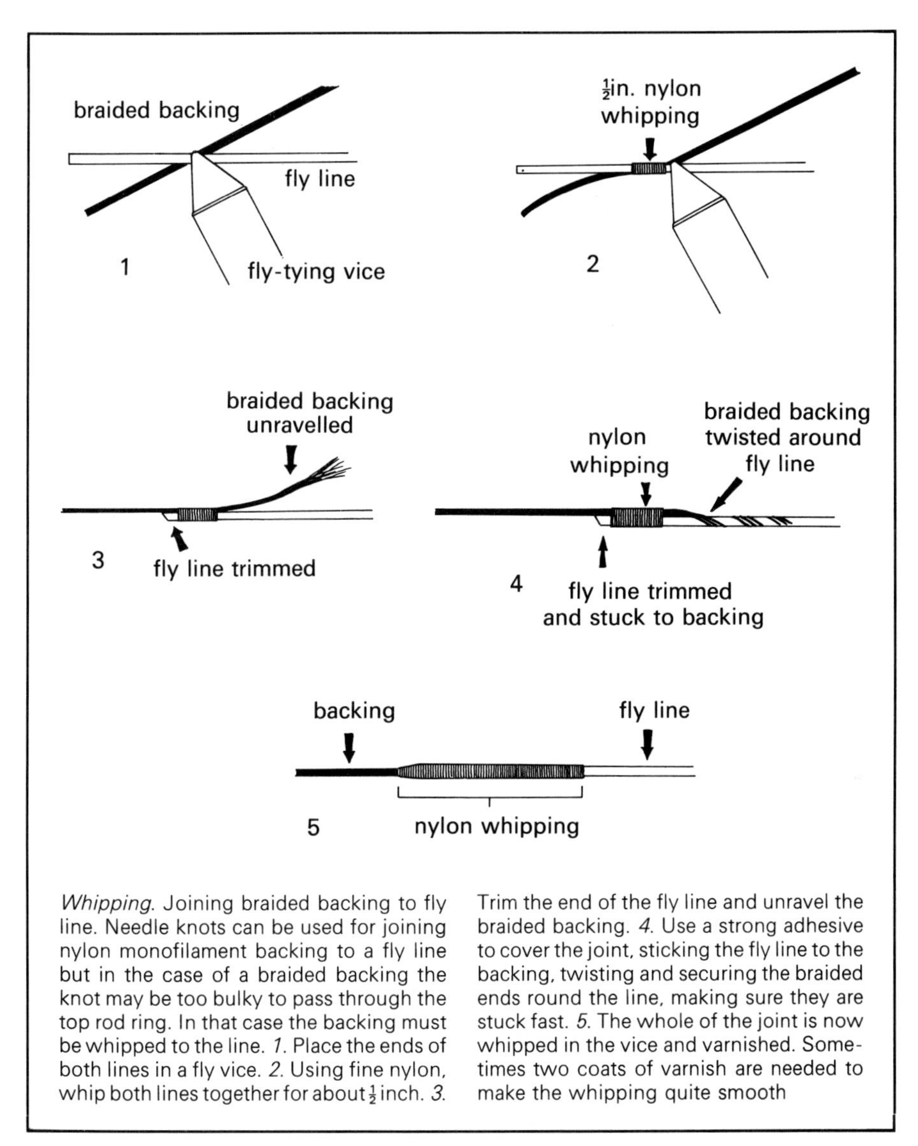

Whipping. Joining braided backing to fly line. Needle knots can be used for joining nylon monofilament backing to a fly line but in the case of a braided backing the knot may be too bulky to pass through the top rod ring. In that case the backing must be whipped to the line. *1.* Place the ends of both lines in a fly vice. *2.* Using fine nylon, whip both lines together for about ½ inch. *3.* Trim the end of the fly line and unravel the braided backing. *4.* Use a strong adhesive to cover the joint, sticking the fly line to the backing, twisting and securing the braided ends round the line, making sure they are stuck fast. *5.* The whole of the joint is now whipped in the vice and varnished. Sometimes two coats of varnish are needed to make the whipping quite smooth

firm of Allcock's of Redditch where he was latterly a director in charge of advertising.

Wilson, Dermot A former regular army officer, Dermot Wilson was awarded the Military Cross during the Second World War. After leaving the army he became a director of J. Walter Thompson, the big London advertising agency, before leaving for the Mill at Nether Wallop where he opened a high-quality mail order fishing tackle business which he ran from 1968 to 1981. He is a former chairman of the Angler's Cooperative Association, a vice-president of the Salmon and Trout Association, and an honorary member of the Theodore

Courtney Williams

Gordon Flyfishers' Club of America. His publications include *Dry Fly Beginnings* first published in 1957 by Douglas Saunders with MacGibbon and Kee, republished by A and C Black in 1970, under the title *Fishing the Dry Fly* with a second revised edition in 1983.

Wiltshire Fishery Association Formed in 1950 by two keen dry-fly fishermen, Colonel George Perkins, who was to become the first chairman, and Mr Norman Rawlence, a partner in the well-known West Country firm of estate agents, Rawlence and Squarey, who became treasurer.

A former chairman of the association, Major John Walker, has summarised its history and objectives:

After the Second World War the chalk streams were in a state of some neglect and disarray. Severe dredging had taken place in the cause of agriculture and tank traps had been dug for defence. At the same time the authority responsible was being changed from river board to river authority and finally to the regional authority – Wessex Water. The founders considered it necessary for riparian owners and other fishermen to have a united voice to state their problems.

The Association's committee includes members with personal knowledge of, and who fish on, the five rivers in its area – the Avon above Salisbury, the Wylye, Nadder, Bourne and Ebble – and also included on the committee are representatives from stillwater angling clubs and the fisheries officer of the Avon and Dorset division of Wessex Water Authority. The Association's representatives sit on local and regional fishery advisory committees so that the voice of fishermen can be clearly heard at all levels.

Dermot Wilson

Help and guidance can be given or obtained in matters of water pollution, abstraction, poaching, netting, electro-fishing, stocking policy, biological investigations and scientific research into all forms of river life. Weed-cutting dates are arranged on behalf of members each year with the water authority, with whom a close relationship is observed on all aspects of river management.

When, as happened in 1969, a major problem arises, in that case the threat of water abstraction from the headwaters of the Wylye at Brixton Deverill, a special fund was opened – the Wiltshire Chalk Streams' Protection Fund – which raised sufficient money to meet the Association's costs at a public enquiry with all its expenses of legal fees and specialist evidence. With generous technical and financial help from the Salmon and Trout Association, the case was won and sufficient modifications introduced to the scheme to ensure the well-being of the Wylye and also to set a precedent in case of any future proposals for water abstraction.

Williams' Favourite A spider-type wet fly designed by Courtney Williams' father, often fished dry in small sizes when it suggests a black gnat or midge. Midland reservoir fishermen with an identical pattern call it a Black Spider. This is Courtney Williams':

Body: black silk ribbed fine silver wire, or thin tinsel in the larger sizes
Hackle: black cock for the dry fly, black hen for the wet
Whisks: none
Hook: 12 to 18

Willie Ross A ghilly at the Altnaharra Hotel, Sutherland, from the early 1930s, through to his death in the 1950s, Willie Ross still has the record for the largest number of fish taken by his rods on Loch Hope and Loch Naver – one of them a 33½lb salmon from Loch Naver. He tied a variation of the Black Pennell – adding a scarlet hackle as a front hackle – which is excellent in small sizes for the wet fly and in large bushy sizes for the dap.

Body: black floss silk or black wool
Rib: fine silver tinsel
Tail: golden pheasant tippet
Hackle: two hackles, black behind and a scarlet hackle in front
Hook: 6 or 8 longshank low water salmon hooks for the dap, 10 or 12 longshank or standard for the wet fly

The fly for dapping should have a thick black hackle going well down the shoulder of the hook.

Woodcock and Green One of several, and probably the best, of the woodcock series – Woodcock and Red, Woodcock and Orange. Useful for rivers and lochs and lakes:

Body: green wool or fur
Rib: fine silver wire
Whisks: a few strands of golden pheasant tippet
Hackle: ginger or red hen
Wing: two slips from the inside feathers from a woodcock's wing
Hook: 14 to 8

Woolley, Roger The author of *Modern Trout Fly Dressings* (1932) Roger Woolley was a professional fly-tier and hairdresser at 5, Marston Road, Hatton, Derbyshire, who was highly praised by many fishermen of his day. He used hackle points for the wings of his dry flies.

Wright, James (1829–1902) A fishing tackle maker of Sprouston on Tweed who tied the first Greenwell's Glory to the design of Canon Greenwell of Durham in 1854. Wright or his family created several well-known salmon flies including the Garry Dog, Stoat's Tail, Durham Ranger and Thunder and Lightning. Authentication is a little uncertain. Wright had three sons and four daughters, died at the age of 73, and is buried in Sprouston churchyard. **Sources include:** Courtney Williams, the Rev. Donald R. Gaddes of Kelso, and others.

Wye (Derbyshire) The Wye, and its near neighbour, the Derwent, are small limestone streams of an excellent quality of water and good weed growth which stand comparison with some of the chalk streams, though the fish are smaller and the banks less trimmed. The waters are clear, the trout have to be stalked. Rainbow trout breed in the Wye, are generally fairly small fish of about a quarter to a half pound though with some well over a pound. Chalk stream patterns do well. On many beats wading is prohibited. The Peacock Hotel at Rowsley and the Cavendish Hotel at Baslow can arrange fishing.

Wye (Herefordshire) A beautiful and powerful river that rises on the Welsh mountains of Plynlimmon and winds through some spectacular scenery (Symond's Yat) to the Severn estuary near Chepstow. It has the deserved reputation of being the finest salmon river in England and Wales and has produced some very big fish.

On 12 March, 1923, Miss Doreen Davy, fishing the Cowpond Pool at Winforton, took a springer of 59½lb. Three years before that a fly fisherman at Whitney was broken by a very large fish which a few days later was found decomposing on the bank. One estimate suggested it might well have weighed nearly 80lb when it was hooked. In those days the average of Wye salmon taken was 18lb but that did not last. By 1980 the average was around 12lb and a 30-pounder comparatively rare.

The Wye is a lovely river to fish. In the lower Wye, boats are needed at times to cover the lies but further up there is good bank fishing and wading. The most popular parts of the river are best avoided at holiday times and some weekends. On the middle Wye a sink tip line is preferred for April and May but after that a floater. The flies are mostly doubles, from size 4 down to 10, especially yellow in coloured water. A middle-Wye fisherman, Mrs Nancy Whitlock, says:

> Tubes are not popular though I have some success with a lightly-dressed black hairwing tube, a half-inch long, in low water conditions. I personally prefer a single fly rather than a double. In a number of places it is necessary to 'work' the fly, a method frowned upon by many, including Scottish ghillies, but assuredly more productive.

Working the fly, by bringing in line with the free hand as the fly swings round in the current is becoming popular in the south of England and in Wales. This may be because the rivers are not so fast as the Scottish rivers, or perhaps more coloured or less disturbed by conflicting flows, but whatever the reason working the fly takes fish well. Possibly in most Scottish rivers the fly itself is adequately worked without a retrieve because of interlinking and diverging flows. All this is purely speculative.

For many years the Wye has been badly poached and heavily wormed and at last has set an example to some of the Scottish rivers. *The Field* reported (28 January, 1984) that the Wye Salmon Fishery Owners' Association had decided at its annual meeting to adopt a voluntary code of practice which would prohibit float fishing throughout the season: the use of worm, prawn and shrimp between 1 September and 1 June; and the use of the gaff after 31 August. It proposed that all hen fish taken after 31 August be returned and that the close season should be lengthened from 10 October to 25 January. The catch should be restricted to three fish per fisherman per day. The Wye association consists of some 111 members who between them represent the ownership of more than 85 per cent of the river fishing.

See also Gilbert, H.A. on page 75 for details about Miss Dabey's 59½lb springer.

Wylye A beautiful little chalk stream rising at Maiden Bradley north of Mere, through Warminster, on to Heytesbury and Stapleford before joining the

Nadder and then the Avon below Salisbury. The Wylye is loved for its wild brown trout, though there is now a little stocking, and if ever rainbows escape from a fish farm, as happens, they are hunted down by grimly determined men who are anxious to keep aliens from their cherished waters.

The native Wylye trout are cunning and there is a good bit of weed for sanctuary so that to take anything over a pound is regarded as skilful handling. Dry fly is pretty well universal but sometimes emerger patterns are used. There are mayfly (*E. danica*) and good hatches of olives and pale wateries. The black gnat abounds and when spinners are on the water Lunn's Particular seems to be in almost universal demand.

Anything over a pound is worth keeping, two pounders are rare, but *The Haig Guide to Trout Fishing in Britain* records that a trout of 7lb 2½oz was taken by Mr Carlton Cross at South Newton in May, 1924. That would have been in the mayfly period and if the ranunculus beds were thickening, as they would be, to land a 7lb fish is a remarkable achievement.

The Salisbury Anglers, the Piscatorial Society, and the Wilton Club all have water.

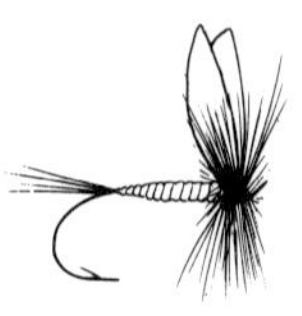

Spiders

I have often seen it said that the spider patterns of the North of England and Southern Scotland are 'exactly like nymphs'. They are not so, except possibly when fished downstream with a drag which makes the hackle hug the body. They are far more probably suggestive of the sub-imago caught and tumbled by the stream in the very act of hatching. The old-fashioned winged patterns with the wings – thin slips of feather – lying close over the back with the hackle sloping back close to the hook, so as to ensure a good entry when fished downstream, or with a drag, were much more like nymphs.

G.E.M. Skues, *Nymph Fishing for Chalk Stream Trout*, 1939

. . . and there is the palmer hackle, or spider, by which name we mean to call it, believing that if it resembles anything in the insect tribe, it is a spider.

W.C. Stewart, *The Practical Angler*, 1857

The North Country softly hackled patterns fished at point are my favourites. These are often loosely called spiders, but anyone who closely examines the colours and materials will have no doubt that they are meant to represent drowned duns or spinners.

T.C. Kingsmill Moore, *A Man May Fish*, 1960

Yellow Torrish A splendid fully-dressed salmon fly for cloudy waters, originally with about nine feathers in the wing, now more like three or four:

Tag: silver tinsel and yellow silk
Tail: golden pheasant crest, up-turned
Butt: black ostrich herl
Lower body: black wool ribbed silver, sometimes just silver
Mid-body: black ostrich herl under a beard hackle of bright yellow feather fibres
Upper body: black wool, ribbed silver
Throat: beard hackle, fairly full, of yellow feather fibres
Wing: dark turkey tail or brown mallard, sided with grey drake, with red, blue and yellow swan, or just red and yellow, topped with golden pheasant crest
Hook: almost any size

Yorkshire Trout Streams No county in England can lay claim to such a variety of trout streams as Yorkshire. In the East Riding are the Costa, Driffield and Foston Beck, chalk streams comparable to the Hampshire rivers; while in the North Riding are the big limestone rivers like the Wharfe; and many others that hold large wild brown trout like the Swale, Ure, Derwent, Aire and Nidd. The rivers of the Dales are great favourites for fishermen in the big northern industrial cities.

See also Wet-Fly Fishing on p 223; Wharfe on p 225, and other entries.

Zulu An excellent black palmer trout fly, named after the head-dresses worn by warriors of Chief Cetawayo, the Zulu king who defeated the British during one of the South African wars of the 1870s:

Body: black wool, ribbed with fine flat silver tinsel
Tail: short stub of bright scarlet wool
Hackle: black cock wound thinly from head to tail, held down by the silvery rib
Hook: 14–10, larger for sea trout

The Blue Zulu is a variation with a blue hackle in front of the black, or by itself; sometimes with a blue wool body as well; an attractive looking fly sometimes used for dapping.

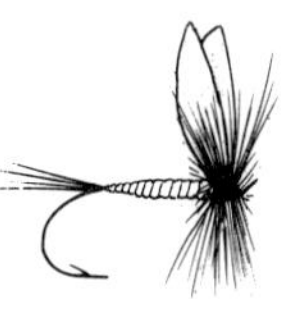

Envoi

The time must come to all of us, who live long, when memory is more than prospect. An angler who has reached this stage and reviews the pleasure of life will be grateful and glad that he has been an angler, for he will look back upon days radiant with happiness, peaks of enjoyment that are no less bright because they are lit in memory by the light of a setting sun.

Viscount Grey of Fallodon, *Fly Fishing*, 1899

Conversion Tables

Length

cm	cm or in	in
2.54	1	0.394
5.08	2	0.787
7.62	3	1.181
10.16	4	1.575
12.70	5	1.969

As a rough guide take 2 inches as 5 centimetres

Breaking strains/fish weights

kg	kg or lb	lb
0.454	1	2.205
0.907	2	4.409
1.361	3	6.614
1.814	4	8.819
2.268	5	11.023
2.722	6	13.228
3.175	7	15.432
3.629	8	17.637
4.082	9	19.842
4.536	10	22.046

As a rough guide, a 1lb trout is a ½kg trout; a UK gallon is 4½ litres (liters); and a mile is 1.6 kilometres (kilometers).

Temperatures

F°	32	40	50	60	70	75	85
C°	0	5	10	15	20	25	30